UNDERSTANDING
POPULAR SCIENCE

ISSUES in CULTURAL and MEDIA STUDIES

Series editor: Stuart Allan

Published titles:

UNDERSTANDING POPULAR SCIENCE

Peter Broks

Open University Press

Open University Press
McGraw-Hill Education
McGraw-Hill House
Shoppenhangers Road
Maidenhead
Berkshire
England
SL6 2QL

email: enquiries@openup.co.uk
world wide web: www.openup.co.uk

and Two Penn Plaza, New York, NY 10121–2289, USA

First published 2006

A catalogue record of this book is available from the British Library

ISBN–10: 0 335 21548 3 (pb) 0 335 21549 1 (hb)
ISBN–13: 978 0 335 21548 5 (pb) 978 0 335 21549 2 (hb)

Library of Congress Cataloging-in-Publication Data
CIP data applied for

Typeset by RefineCatch Limited, Bungay, Suffolk
Printed in the UK by Bell & Bain Ltd, Glasgow

For Barbara

CONTENTS

SERIES EDITOR'S FOREWORD

'The work of creating science has been organized for centuries,' Edward Livingston Youmans observed in 1872, yet the 'work of diffusing science [. . .] is clearly the next great task of civilization.' The occasion for Youmans's observation was the formal launch of the magazine *Popular Science Monthly*, of which he was the founding editor. His longstanding experiences as one of the first scientists striving to popularize evolution in the US meant that he was hardly distracted by the bitter attacks waged by critics against his new magazine (several of whom disparaged it as the devilish labour of atheists, amongst other colourful descriptions). Youmans was convinced that his 'experimental' undertaking would succeed, perceiving at the time a 'growing sympathy, on the part of men of science of the highest character, with the work of popular teaching, and an increasing readiness to cooperate in undertakings that shall promote it.' Moreover, he added, there is, 'in fact, growing up a valuable literature of popular science – not the trash that caters to public ignorance, wonder, and prejudice, but able and instructive essays and lectures from men who are authorities upon the subjects which they treat.' Hence his firm belief that publications such as *Popular Science Monthly* would perform the task of 'systematically disseminating these valuable productions' for those readers willing and able to meet the challenges of 'self-instruction in science.'

From the vantage point of today, these words sound anachronistic – not least Youmans's use of the male pronoun to describe scientists – and yet, rather tellingly, all too familiar. Thanks to the broad sweep of its historical purview, Peter Broks's *Understanding Popular Science* offers a compelling analysis of precisely these sorts of tensions. The discussion begins with the premise that while science is a defining feature of the modern world, it is through what we have come to call 'popular science' that most of us make sense of this fact. In the course of tracing a cultural history of popular science over the past two hundred years, Broks elaborates a framework to help discern the ways in which it has been invented, redefined and fought over. In the course of showing us why this history matters today, he proceeds to address a range of contemporary concerns that go to the heart of current controversies about the relationship between science and its public. In so doing, he raises questions not only about its authority but, crucially, its very legitimacy as well. It is Broks's view that we need to move beyond the usual top-down models of expertise so as to better theorize how popular science can be recognized as a 'conceptual space' for the construction, proliferation and negotiation of meanings inflected in public debate. Such an approach, we soon discover, provides us with a rich array of intriguing – and unexpected – insights.

The *Issues in Cultural and Media Studies* series aims to facilitate a diverse range of critical investigations into pressing questions considered to be central to current thinking and research. In light of the remarkable speed at which the conceptual agendas of cultural and media studies are changing, the series is committed to contributing to what is an ongoing process of re-evaluation and critique. Each of the books is intended to provide a lively, innovative and comprehensive introduction to a specific topical issue from a fresh perspective. The reader is offered a thorough grounding in the most salient debates indicative of the book's subject, as well as important insights into how new modes of enquiry may be established for future explorations. Taken as a whole, the series is designed to cover the core components of cultural and media studies courses in an imaginatively distinctive and engaging manner.

Stuart Allan

ACKNOWLEDGEMENTS

I know this is one part of a book that tends to be skipped over, but there are some people I really would like to thank. I shall forsake a lengthy list of names and instead mention those who, in whatever way, have made a difference. Thus my brevity should be taken as an indication of sincerity. First mention must go to the Faculty of Humanities and Social Sciences at the University of the West of England, Bristol, for providing me with research leave to write the book: it would not have been possible otherwise. I am also grateful to Chris Cudmore at the Open University Press and series editor Stuart Allan for their patience and understanding in waiting for a manuscript that was long overdue. For reading early versions of different chapters and for their general encouragement I want to thank Peter Bowler, Paul Broks, Michelle Henning, Bernie Lightman and Felicity Mellor. The ideas in Chapter 7 were helped by discussions with Kuruvilla Pandikattu in Pune and with participants at the international conference on Public Communication of Science and Technology held in Barcelona. My principal thanks, however, must be reserved for my family: Ilizane and Lara for appreciating my need to spend so much time in front of the computer, and especially Barbara who supported me with a regular supply of smiles, gourmet meals and constructive criticism. Without you this book would not be what it is and so it is to you that it is dedicated with love and thanks.

INTRODUCTION

This is a book about popular science. The culture we live in is saturated with science; indeed, it might be taken as a defining feature of the modern world. Popular science is where most of us make sense of that fact and this book tries to make sense of popular science.

However, part of the aim of the book is to show how that opening sentence may not be as simple as it first appears. Indeed, it has been suggested that 'popular science' is an 'unworkable analytical category' and that it would be best if it were abandoned (Topham 1998; Secord 2004). This need not trouble us unduly since an array of other possible terms and combination of terms is at hand so that, if we wish, we might prefer to examine the public, pop, common, low, plebeian, banal, indigenous, vernacular or democratic forms of science, knowledge, epistemology or world-view. Similarly, we can avoid using the term if we wish to shift our attention from the content of popular science as a body of knowledge to examine the relationship between science and the public. In this instance we might prefer to talk about lay–expert and amateur–professional dimensions, or direct our scholarly gaze at the popularization of science, the communication of science, the diffusion of knowledge, the public understanding of science, and knowledge transfer.

Even so, apart from losing a perfectly good term that is in common usage I think we would be missing a great opportunity if we studiously avoid referring to 'popular science'. I would like to reclaim the term and, rather than see it as problematic, see it as encompassing a set of problematics. By accepting a comprehensive sense of the term not only do we avoid a myopic focus on the diffusion of science, but we are also encouraged to pay attention, amongst other things, to a whole range of participatory and indigenous forms, of practitioners, knowledge producers, knowledge consumers, commercial interests, political aspirations and social fears. The very fact that it covers such a diversity of beliefs, practices, artefacts and contexts forces us to acknowledge the complex interrelationship of knowledge, culture and society. Furthermore, in recognizing that the needs, purposes and models for popular science change we can encompass those changes within our set of problematics and include them within our object of study too. Indeed, far from accepting 'popular science' as a natural category, a major theme of this book is that what we take to be popular science is constituted by the struggles around it and the questions we ask about it. We could even push this further and say that how we understand popular science is part of the struggle within it.

With all that in mind, the first four chapters of this book show how popular science has been invented, redefined and fought over; how it has been a force for social revolution and for social control; and how it has both legitimated the authority of science and raised fears of an anti-science movement. Drawing on that history, the next two chapters raise questions about the relationship between science and the public, the nature of expertise and the ways of thinking about popularization. The final chapter is not so much a conclusion as a speculative suggestion for how we might think about popular science. More particularly, a brief overview of chapters looks like this:

- **Chapter 1** looks at how the cultural meanings of popular science were fiercely contested. Focusing on the first half of the nineteenth century, it shows how radical artisans were using science as a weapon against the established authorities of church and government, and how a frightened middle class used science in a vain effort to instil their own values into the labour aristocracy. Beyond the legitimation of radical and bourgeois values, the chapter also examines appeals to the usefulness of science and, more particularly, the usefulness of scientists. This was the period in which scientists sought to develop their own self-identity as a group, a process through which excluding the public became a defining feature of what it meant to be scientific.
- The idea of exclusion is picked up in **Chapter 2**, which moves the story on into the second half of the nineteenth century and the professionalization of science. Whereas before popular science had been permeated by an ideology of participation in a 'Republic of Science', by the 1860s the emphasis was shifting to the public being called upon as supporters for the professional scientists. The chapter shows how scientists were presented as the heroes of the modern age and how technological utopianism fostered a widespread belief in future progress. Moreover, the belief in progress seemed justified by evolutionary theory, and the chapter concludes with an examin-

ation of popular responses to Darwin's theory of evolution by natural selection.

- In the twentieth century, science would be inextricably entangled with all the hopes and fears of modernity. **Chapter 3** examines the relationship between science and modernity, with particular attention being paid to efficiency and control as commonly held values. The appeal of these values was felt across the political spectrum, and the chapter shows how the popularization of science was, in effect, the popularization of modernity. More particularly, the chapter looks at Fordism, eugenics, and H.G. Wells's vision of a technocratic utopia as well as representations of science in popular magazines. Presenting previously unpublished research, the chapter gives the final voice to the men and women recorded in the files of Mass Observation, the social research organization set up in the 1930s to investigate the everyday lives of people in Britain.

- In the period after the Second World War examined in **Chapter 4,** once again we see the cultural meaning of science openly contested. Public attitudes towards science appear deeply contradictory: rejoicing in the role that science had played in winning the war, but still coming to terms with the new atomic nightmare; enjoying a technology-based consumer boom, but voicing concerns about the effect on the environment. The chapter discusses the new critical tone and shows that it was not so much simple opposition as a new concern for accountability and responsibility. Following an examination of 1960s counter-culture and the rise of postmodern theory, the chapter explores what seems to be the greatest contradiction of all: the late twentieth-century boom in popular science amid rising fears of 'anti-science'.

- Bringing this history up to the present day, Chapters 5 and 6 engage with current debates about science communication and the Public Understanding of Science (PUS). **Chapter 5** begins with an account of C.P. Snow's Two Cultures and post-war concerns over science literacy. It discusses the problems of defining and measuring science literacy as well as how the 'deficit model' was a structuring principle of PUS. The chapter explores the idea of the PUS movement being a search for legitimation and uses this idea as a way to understand the 'science wars' of the 1990s. The problem for scientists was how to reconcile their authority (setting themselves apart from the public) with a need for legitimation (through an appeal to the public). The chapter argues that it is in the domain of popular science that this delicate balancing act is carried out.

- In recent years the dominant view of science communication as represented by PUS and the deficit model has been increasingly called into question. **Chapter 6** exposes some of the deficiencies of this dominant view before considering alternative models that have been put forward. In particular it looks at recent calls for a 'dialogue' between science and public, examining the asymmetrical nature of that dialogue and suggesting that we acknowledge the experiential expertise of the lay public. More importantly, the chapter highlights the shift from information transfer to meaning construction as the essential feature of developing a new Critical Understanding of Science in Public (CUSP). The chapter concludes with some examples of a 'CUSP' approach.

- **Chapter 7** suggests a new model to give a critical account of the construction, proliferation and negotiation of meanings within popular science. In taking seriously the spatial imagery that is often employed in discussing ideas, a model of 'conceptual space' invites us to think of popular science not as a thing to be passed from one person to another but rather as contextualized interactivity in a network of relationships. The chapter also takes this spatial imagery to address the problem of science and democracy with discussions of the 'public sphere' and the '*agora*'. It concludes with a speculation about creating a 'demosophic' society with formal and informal institutional machinery for sharing knowledge.

So, this is what the book is about: not just the diffusion of knowledge but the struggle over meaning; the separation of professional expertise from public experience; the relationship between science and democracy; the legitimation of the scientific enterprise; and the ways that our understanding of populariza-tion are framed by the questions we ask about it. In this way, this is a book about popular science.

1 | UNCERTAIN TIMES

It is sometimes said that history is the collective memory of a society. The art of the historian, however, is the art of forgetting – forgetting that we know how things turn out in the end. Similarly, knowing how things turn out often blinds us to how things might have been different or were different. 'It doesn't have to be like this' may be a cry of despair, but it is also a useful reminder of the nature of historical contingency and prompts us to ask why it is like this if it does not have to be. Such is the case with popular science.

In the first half of the nineteenth century much of what we now recognize as British (or more particularly English) social and cultural life was 'in the making'. One of the classic studies of social history looks to these years for 'the origins of modern English society' in the shift from 'an open aristocracy based on property and patronage' which generated the Industrial Revolution to the 'triumph of the entrepreneurial ideal' which exploited it (Perkin 1969). Most famously, perhaps, is E.P. Thompson's (1968) account of the 'making of the English working class' in the period between the French Revolution and the Great Reform Act of 1832. The outstanding fact of the period, says Thompson, is the formation of the 'working class' revealed in the growth of class consciousness, 'the consciousness of an identity of interests as between all these diverse groups of working people and as against the interests of other classes' (212). Equally, this period saw the making of the English working scientist when diverse groups of practitioners in science came to feel an identity of interests between themselves and against, not so much their rulers and employers, but rather against everyone who were not scientists – the public at large. Indeed, it is in the first half of the nineteenth century that we find the emergence both of the term 'scientist' and the modern usage of the term 'popularization'.

This first chapter will examine this formative period and look at the diverse meanings of science, the institutional attempts to control such diversity, and the creation of new audiences for the new knowledge. In those uncertain times we will see the construction of what we have come to understand as 'science', 'the public' and the relationship between them.

Radical, safe and useful

Describing science as 'revolutionary' is now so commonplace that it verges on cliché. We now have a stock of well-worn phrases about the computer revolution, the genetic revolution, the biotech revolution, as well as the 'revolutions' brought on by the impact of technology upon society. In the early nineteenth century the idea that science was 'revolutionary' had much more explicitly political connotations. Romantic associations between storms and revolution suggested that 'liberty was a natural and hence ultimately irresistible force', and it was the man of science that had control of those forces (Schama 1989: 46). In the standard iconography of Revolutionary France, for example, the forces of nature were presented as being at the command of one man in particular: Benjamin Franklin, the 'Electrical Ambassador'. Famous for his experiments flying kites in thunder storms and for his role in the American Revolution, the popularized image of Franklin has him drawing down bolts of lightning from the heavens and brushing aside tyrannical regimes (like that of the British). Such was Franklin's celebrity status in Paris that it brought fellow revolutionary John Adams to comment, 'It is universally believed in France that his electric wand has accomplished all this revolution' (Schama 1989: 44).

Across the channel in England, science was equally amenable to radical thought. It was because of his enthusiasm for the French Revolution that the physician Thomas Beddoes found it necessary to give up his readership at Oxford. His Pneumatic Institution was finally established in the Hotwells area of Bristol which would have been more sympathetic to his radical politics. Nevertheless, his medical work on respiratory disorders still earned him a hostile notice in *The Anti-Jacobin Review and Magazine*, while his attacks on the rich and the government brought him under investigation for sedition (Russell 1983: 136–7; Levere 1984). Beddoes's network of correspondents and fellow travellers included the non-conformist preacher, political reformer and chemist Joseph Priestley. In Birmingham a 'Church and Country mob' destroyed Priestley's laboratory and library. By Priestley's own account the crowd's anger was provoked by his celebrations at the fall of the Bastille. For critics of the revolution such as Edmund Burke, science was seen as a threat and Priestley was the embodiment of everything that was detestable about the French and their philosophy (Crosland 1987).

Radical politics and science were also closely linked in the street literature studied by Adrian Desmond (1987). In these deist, atheist and socialist penny prints Desmond found a 'faith in the socially regenerative properties of **materialistic** science and a utopian belief in its liberalizing force' (1987: 82). Science was projected as egalitarian and promoted as a weapon to attack institutions like the established church. Deism, says Desmond, was part of working-class republican ideology. Not surprisingly, deism (the belief that nature is self-governing and needed no intervention from God) could easily slip into atheism (the belief that there is no God), and the greater the militancy the more pronounced the atheism. This is certainly true, for example, with the penny print *The Oracle of Reason* (1841–43) and its 'aggressively confrontationist atheism' (1987: 86). It was deliberately crude and as offensive as possible, resulting in a succession of editors being imprisoned for blasphemy. It is in publications such as this that Desmond explores 'the materialist science that artisans believed best served their republican interests' (1987: 78). It was a pragmatic attitude, 'a crudely effective functional ideology of science'; as far as these mid-century socialists were concerned, science 'was what worked politically' (1987: 89). What worked included: geography to promote ideas of cultural **relativism**; natural history to show man's status as a natural being; astronomy to replace the old myths with faith in natural law; and chemistry which could provide materialist ammunition for anti-clerical attacks. Of particular importance was the environmental determinism to be found in Lamarckian ideas of transmutation.

In many respects Jean-Baptiste Lamarck was a product of the French Revolution. Holding a junior position at the *Jardin du Roi* prior to the revolution, he emerges as a major figure after the Jacobin upheaval. In the reorganization of the *Jardin* into the French Natural History Museum Lamarck was given special responsibility for the study of worms and insects, or 'invertebrates' as he came to call them. His ideas on transmutation (i.e. that species can change) first appear in his lectures in 1800 and published in his *Philosophie Zoologique* (1809) and the first volume of his *Histoire Naturelle des Animaux sans Vertèbres* (1815). Although not translated into English until 1914, Lamarck's evolutionary ideas were often popularized by the many attempts to refute them, most notably in Charles Lyell's *Principles of Geology* (1830–33). He is, perhaps, now most often remembered for the notion of the inheritance of acquired characteristics which is supposed to distinguish his theory of evolution from that of Charles Darwin, even though Darwin himself later held to a modified form of the idea. More important, and more shocking for many Victorians, were the other elements of Lamarck's theory. At the heart of the theory was environmental determinism, the idea that all organisms are adapted to their environment and that changes in the environment invoke corresponding changes in the organism. Species, therefore, are not fixed, immutable entities – as created by God – but are constantly in a state of flux, a process of transmutation, adapting to changing circumstances. More shocking still was Lamarck's inclusion of mankind into the evolutionary scheme, even to the extent of seeing the human mind as a product of such natural processes.

Though shocking for some, for others such evolutionary or 'progressionist' ideas 'provided a potent legitimation of artisan demands for democratic change' (Desmond 1987: 110). Lamarckian ideas of evolution 'drove out the deity and legitimated the republican struggle by providing a model of social ascent power-driven from below' (102–3). There was a natural affinity between the science and political aspiration:

> The strong metaphoric congruence between a self-emerging physical and mental organization and the democratic ideal made a **reductionist** philosophy attractive to artisan and bourgeois radicals: the sum of the parts made up the whole, and power and sovereignty resided at the base, with the individual. Authority did not delegate downward but was mandated from below . . . The inherent power of the mass (matter in physics, the crowd in politics) became the cornerstone of radical working-class philosophy . . . It is not surprising, therefore, that a reductionist biology of emergent organic change dominated the republican, atheist, and prosuffrage street literature.
> (Desmond 1987: 97)

Moreover, by recontextualizing Lamarckism as a 'progressive antiestablishment science' Desmond is able to give a political dimension to understanding attacks on Lamarckism from Oxbridge dons and learned societies, a social dimension to anti-religious sentiments and materialist ideas, and a class framework to help understand rival evolutionary theories – Darwin's natural selection may be seen as a 'reification of bourgeois utilitarian **Malthusian** doctrines' and Lamarck's social environmentalism as part of a more general 'levelling' strategy for social and economic reconstruction (1987: 79).

However, the legitimation of radical politics by progressionist theories was only one of a number of possible meanings given to scientific ideas. The fine-tuning of organism to environment was equally important to those who wished to show the beneficence of God rather than his non-existence. The clearest and most popular expression of such ideas is to be found in the Reverend William Paley's *Natural Theology* (1802).

Paley made no claims for originality in his books. The argument from design had been one of the most persistent proofs for the existence of God since Aquinas in the thirteenth century or back to Cicero for a pre-Christian version. Particularly in England there had long been a tradition of **natural theology**, not simply as a form of Christian apologetics but as a way in which the scientific community could assert its legitimacy. From the seventeenth century onwards 'the culture of natural theology was one of the main vehicles by which scientists addressed the public and advertised the cultural and moral goods that scientific activity might deliver' (Shapin 1990: 999). There was, therefore, nothing much new in Paley's book; rather his success lay in the simple, clear style with which it was written. The book is a delight to read. It opens with the familiar analogy between God's creation and a watch – in each case 'there cannot be design without a designer; a contrivance without a contriver' (Paley [1802] 1837: 437) and step by step unfolds a steady accumulation of evidence to show not only God's handiwork but also his unity, omnipotence and beneficence. Thus, the parts of animals are marvellously constructed for their particular purpose (the eye is Paley's favourite example), and the function of each part is exquisitely suited to the particular circumstances of each animal. More than that, to the simple necessary functions of animal sensations God in His goodness has superadded pleasure – small wonder that Paley was to write, 'It is a happy world after all' (Paley [1802] 1837: 534).

By the early 1820s the book was already regarded as a classic and throughout the century new editions kept it relevant enough to appeal to new audiences, popularizing science for a non-technical readership and showing science and religion could be in harmony. Fresh editions appeared long after Darwin was supposed to have destroyed the central idea upon which it was based (Fyfe 2002). Not surprisingly, with such success it was singled out for attack by radicals for whom 'breaking the propagandist image of Paley's happy world was an integral step to altering the collective perception of the masses' (Desmond 1987: 88). It was, however, a view of the world that was remarkably robust and endurable, in part, at least, because it was so ambiguous and flexible. For Paley the argument from design not only gave independent proof of God's existence but also showed His wisdom through his Creation. For Deists, on the other hand, an appeal to design was useful because the more that could be known of God through reason the less need there was for reliance on revelation and Biblical authority. Indeed, this was the approach taken by Tom Paine in his attacks on organized religion (Brooke 1991: 193). Paine might be an extreme example but this does give some indication of the range of possible positions that the design argument was able to offer.

As a way of looking at the world, natural theology was probably the shared viewpoint of most Victorians. For most people it was something that could be agreed upon even though it might be difficult for them to come to an agreement over just what it was that they were agreeing about. As John Brooke has argued, this was the greatest strength of natural theology which 'performed a mediating function between different religious traditions; at a time when religious differences were associated with marked social and political consequences. Design arguments were well equipped to fulfil this mediating role precisely because they were doctrinally so imprecise' (Brooke: 1979: 42). In the turbulent 1830s and 1840s the ambiguities of natural theology provided 'the lowest common denominator for men whose primary interest was the pursuit of science' (Brooke 1991: 211), enabling them to avoid religious and political discord and helping them to 'dissociate science from fears of atheism and spasmodic fears of revolution' (Brooke 1979: 52). It has also been argued that at a more mundane, everyday level this mediating function was 'most critical' in polite conversations, smoothing over awkward social situations and avoiding unseemly quarrels over doctrine with shared religious sentiments 'as a kind of sublime version of discussing the weather' (Secord 2000: 162). For all its deistic dangers this was 'safe science' (Topham 1992).

Not only did natural theology provide common ground for diverse opinions but, according to Robert Young, it also provided the common context for the debate over our place in nature. In his examination of Victorian periodicals Young found a 'relatively integrated common culture of issues and publications' in the first half of the nineteenth century, a common intellectual context that was fragmenting by the 1870s:

> In the period from about 1800 to 1880, it seems to me that the role of theology seems to change from that of providing the *context* for the debate to that of acting as the point of view in a *conflict*. In the early debate the effort is to retain harmony between science and theology; after about 1850 increasing efforts are made to *separate* them or to make the claims of theology so abstract that they cannot come into conflict with the discoveries of science.
>
> (Young 1980: 76, original emphasis)

Questions about the fragmentation of a common culture and the conflict/ separation of science and religion will be returned to in the next chapter. For now, I want to stay with the earlier period and Young's claims about natural theology as the common context for debate. In accepting the general hypothesis there are, nevertheless, two caveats that need to be added. First, focusing on the later fragmentation can give a false impression of natural theology's previous unity (Brooke 1991; Yeo 1993). This does not undermine the idea of natural theology's commonality, but does emphasize its capacity to mediate between otherwise disparate intellectual positions. Secondly, Young's 'common' culture extends no further than the Victorian intelligentsia and its highbrow quarterly reviews. He explicitly sacrifices 'the social history of ideas conceived as the study of low-brow popular opinion' (Young 1980: 73). However, this is just the kind of social history that has been embarked upon in the years since Young's paper (see below).

The situation in the United States was slightly different. Americans were more concerned with consolidating a revolution than in fomenting or avoiding one, channelling their energies into building a boisterous democracy and expanding westward. As a consequence, although there were appeals to natural theology the primary justification for science was its utility. Not that the early nineteenth century was a great age for popular science in the US. In Jefferson's day science books only had a limited circulation and there was only a small demand for public lectures. The situation was particularly dire in the South where the population was poorly educated (that is, the section of the population that was allowed to be educated) and itinerant lecturers found travel difficult, towns small and crowds hard to gather. What science there was tended to focus on developments in Europe where many leading scientists were to go on individual pilgrimages. Nevertheless, some attempts were made to cultivate a taste for science among the educated classes 'by appeals to patriotism and civic pride, to natural theology and the utilitarian spirit of the age' (Greene 1958: 25). It was the 1830s and 1840s that first saw the rapid diffusion of science in the belief that science and democracy were natural partners for the Jacksonian 'common man' (Zochert 1974). The **Lyceum movement** of the 1830s which organized lectures across the country (though it was strongest in New England) gave about one fifth of its platform to public lectures on science, and on one occasion 5000 went to hear Louis Agassis speak in Boston (Bruce 1987: 116). Likewise, the Lowell lectures with their required theme of natural theology were very popular in the 1840s. However, developments were patchy and the North remained the home of American science – in 1850 Massachusetts printed five times as many copies of science periodicals than all the slave states put together (Bruce 1987: 59). Always the mix was the same: piety and utility.

By mid-century appeals to the usefulness of science had become a matter of faith that it would bring technological progress:

> The notion that science might sometimes yield material benefit was, of course, far from new . . . What was new was the dubious but spreading popular assumption that everything in technology was rooted in science . . . Professional scientists and technologists, who surely knew better, heartily endorsed the delusion, presumably because they wished it were true, hoped it might be some day, and in any case knew it to be in their interest.
>
> (Bruce 1987: 128)

It was mostly on utilitarian grounds that the US scientific community argued for public support. 'Pure science, it was repeatedly said, would ultimately yield applied science and economic benefits. In a democratic society, the state was justified in spending public money on these grounds and on no others' (Shapin

1990: 1004). Public money, however, also meant public accountability. The easy equation of science with democracy is shadowed by a less than easy relationship between the scientist's desire for autonomy and the public's desire for control. It may have been particularly acute in America, but it was to become a dominant theme in public science elsewhere – the tension between the democratic ideals of openness and freedom as core values of science and equally democratic public appeals to such values to make demands upon science. In different guises it will be a theme that recurs in the chapters that follow.

Science and social control

Education is a dangerous thing – at least, it should be if it is done properly. In a general sense, it can be seen as a revolutionary force with the power to transform lives, open minds and create a society filled with free-thinking, independent individuals. In a more specific sense, for early-nineteenth century Tories, Anglicans and aristocrats it could be seen as a revolutionary force of the godless French variety. As one magistrate was to put it succinctly, 'science and learning, if universally diffused, would speedily overturn the best constituted government on earth' (cited in Cardwell 1972: 38). On the other hand, science and education were said to be essential ingredients for a modern industrial nation (a familiar political mantra even today and another recurring theme for the following chapters). This posed a dilemma for reformers trying to cope with (or exploit) the problems of rapid industrialization and an emerging class structure: how to balance utilitarian ideals with middle-class fears. Pragmatic appeals to the utility of science were as common in Britain as they were in the US, but, as we shall see, there were more ways than one that science could be 'useful'.

The making of a class society was an active process – class identity being forged out of class conflict and class conflict sparked by developing identities. In Thompson's dynamic model we can see class not as a thing, but as a relationship arising from common experiences and defined by people as they live their own history (Thompson 1968: 9–11). The growing recognition of class interests was an educational and moral struggle – on the one hand, towards class consciousness, and on the other, the imposition of one's own class values upon the rest of society. As Perkin says, 'the primary conflict in the newly born class society of the early nineteenth century was a struggle for the minds and hearts of men' (Perkin 1969: 220). In the main, it was a struggle between the aristocratic, entrepreneurial and working-class ideals. However, there was also the 'forgotten' professional middle class of lawyers, doctors, public officials, journalists, professors and lecturers which played a part 'out of all proportion to its numbers' (Perkin 1969: 252). The efficient satisfaction of human needs through the application of expertise was the central dogma of the professional ideal and Jeremy Bentham was its apotheosis. His principle of utility ('the greatest happiness of the greatest number') was widely accepted, even by anti-Benthamite professionals (Perkin 1969). Conveniently, in tackling society's problems the pursuit of happiness through progress and efficiency needed just the sort of objective, disinterested solutions that could be provided by an emerging class whose profession was disinterested objectivity.

This professional sense of useful science is to be found in the early years of the **Royal Institution**. The ideal of the landed aristocrat was to be found in the gentleman amateur tradition of the **Royal Society** dating back to the seventeenth century. By contrast the first decades of the Royal Institution (RI), founded in 1799, were to see a shift from science as polite knowledge or agricultural improvement to science as a professional tool for an organized society. 'The impact of the Institution', says Morris Berman, 'was to articulate and consolidate ideologies of science which would ultimately usurp the aristocratic one . . . By bending science to entrepreneurial and professional purposes, the RI was the opening wedge in a major ideological shift' (Berman 1978: xxi). This new 'legal ideology of science', to use Berman's phrase, was the belief that science was a tool for the construction and maintenance of an orderly social machine. 'England, on this view, did not have social problems. Rather, it had "technical difficulties", and thus the various facets of the condition-of-England question and the modernization of the nation were scientific matters, amenable to scientific treatment. Thus was born, as a political force, the technological fix' (Berman 1978: 109). The scientific management of social problems marked a 'crucial reorientation in the public conception of science' and was given legitimacy through a range of activities at the RI such as concern for urban improvements like better water supplies and gas lighting as well as testimony in courts and to government inquiries (Berman 1978: xxi and 155). However, the application of professional expertise, says Berman, bestowed an 'aura of objectivity on a very biased status quo' and, in turn, science was 'recreated in capitalism's image' (189). It is through his examination of the social processes at work at the Royal Institution that Berman sees how science came to serve as 'the grammar of industrial society: its set of rules, its ideology' (xviii–xix).

The legal ideology of science that Berman writes about is most clearly expressed in Bentham's philosophy. For the Tories, Church and aristocracy education might be seen as dangerous, but for Bentham 'useful knowledge' could help foster social stability. This was the basic premise behind the work of the **Society for the Diffusion of Useful Knowledge** (SDUK), set up in 1826 and one of a number of Benthamite initiatives driven on by the circle of Whig reformers grouped around Henry Brougham. Through publications such as the *Penny Magazine*, the *Penny Cyclopaedia* and the *Library of Useful Knowledge*, the SDUK sought to counter the forces of dissent with cheap reading material. For example, at the height of the Reform crisis in 1832 the *Penny Magazine* tried to swamp out the seditious press with more wholesome material as part of the SDUK's attempt 'to divert the attention of working-class readers from revolutionary radical prints to more "rational" pursuits' (Topham 1992: 419). Much of what was deemed 'useful' was drawn from the natural sciences and there was also a heavy emphasis on science in a second Benthamite educational initiative. Established in the same year as the SDUK, London University was founded as a secular and progressive alternative to the Tory–Anglican domination of Oxford and Cambridge. From the start it offered courses in subjects that were largely neglected at the old universities, including chemistry, physics, botany and geography. Again Henry Brougham was a key player, and there was a large overlap of personnel between the university, the Royal Institution and the SDUK (Bentham still makes appearances at the university where his mummified body is wheeled out on special occasions).

In 1825 Brougham published a pamphlet, *Practical Observations on the Education of the People*, which was influential in the creation of the SDUK. It also provided the blueprints for other organizations which the SDUK saw itself as in command of – the mechanics' institutes. There had been a small number of institutes for artisans before, but in the mid-1820s, in part guided by Brougham, mechanics' institutes proliferated across the country to the extent that there was hardly a large town that did not have one. Naturally, with so many institutes one should expect a great diversity reflecting local circumstances, but a general pattern does emerge; institutes were set up by the middle classes for the working classes. Organized by physicians, merchants and 'enlightened' manufacturers, the institutes were intended as a medium for the dissemination of the entrepreneurial ideal and middle-class morality. For Steven Shapin and Barry Barnes in their important study of the institutes, the intention is quite clear. Like most British educational policy in the early nineteenth century, the founding of the mechanics' institutes 'was mainly informed by an interest in social control' (Shapin and Barnes 1977: 32). Faced with the problems of urbanization and industrialization (crime, irreligion, immorality, improvidence and, most importantly, drunkenness) the institutes' organizers felt the need for some form of active control as old certainties seemed to crumble around them. The end of the Napoleonic wars not only brought an economic slump but also the loss of a sense of solidarity in the face of a foreign threat. At the same time the Church, the traditional source of moral authority, could not keep up with the rapid pace of urbanization. Clearly something new was needed. Mechanics' institutes with their Benthamite emphasis on education seemed to offer a solution. Social stability would be promoted through the transformation of working-class values. The strategy was to target the labour aristocracy of mechanics and artisans so that they would affiliate themselves with the higher orders and, in turn, would influence the rest of the working class with their newly acquired middle-class values.

Science had a key part to play in the strategy. Examining the public statements of the movement's leaders, Shapin and Barnes show how it was believed that 'a regimen of scientific education for certain members of the working class would render them, and their class as a whole, more docile, less troublesome and more accepting of the emerging structure of industrial society' (1977: 32). How was science expected to do that?

> The study of nature would point out laws, relationships and the presence of design of which the worker would otherwise be unaware, and in being thus brought to perceive this rational organisation of nature would perceive (metaphorically or directly) the rational organisation of society also, in its harmonious relationship with the natural world. The effect of this perception would be to render behaviour and values more stable.
>
> (Shapin and Barnes 1977: 36)

Moreover, for science to gain credibility it had to be seen as 'value neutral' and 'objective'. This would also ensure common ground between the middle and upper classes, unlike contentious subjects like political economy. Likewise, the science presented avoided theory and conjecture (which would weaken its credibility) and instead emphasized the demonstration of facts and laws (i.e. showing how things 'really are'). This also accorded with the belief that the lower orders were incapable of grasping abstractions, a belief founded on a perceived correspondence between mental capacities and social order. At the top men were rational, profound and contemplative while the lower orders were sensual, impressionable and only capable of fragmentary thought. In the right environment this made them suitable material for control; in the wrong environment it left them open to all kinds of mischief. Much better to have a sober lecture on physics in the local institute than a drunken discussion of politics in the local pub (Shapin and Barnes 1977).

The extent to which the institutes were such instruments of social control might be questioned (Russell 1983), but historians are generally agreed upon one thing; given the stated aims of the institutes' founders and the clientele that they targeted, the movement was a failure. It might be seen as testimony to the strength of working-class autodidact culture that so many workers did actually turn up at the institutes, but could it really be expected that studying science would be their first choice of recreation after a hard day's toil in the factory? Not surprisingly, by the mid-1830s it was evident that increasingly those who went to the institutes were those who had more leisure, such as lower middle-class clerks and shopkeepers. Consequently, in response to popular taste, programmes of lectures went into decline and institute libraries began to stock more light fiction. Moreover, not only were the institutes losing the class for which they were intended, but those same mechanics who were targeted failed to respond to the social message that the institutes tried to convey. As Shapin and Barnes put it, the lower orders 'were evidently as well able as their betters to sniff ideology and reject it' (1977: 64).

If this were the case, then maybe one should look for a 'scentless ideology' as the key to maintaining hegemony. This is precisely the strategy taken by Roger Cooter in his study of early-nineteenth century **phrenology** where he aims to fill what he calls the 'wasteland between the sociology of collective behaviour and the history of scientific ideas' (1984: 2). Originally developed by Franz Joseph Gall at the end of the eighteenth century, phrenology drew a correlation between skull shape and mental faculties – the bumps on a person's skull corresponding to the development of the brain beneath it. The ideas were popularized in Britain with the publication in 1835 of George Combes's *Constitution of Man*, which was immediately seized upon as a vehicle for liberal social reform. By and large what distinguished those attracted to phrenology 'was their recently heightened sense of social worth being incommensurate with their place and power in the social process' (1984: 47). Phrenology was not simply a justification of the new socio-economic order but rather 'naturalised the emergent structures and relations of industrial capitalism by casting them into the descriptive and explanatory language of mental organisation and mental function' (113). The internalization of appropriate attitudes and behaviours was promoted by phrenology's inherent individualism and functionalism wrapped up in a language of self-help akin to that of the moralist Samuel Smiles. Much like modern schemes for self-improvement, it encouraged changing oneself to fit the system and made a deep impression among a self-improving section of the working class. In the 1830s and 1840s, says Cooter, there was a confluence of interests between those trying to popularize phrenology ('the ideological vanguard of the professionalising lower middle class') and literate artisans seeking an individualist rationale for the uncertainties brought by industrialization. For the artisans, however, the rhetoric of phrenology seemed egalitarian, democratic and anti-clerical. A phrenological map was as open to showing common structures as it was individual differences. It would be wrong, therefore, to see phrenology simply as a tool of bourgeois oppression, but rather as a way that reality was delimited to a common perspective – a 'mystified mediation of ideology' which in turn requires a 'deeper-than-normal demystification' for us to understand bourgeois hegemony (192, 165).

But the lower orders were able to do more than just resist ideological manipulation or negotiate 'aberrant' meanings of science. 'Halls of Science' and

Secular Sunday Schools, for example, were established as alternatives to more orthodox education. Moreover, workers showed that they were as well able to appropriate mechanics' institutes as they did other aspects of culture provided for them such as working men's clubs and organized sport. This is certainly what John Laurent shows in his study of mechanics' institutes in Yorkshire where the movement was most vigorous. Most studies of institutes have tended to focus on the period before 1850 and simply accepted that they were in decline afterwards. Laurent, however, made a careful study of institutes in Yorkshire in the second half of the century and what he found was far from the middle-class ideals of their founding fathers. The workers were there, but on their own terms:

> . . . the scientific education offered through Mechanics' Institutes was used by working-class people for their own purposes – namely, the development of an alternative social and economic philosophy. Specifically, this same scientific education fostered the growth of evolutionary socialism.
>
> In other words, through their own initiative the working classes used the scientific education offered them to transform agencies designed for social control into instruments for emancipation.
>
> (Laurent 1984: 586)

In the early part of the nineteenth century amongst radical artisans 'there was a strong belief that gentlemen naturalists had prostituted their gifts, that the upper classes had hijacked science and incorporated it into the apparatus of class enslavement' (Desmond 1987: 89). Science 'rightly understood' would bring social transformation. Consequently, from a radical perspective the educational initiatives of Henry Brougham were to be treated with suspicion, if not contempt (the Society for the Diffusion of Useful Knowledge was frequently ridiculed in the radical press). For radicals what was more important was an understanding of economic exploitation, social domination and the class character of the state; in short, the construction and diffusion of their own '*really* useful knowledge' (Johnson 1979).

Inventing 'popular science'

So far we have looked at the variety of meanings attached to popular science, attempts to control those meanings as a way of transmitting middle-class values and the resistance to such attempts. However, the importance of this period lies not just in the egalitarian rhetoric of radicals nor in bourgeois ideological manipulation, but in the science that artisans did for themselves. For example, like phrenology, one of the great attractions of **mesmerism** or 'animal magnetism' was its accessibility; its raw material (another person) was readily available and no expensive equipment was needed. Moreover, as Alison Winter has argued, it was not at all clear who controlled this 'new science'. For men such as John Elliotson, Professor of Practical Medicine at University College London, mesmerism was seen as a branch of materialist physiology to be used in an attack on 'superstition'. For the numerous itinerant lecturers, however, 'science, reform and progress were as much the property of artisans, provincials and travellers as they were of the middle-class metropolitan professionals' (Winter 1994: 330). Representing themselves as validators of the 'common man', they struggled to establish the industrial towns of the provinces as new authoritative sites. The work of lecturers such as Spencer Timothy Hall was 'grounded implicitly in a natural world which was fully accessible to the general public, should they choose to make their own experiments' (332). We should not dismiss mesmerism, says Winter, simply as 'fringe' or 'popular', but instead should shift our attention 'towards a history of the politics of appropriation and participation' (337). Such a history would also highlight the uncertainties of the period:

> ... rather than portraying a collection of elite scientists and doctors asserting their expertise in the face of a fringe counter-culture, a picture emerges of orthodoxy and fringe emerging *together*, constructed and reconstructed during a period of cultural turbulence, when the nature of orthodox knowledge was, to varying degrees in different branches of science and medicine, ambiguous.
>
> (Winter 1994: 338)

Such ambiguities are also to be seen in the position of the artisan botanists studied by Anne Secord (1994), not so much in the knowledge they possessed but in their right to participate in the scientific enterprise, in their right to claim that they were *botanists*. Their activity was just the type of rational recreation that middle-class reformers encouraged but, like many other working-class activities, societies usually met in pubs, the location for just the sort of immorality that the rational recreation was supposed to replace. Secord sees the artisan botanists as an 'intersection of "popular" and "elite" culture' (270) existing in a social network of gentleman botanists, medical botanists, herbalists, gardeners, nurserymen and plant dealers. At a time when particular trade skills were being undermined by industrialization, botanical skill could restore a sense of status and respectability, but this 'property of skill' was also part of a collective craft; as one artisan botanist put it, 'we instruct one another by continually meeting together; so that the knowledge of one becomes the knowledge of all' (cited 280). Such collective practice, seeking only a fair exchange of plant and information, was at odds with the more individualist practices of the gentleman botanists (who had increasing control over botanical knowledge through their control of print media) and the plant dealers (always with an eye on profit). In the end, these ambiguities would be resolved by the marginalization of popular practice:

> Science was contested territory in the first half of the nineteenth century. For many, including some in the scientific elite, the contest revolved around the issue of whether science should be popular, in the sense of being open to a wide range of participants (including women and artisans) who could contribute to and benefit from the production of knowledge. Increasingly, however, the term 'popular science' was used by the dominant culture to signify bodies of literature and scientific activity that had little or no interaction with elite science . . . More than any other area of knowledge production, scientific practice became increasingly associated with specific sites from which 'the people' were excluded.
>
> (Secord 1994: 297)

In short, the contest was about who could participate and on what terms. The result of the contest, as Secord says, was 'the redefinition of popular science' (299).

This redefinition was at the expense of a much more inclusive, participatory form of popular science, what Susan Sheets-Pyenson (1985) calls 'low science'. In her examination of mid-century popular science periodicals she found that often the editors were 'not mere popularizers of high scientific activity, but rather the architects of an alternative "low scientific culture" ' (552), encouraging amateur activity and emphasizing the universal accessibility of science. Promoting an experiential and inductivist philosophy of science, the magazines called on all their readers to become members of what was seen as the 'Republic of Science' where no specialist knowledge was needed, only an eagerness to collect facts based on simple observations. Again, however, we find the same shift in what was meant by popular science. Where once the magazines sought to develop their own domain of criticism and investigation, often in opposition to the 'high' scientific establishment, by the 1860s 'a younger generation of scientists began to try to mould the Republic of Science's amateur practitioners into sympathetic supporters of professional high science' (563). The magazines became, in Sheets-Pyenson's words, 'accomplices of the high scientific community' and she draws on Perkin's account of the changes in British society when she writes of the periodicals 'replacing the "entrepreneurial ideal" of the self-made science worker with the "professional ideal" of the scientific expert' (555; see also Barton 1998a).

To the ambiguities surrounding popular practices we must also add the proliferation of texts. This was the age of 'steam reading' when the application of steam power to printing and transportation revolutionized the production and distribution of books and periodicals. The early decades of the nineteenth century, says Secord:

> witnessed the greatest transformation in human communication since the Renaissance. Mechanised presses, machine-made paper, railway distribution, improved education, and the penny post played a major part in opening the floodgates to a vastly increased reading public. Only now, with the advent of electronic communication, are we undergoing a period of equal change.
>
> (Secord 2000: 2)

This is especially important when we consider the periodical press which was by its very nature open-ended and ephemeral, making it particularly suited to the contestation of ideas, public dialogue and controversy (see Henson *et al*. 2004). In recent years the importance of science in Victorian periodicals has been recognized by historians and much good work has been done including the setting up of an online resource[1] (Cantor *et al*. 2004; Cantor and Shuttleworth 2004). What is clear in many of these studies is that with the diversity and proliferation of texts we must also expect a corresponding diversity and proliferation of readings.

However, so far very little work has been done on how texts were read. What is required, says Jonathan R. Topham, 'is an approach that, while taking seriously the attempts of authors and publishers to police the reading of the text, also recovers the agency of readers themselves' (Topham 1998: 235). In trying to go 'beyond the common context' proposed by Robert Young, Topham adopts the 'communication circuit' suggested by Robert Darnton (1990) to see how the contested meanings of science amongst a diversity of readers fed back into the production of fresh scientific texts. In the main, his attention has been focused on the *Bridgewater Treatises*, a series of volumes 'on the Power, Wisdom and Goodness of God as manifested in Creation' written by seven prominent scientists together with one theologian and published 1833–6. Although this was a single publishing venture funded at the bequest of the eighth Earl of Bridgewater there was no common purpose amongst the authors and, more importantly, several of the authors intended their work to be read at different levels, often presenting original research to lay readers:

> Thus we have not only to contend with *readers* who actively multiplied the meanings of these works, but also with the *authors* who intended their meanings to be multiple. Moreover, the ambiguities inherent in the Bridgewater Treatises are particularly profound: these were works the genre of which could not easily be defined. They were widely reviewed

both in religious and in specialist journals; and they were read both by scientific experts and by laypeople.

(Topham 1998: 239)

Read in a variety of contexts the books could carry radically different meanings – as specialist science and subjects of fashionable conversation, topics for domestic intercourse or public controversy, a reputable compendium of science and an appropriate theology of nature. The authors and publishers may have been surprised at the success of the series, but its ability to encompass such divergent reading contexts did show the potential for a new genre of 'popular science' book.

That potential was fully realized in what was quite possibly the most sensational book published in Victorian Britain: *Vestiges of the Natural History of Creation*. It is a delightful book, a lucid, stimulating and comprehensive guided tour of God's creation from the formation of the solar system through the geological history of the Earth to the origin and development of life upon it. Written by Robert Chambers, the book was published anonymously in 1844 and very quickly went through several editions. In an impressive study of the book and its readers, James Secord stresses that *Vestiges* was 'a literary hybrid . . . whose status within accepted genres of fiction, science and philosophy was indeterminate' (Secord 2000: 522). Using progressive development as its central structuring idea enabled the book to meet a popular demand for works of general synthesis, yet at the same time its narrative form made it akin to a novel (which in turn might make it more readable but less credible). Indeed, the distinction of form and content is blurred in the act of reading which affirms progress in nature through causal language, a temporal sequence and the forward-directed process of page turning (2000: 101). This indeterminacy of genre and form, of course, would have been compounded by the anonymity of the author which denied the reader any clues as to how the book should be read. Without a fixed point of reference the text was more open to variant readings and its 'deep anonymity meant that *Vestiges* remained an "open" text for a very long time' (24).

Chambers once said that he wanted to be 'the essayist of the middle class' and in his journalistic writings for his own *Chambers' Edinburgh Journal* he assumed the character of an intimate acquaintance on a weekly visit (2000: 97–8). This style is carried over into the anonymous *Vestiges* where the narrative voice is that of a patient and modest companion. The delicate balance between informative authority and friendly visitor is carefully struck in the opening sentence:

It is familiar knowledge that the earth which we inhabit is a globe of somewhat less than 8000 miles in diameter, being one of a series of eleven which revolves at different distances around the sun, and some of which have satellites in like manner revolving around them.

(Cited in Secord 2000: 98)

Thus the book begins with a declaration of facts, but presented as 'familiar knowledge' shared with the reader and avoiding blunt didacticism with a disarming imprecision when it comes to figures ('somewhat less than 8000'). This was a new voice for a new genre, something which Chambers accomplished by drawing on his journalistic experience, reflexive writings on science that were popular in the 1830s and also, in part, the historical novels of Walter Scott for their narrative structure:

> Reintroducing a causal account of all natural phenomena demanded the creation of an appropriate literary form. Any direct debts to the historical novel had to be muted, lest controversial claims be dismissed as imaginative fantasies (which some readers did anyway). Univocal modes of address typical of law, mathematics, or physics would be equally inappropriate. Chambers needed to create not only a new vision of creation, but a narrative voice through which to speak to potential readers.
>
> (Secord 2000: 97)

Chambers demanded a high level of trust from his readers. Many of the ideas he was putting forward in *Vestiges* would have been profoundly shocking to some of them. For example, as we saw earlier there was a close association between the idea of progressive development and radical, even revolutionary, politics. 'Progress' might provide a convenient narrative structuring device, but if not handled carefully could be read as making humans no more than beasts or supporting the Enlightenment ideal of perfectibility (and see what that led to in France). Moreover, as Secord writes, 'systematic treatises downplayed or rejected the evolutionary implications of philosophical anatomy because it could be so readily associated with infidelity, pornography or the unstamped press' (2000: 64) – small wonder that Darwin delayed publishing about evolution for so long (see next chapter). It was essential, therefore, for Chambers to build a sense of trust, and the growing relationship between implied narrator and reader runs as a sub-plot throughout the book (98). This becomes crucial at the more speculative and controversial moments in the story, such as trying to explain the origin of life. However, having established that trust and giving due weight to scientific authority, Chambers was able to invite the reader, as a friend, to share in a confidential discussion and go beyond established knowledge (101–5).

It was, perhaps, this combination of being friendly and speculative that made *Vestiges* so popular, but which also provoked the fiercest attacks from its critics.

The most famous attack appeared in the *Edinburgh Review* in a piece written by Adam Sedgwick, a professor of geology who thought the book's author seduced female readers 'with the serpent coils of a false philosophy . . . to talk familiarly with him of things without raising a blush upon a modest cheek' (cited in Gillispie 1959: 149–50). Sedgwick, however, was at his most vitriolic in his private correspondence where he confessed to having thrown the book down in disgust:

> If the book be true, the labours of sober induction are in vain; religion is a lie; human law is a mass of folly, and a base injustice; morality is moonshine; our labours for the black people of Africa were works of madmen; and man and woman are only better beasts!
>
> (cited in Gillispie 1959: 165)

Faced with this abhorrent example of 'gross credulity and rank infidelity joined in unlawful marriage, and breeding a deformed progeny of unnatural conclusions' (cited in Gillispie 1959: 165), the task of the reviewer, thought Sedgwick, was to stamp with 'an iron heel upon the head of the filthy abortion, and put an end to its crawlings' (cited in Secord 2000: 242). For Sedgwick, *Vestiges* was an abomination not least because he suspected it had been written by a woman. Science was a masculine activity – 'the ascent up the hill of science is rugged and thorny and ill-fitted for the drapery of a petticoat' (cited in Secord 2000: 243) – and original science did not come from drawing rooms and dinner parties, newspapers and lectures. However, we should not dismiss Sedgwick as the kind of narrow-minded reactionary we are often too quick to see as being typically Victorian. He was a leading scientist who had done much to establish the study of geology at Cambridge and supported efforts at popular education such as the SDUK and the mechanics' institutes. Nevertheless, what was clearly important for Sedgwick was who was entitled to do science and how it should be done.

The most common description in the attacks on *Vestiges* was 'dangerous'. It was seen as a threat not just to the natural order of the social world, but to science itself. The authority of science was a significant issue because of the insecure status of science at a time when it still had a close relationship with general culture. Leading scientists spent an extraordinary amount of effort dismissing a book they all thought was worthless in part because what was at stake was the meaning of their own scientific practice. As Richard Yeo argues, '. . . to preserve the religious and social respectability of science, it was crucial to show not only that the theories in the book were false and dangerous, but that the work itself could not be classified as "science" ' (Yeo 1984: 11). By appealing directly to the public, Chambers had frightened the scientific community with the prospect that 'the criterion of popularity would come to decide the acceptability, and even the truth, of ideas' and, to make matters worse, the very popularity of *Vestiges* reinforced anxieties that the reading public were ill-informed and unscientific (1984: 7). More specifically, as a work of grand speculation by an unrecognized amateur, *Vestiges* violated the principle that theory should be left to professionals whose status as theorists was sanctioned by their institutional positions. By appealing to 'ordinary readers' to participate in a broad, speculative natural philosophy 'Chambers challenged the right of scientific authorities to restrict the scope of conjecture in science and proclaimed the right of the lay person to speculate in the field of knowledge' (27).

Thus, excluding the public became a defining feature of what it meant to be 'scientific'. In this chapter we have seen a bewildering array of meanings of science: radical, materialist and atheistic; inspired or tainted by the French Revolution; an expression of utilitarianism or natural theology; useful knowledge for social stability and really useful knowledge for social transformation; safe science and dangerous science. The language has been of ambiguities, diversity, the proliferation of texts and the plurality of readings. Alison Winter has written of the 'dizzying variety' of arenas for the practice and communication of science in the early Victorian period, a 'fluid chaotic state of affairs' when science was 'less defined' (Winter 1997). It was in an attempt to define science that William Whewell coined the term 'scientist' in 1833. For Whewell, science was not defined by its content but rather as a particular type of knowledge, and by focusing on the practice of the sciences it could show their underlying unity at a time when they were characterized by increasingly specialized languages, journals, institutions and equipment. Excluding the public can be seen as part of this felt need for unity amongst practitioners with the growing self-consciousness of themselves as a group. However, excluding the public also means that the term 'popular science' becomes an oxymoron, a self-contradiction, since something cannot be both public and scientific. In seeking to define science, 'popular science' had to be redefined. No longer could it properly stand for that egalitarian participation in the Republic of Science, but rather it was to be the science which is popularized, and in this new sense emerged as a stable publishing genre. 'Scientist' and 'popularization' was a twin birth; each helps us to understand the other. Inventing 'popular science' helped to define what science was.

Note

1 The SciPer project based at the Universities of Leeds and Sheffield set up an online resource at *www.sciper.org*.

Further reading

Cooter, R. (1984) *The Cultural Meaning of Popular Science*. Cambridge: Cambridge University Press.

Desmond, A. (1989) *The Politics of Evolution: Morphology, Medicine and Reform in Radical London*. Chicago, IL: University of Chicago Press.

Morrell, J. and Thackray, A. (eds) (1981) *Gentlemen of Science: Early Years of the British Association for the Advancement of Science*. Oxford: Clarendon Press.

Secord, J.A. (2000) *Victorian Sensation: The Extraordinary Publication, Reception, and Secret Authorship of Vestiges of the Natural History of Creation*. Chicago, IL: Chicago University Press.

Yeo, R. (1993) *Defining Science: William Whewell, Natural Knowledge, and Public Debate in Early Victorian Britain*. Cambridge: Cambridge University Press.

2 | PROGRESS AND PROFESSIONALISM

In the nineteenth century advances in science and technology became embodiments of the Enlightenment idea of Progress. Moreover, the advance of science was matched by the advance of the scientist. It is to the third quarter of the nineteenth century that Robert V. Bruce (1987) looks for the 'launching of modern American science', while in Britain previous developments in the organization of science were, as Cardwell puts it, only a 'preface' for what was to come (1972: 70). This chapter will look at the professionalization of science and the public's belief in progress. Together these constitute not just a faith in the scientist but also a confidence in the historical process, a process that increasingly appeared in evolutionary guise. It was, moreover, a confidence not to be shaken by major restructuring in the economies on both sides of the Atlantic, and a bloody civil war in the US.

From 1861 to 1865 the United States did its best to tear itself apart. The Civil War was the bloodiest war in American history, claiming more American lives than all other wars put together – including the Second World War and Vietnam. The scale of the slaughter in large part arose because of the combination of old military tactics (such as massed formations) with new military technology (such as breech-loading rifles and machine guns). It was also due to the scale of the manufacturing for that new technology. Modern mass armies need modern mass production to supply them and the Civil War was the first to show the deadly potential of that simple fact. The factory system, particularly applied to the manufacture of textiles, had already shown what was possible when all aspects of the production process were brought together under one roof. This rationalization was pushed a step further by what became known as the American System of manufacture. Where once a single item might have been made by a skilled worker (or even several skilled workers), under the American System an unskilled or semi-skilled workforce would fit together vast quantities from a collection of machine-made, standardized and interchangeable parts. The first industry to benefit from this system was the American armaments industry: the first war to feel its consequences the American Civil War.

After the war the system was extended to the manufacture of other goods in other countries and the late nineteenth century saw the mass production of such things as sewing machines, bicycles, phonographs and eventually auto-mobiles (see next chapter). This mass production of new technologies was a typical feature of what some historians call the Second Industrial Revolution. Whereas in the eighteenth century the first wave of industrialization had princi-pally been low-tech and driven by a multitude of small-factory owners, in the latter half of the nineteenth century the second wave was much more techno-logically dependent and concentrated ownership into the hands of a few big businesses. Previous industrialization had relied on technologies that could be developed by skilled workers with little scientific knowledge. Now, not only were many consumer goods essentially the products of applied science, but whole new industries such as the chemical and electrical industries were entirely science-based. Consequently, this second phase required a much closer relation-ship between industrialists, technologists and scientists, and as business became consolidated into ever larger corporations (Hobsbawm 1977 and 1987; Brogan 1999: 383–93), so too the scientific community became consolidated into pro-fessional institutions (Cardwell 1972; Russell 1983). The restructuring of capit-alism was matched step by step with the restructuring of science; both were transformed in the third quarter of the nineteenth century so that by the 1880s the strength of each could be seen in the increasing concentration of capital, labour and control (Bruce 1987). For the public, such concentration meant that science was increasingly something that was best left to the professionals.

The rise of the expert

At the end of the eighteenth century, for radicals like Priestley and Beddoes the importance of chemistry was as a part of a programme of social and intel-lectual progress. As Jan Golinski has shown, the rhetoric of Priestley's work 'was aimed at diffusing factual knowledge among as wide an audience as pos-sible by allowing them to witness, or if possible to replicate, experimental findings'. Through 'direct experience' people would be freed from the 'ignor-ance on which corrupt authority was founded' (Golinski 1992: 8). In contrast, at the start of the nineteenth century, in his presentations at the newly formed Royal Institution Humphrey Davy used a rhetoric that 'described experimental science as a genteel, theologically safe, and socially conservative activity' (1992: 285), projecting an image of the scientific genius to an admiring audience. 'The form of public science that Davy constructed', says Golinski, 'was in marked contrast to that favoured by Priestley. Far from being invited to share in the production of scientific knowledge by replicating experiments, Davy's public audience was expected to remain entirely passive, awed by the power of the philosopher and his instruments, and accepting his interpretation of phenomena' (1992: 9). The differences between Priestley and Davy encapsulate the distinction between the Enlightenment ideal of 'experience' and the early nineteenth-century construction of 'expertise'. For Davy, new – and expensive – instrumental resources and refined experimental practices needed specialist expertise built on intensive practical training and exclusive knowledge. The formation of a new disciplined community of chemists 'became embodied in instruments, techniques, and modes of discourse' which in turn meant less direct involvement from the lay public (1992: 9–10, 284).

What happened in the second half of the nineteenth century was the institutionalization of this exclusivity, thereby transforming the idea of expertise into that of the professional expert.

In the previous chapter we noted Perkin's account of how entrepreneurial, aristocratic and working-class ideals had struggled for moral and cultural supremacy in the early formation of a class society in Britain. We can now pick up this story and take it into the mid-Victorian decades, a key period not only for the triumph of the entrepreneurial ideal, but also for 'the emergence and consolidation of the leading professions, and for the crystallization of the professional ideal as a separate entity' (Perkin 1969: 428). The central dogma of the professional ideal, it will be recalled, was a Benthamite faith in the efficient application of disinterested expertise as a solution for social problems, and at first the two ideals worked closely together. 'The cheap efficient government demanded by the entrepreneurial ideal could only be provided by expert professional administrators selected by merit' (320). Yet the success in bringing about governmental reform exposed a tension between the businessman's desire for *laissez-faire* cheapness and the professional's desire for interventionalist efficiency. The 1860s proved to be a turning point, with more state intervention and regulation in various aspects of Victorian life – factory inspections, sanitation, food standards, pollution from chemical factories, contagious diseases – all of which needed some form of professional expertise and in most cases some form of scientific training. Not surprisingly, in the mid-Victorian period professional occupations constituted a substantial and growing part of the middle class. Between 1841 and 1881 while the general population had increased by two thirds, the number of people in professional occupations had trebled (429).

New demands on science meant also a stronger desire on the part of scientific practitioners to protect the integrity and status of their practice. Earlier scientific societies had often recruited their members largely on the basis simply of having an interest in science (or merely a desire to socialize with scientists). The pattern in the second half of the century was the formation of professional institutes, entry into which was restricted to those possessing the necessary scientific ability.

> Beginning with the British Medical Association in 1856 a new and much larger wave of professional institutions came into existence for doctors, dentists, mechanical, mining and electrical engineers, naval architects, accountants, surveyors, chemists, teachers and others, expressly to exclude quacks and charlatans who put profit before professional service.
>
> (Perkin 1969: 429)

The position of chemists in Britain provides a good example. Increased state interest in issues such as food adulteration and pollution had increased demand for chemical analysts, but there were numerous cases where the people employed to carry out the analyses had little or no relevant training. In response chemists formed the Institute of Chemistry in 1877. Its objectives were not only to promote the study and application of chemistry, but also 'To ensure that persons practising as Consulting Chemists, or as Analytical Chemists, are qualified by study and training for the competent discharge of the duties they undertake' (cited in Russell 1983: 229).

The work of Frank M. Turner (1974, 1978 and 1980) is especially useful in providing a framework to help us understand this process of professionalization and exclusion. Scientists, says Turner, need to present a public justification for their activities since they are part of a larger social order and dependent upon institutions for their good will, patronage and support. 'The body of rhetoric, argument, and polemic produced in this process may be termed *public science*, and those who sustain the enterprise may be regarded as *public scientists*' (Turner 1980: 589). According to Turner, 'the nineteenth and early twentieth centuries constituted the premier age of British public science' (590) and can be divided into three phases:

1   *up to mid-century* when public scientists urged 'the importance of science as a mode of useful knowledge, an instrument of self-improvement, an aid to profitable, rational, and usually individualistic economic activity, and a pillar of natural religion';

2   *mid-1840s to late 1870s* when public scientists used science 'to challenge the cultural dominance of the clergy, to attack religion and metaphysics in scientific thought, and to forge a genuinely self-conscious professional scientific community based on science pursued

according to strictly naturalistic premises. They repeatedly equated the progress of science with the progress of civilisation';

3   *approximately 1875 onwards* when '. . . science came to be portrayed as a means to create and educate better citizens for state service and stable politics, and to ensure the military security and economic efficiency of the nation . . . politicians and complacent manufacturers replaced priests and obscurantist clergy as the primary perceived enemy of the progress and application of scientific knowledge'.

(Turner 1980: 591–2)

Much of what Turner says about phase one was looked at in Chapter 1. Much of what he says about phase three will be discussed in Chapter 3. It is phase two that concerns us at present. Moreover, although Turner's work is based principally upon science and culture in Britain we can see from Robert V. Bruce's work that a similar case can be made for the 'launching of American science' between 1846 and 1876 (Bruce 1987).

'During the early stages of professionalism', writes Turner (1978), 'an elite from the emerging professional group attempts to project a new public image by formulating codes of ethics, strengthening professional organizations, establishing professional schools, penetrating existing educational institutions, and dispersing information to the general public' (359). Inevitably this leads to conflict both within and outside the professionalizing group.

Within the group they must raise standards of competence, foster a common bond of purpose, and subject practitioners to the judgment of peers rather than external social or intellectual authorities. Outside they must establish the independence of the would-be professional group, its right of self-definition, and its self-generating role in the social order.

(360)

We can see this process at work from the 1840s onwards when 'the size, character, structure, ideology, and leadership of the Victorian scientific world underwent considerable transformation' (361). For example, between 1850 and 1880, the number of faculty members teaching physics at universities in the UK rose from 19 to 50, and the total membership of major scientific societies more than doubled. Moreover, at the same time a group of ambitious young scientists took up the public championship of professionalized science. The 'X' Club was a small, informal group of friends that set itself the task of raising the public profile of science and furthering the cause of science education. (The American equivalent would be the 'Lazzaroni' centred upon Alexander Dallas Bache and Joseph Henry – see Bruce 1987.) By the 1870s its members – including T.H. Huxley and John Tyndall, two of the great popularizers of

Victorian science – were to establish themselves as a 'major segment of the elite of the Victorian scientific world' (362). Not only did they hold key positions in various leading scientific societies (three were to become presidents of the Royal Society) but they also helped to found the periodical *Nature* (still the world's leading scientific journal), wrote text books, gave popular lectures, advised government commissions, and campaigned for technical education and the endowment of research.

Establishing the professional status of the scientific community meant also asserting its independence. From the 1850s onward the scientists' conscious move toward greater professionalism involved their 'social and intellectual emancipation from theology and financial independence from aristocratic patronage' (Turner 1974: 12). Science had once looked to religion for legitimation, but now that the scientific community was more firmly established many scientists saw religion as a rival. What was at stake was the cultural leadership of Britain. Science and religion may not necessarily be opposed (see for example Brooke 1991; and Lindberg and Numbers 1986 and 2003) but there was, as Turner says, a 'professional dimension' to the conflict. For Huxley and Tyndall, being members of the X Club, attacking religion and popularizing science were all part of the same drive to replace the Christian metaphysical foundations for society with ones that were rational, scientific and secular. As far as science was concerned the triumph of the professional ideal was also the triumph of Victorian scientific naturalism.

Rejecting supernaturalism and metaphysics, scientific naturalism instead sought to explain nature and society with, and only with, the methods and laws of empirical science. 'By claiming their own **epistemology** as the exclusive foundation for legitimate science and as the correct model for knowledge generally, the professionalizing scientists sought to undermine the intellectual legitimacy of alternative modes of scientific thought and practice' (Turner 1978: 364). Quite naturally this brought them into conflict not only with the supporters of organized religion but also with the religiously minded within their own scientific community. Indeed:

> . . . much of the harshest rhetoric stemmed from the determination of the aggressive, professionally minded scientists to exorcise from their ranks clergymen–scientists and lay scientists who regarded the study of physical nature as serving natural theology or as standing subordinate to theology and religious authority.
>
> (Turner 1978: 364)

It was, to all intents and purposes, a turf war. Tyndall made this clear in 1874 with his notorious presidential address at the Belfast meeting of the **British Association for the Advancement of Science**. Men of science, he said, 'claim, and . . . shall wrest from theology, the entire domain of cosmological theory. All schemes and systems which infringe upon the domain of science must, in so far as they do this, submit to its control, and relinquish all thought of controlling it' (cited in Turner 1978: 373).

As far as the public were concerned Tyndall may have gone a little too far in his Belfast address. He was quickly branded as a materialist by the press and there were calls for him to be tried for blasphemy. As Bernard Lightman has shown:

> In the eyes of his detractors Tyndall symbolized everything that was wrong with modern science, especially the pretensions of scientific naturalists to replace the Christian clergy as members of the cultural elite. After Belfast, the periodical press became a significant site of resistance to the cultural authority of scientific naturalists, part of a growing disillusionment with the attempts of Tyndall and his allies to dominate science, and through it, the fate of British society.
>
> (Lightman 2004: 230)

When scientific naturalism excluded religious thinking from the scientific enterprise those features that were held in common between religion and the public (in particular **anthropomorphism, anthropocentricism** and **teleology**) were excluded with it. In doing so it tried 'to eject from what counted as scientific thinking those elements that had previously linked public and scientific culture' (Shapin 1990: 996). As a result, scientific naturalism is as significant for science–public relations as it is for those between science and religion, 'establishing and validating important modern social and cultural boundaries between science and the public' (Shapin 1990: 991). Steven Shapin has written:

> Scientists (now properly so called) were the only experts with a legitimate interest in, and with legitimate rights to pronounce upon, the domain of secularised nature. The public were told to expect substantial utilitarian benefits from the activities of authentic scientists (indeed, they were told that they had already enjoyed such benefits); but they were at the same time instructed that the only proper role that could be served by the public was to encourage and support the programmes of work and conceptions decided upon by autonomous scientists.
>
> (Shapin 1990: 1000)

It is worth recalling from Chapter 1 that popular science magazines at this time were to shift from encouraging activity in 'low science' to promoting support for 'high science'. The magazines became, in Sheets-Pyenson's words, 'accomplices of the high scientific community' and she draws on Perkin's account of the changes in British society when she writes of the periodicals 'replacing the "entrepreneurial ideal" of the self-made science worker with the "professional ideal" of the scientific expert' (Sheets-Pyenson 1985: 555; see also Barton 1998b).

Popular culture, popular press, popular science

It would seem that the role expected of the public was simply to cheer from the sidelines. This would be in line with other aspects of popular culture in late Victorian Britain (for a more detailed account of what follows see Broks 1996: 1–52). Of particular significance is the commercialization of both popular culture and the popular press. For many workers the second half of the century had seen a steady reduction in working hours and a rise in real wages. At the same time cheap imported foods, though they may have been seen as a threat by farmers and landowners in the Great Depression of the 1880s, were a godsend for the masses on low incomes. By modern standards the changes might seem modest but to the people involved it could mean a substantial improvement to their quality of life – a change from a life of mere subsistence to one which opened up the possibility of simple luxuries and simple pleasures such as a bicycle, a sewing machine, a day at the seaside, or going to the music hall. As leisure became an increasingly important part of popular culture, so new and powerful leisure industries grew to meet demand. The scale of these industries resulted in a spiral of commercialization to meet the increased costs. For example, this is the period when professional football was developed – bigger stadia had to be built to accommodate the larger crowds who were needed to pay for the professional players who drew in larger crowds who increased profits and helped pay for the bigger grounds. The same was true for the professionalization and commercialization of the Victorian music hall. The role of the public was to pay up and watch.

Thus, we can see how the commercialization of popular culture was transforming the British public from participants to consumers. A similar story can be told for the commercialization of the popular press. The growth in periodical literature – and in particular the growth of mass circulation family magazines – was very much part of the late nineteenth-century consumer revolution. One consequence of this was a corresponding revolution in the economic basis of the press – the greatest profits were to be found in advertising revenues. Publications were now driven by a need to increase circulation as a way of attracting advertisers and as the market expanded and running costs went up so the traditional small-scale proprietorial structures were replaced by large-scale groups of newspapers and magazines. The flotation of such corporations as public companies completed the transformation of periodicals from public servants or instruments of political influence into financial investments. The bottom line was what mattered and once again the public's role was to pay up and consume.

The transformation of the popular press is especially important for our understanding of popular science since it was through the new commercialized mass media that most people viewed most of the world, including science. With circulation the *sine qua non* of commercial success it was necessary to please, or at least avoid offending, as many readers as possible. The result was the reproduction of conventional opinion and this is what makes the popular press so important for the historian since 'it represents and articulates, as nothing else does, what was ordinary about Victorian Britain' (Shattock and Wolff 1982: xv). On this basis we should be able to look to the mass circulation periodicals for conventional opinions on science.

The ordinariness of mass periodical science is further highlighted when we consider who wrote it. Although there was a rich diversity of contributors which makes a nonsense of trying to construct a single 'type' of science contributor, in most cases one thing was clear: they were historical nonentities. The popularizers of science seemed to have been very ordinary themselves; literary hacks who have failed to leave a trace in any biographical dictionary, catalogue of books or index of articles. They are the wraiths of the reading room at the British Museum – so vividly captured in George Gissing's novel *New Grub Street* – mechanically producing their quota of words in a desperate effort to maintain at least a shabby gentility. Ignorance was often taken to be a necessary prerequisite. The editor W.T. Stead gave the following advice:

> In editing a newspaper, never employ an expert to write a popular article on his own subject, better employ someone who knows nothing about it to tap the expert's brains, and write the article, sending the proof to the expert to correct. If the expert writes he will always forget that he is not writing for experts but for the public, and will assume that they need not be told things which, although familiar to him as ABC, are nevertheless totally unknown to the general reader.
>
> (Stead 1906: 297)

One contributor put it more succinctly. He always asked people lots of questions, he said, because, 'a healthy ignorance is useful to the purveyor of hastily collected facts' (cited in Broks 1996: 34). For a 'scissors and paste' production such as the immensely popular *Tit-Bits*, the journalists' role was reduced even further – they simply had to find a journal article, cut out the final paragraph and then reprint it. In this way the whole process of science would, quite literally, be cut down to the results, the 'facts', that it produced. Much of what can be found in the late Victorian popular press can be put under the heading of 'new journalism', a term coined by Matthew Arnold and which quickly became the conventional description for developments in the press from the 1880s onwards. Typographically, innovations included shorter paragraphs, bigger headlines and the use of more illustrations. Journalistically, it was characterized by a concentration on the human interest story and, possibly its most significant feature, the interview. It included an almost prurient fascination with the private lives of the rich and famous, presenting the personal minutiae about royalty, statesmen, music hall stars, and also of scientists. Although scientific practice may have valued the absence or anonymity of the scientist in the pretence of objectivity, 'by creating "public figures" and "personalities", the new journalism helped to personalise an otherwise impersonal process' (Broks 1996: 47).

Readers were rarely invited to participate in science (Broks 1996: 37), but we must be careful before we dismiss them simply as *passive* consumers. As Gowan Dawson (2004) argues in his study of the *Review of Reviews*, which saw itself as the flagship of the new journalism, 'interviews and other personality-based journalism . . . were not merely passive and trivializing modes of popularization'. For W.T. Stead, editor of the *Review of Reviews*, the format of the interview 'afforded a further means of critiquing the increasingly hierarchical nature of professional science, and formed part of a wider campaign against the alleged arrogance of scientific experts' (2004: 192). In similar vein, readers were encouraged to send in their own observations (of ghost sightings) to counter the 'condescending and intolerant scepticism exhibited by professional scientific experts' (193). For Dawson, the innovative methods of science popularization offered by the new journalism 'make it clear that the growing division between "elite" science and public discourse in the final decades of the nineteenth century was contested much more actively than has generally been recognised' (194–5). It is also worth recalling that, as we saw in Chapter 1, even if readers are not encouraged to engage in scientific activities they are never passive with respect to the construction of meaning. 'The mass-communications industry never created a passive homogeneous audience: it stereotyped books and newspapers, not readers' (Secord 2000: 525).

The possibility for alternative non-professional constructions of nature is also raised by Bernard Lightman (1997) in his study of those knowledgeable amateurs and journalists who produced books for the mass market. 'Prolific and wildly successful' but seldom mentioned by scholars, 'these popularizers of science may have been more important than the Huxleys and Tyndalls in shaping the understanding of science in the minds of a reading public composed of children, teenagers, women and non-scientific males' (188). More importantly, the perspective offered by writers such as Margaret Gatty, Eliza Brightwen, Arabella Buckley and the Reverend J.G. Wood provided an alternative to the scientific naturalism that was on offer from professional scientists. Those elements of religious thinking that, as we saw earlier, scientific naturalism had tried to exclude from science were just those elements which Lightman's group of popularizers were at pains to include. Consequently, far from breaking the link between scientific and public culture by cleansing scientific thought of anthropomorphism, anthropocentrism and teleology, these popularizers were able to maintain the link through employing them. By catering to the public's interest in nature's religious and moral lessons the popularizers 'continued to give the public a sense that they participated in the production of knowledge. The publishing success of popularizers indicates that there was resistance to the claims of professional scientists to provide the only legitimate voice of nature and to their attempt to secularize science' (191). As Lightman says, it was not ignorance or simplification that brought these writers to emphasize the teleological, aesthetic, moral and divine quality of nature, 'it was an intentional refashioning of recent scientific discovery into a form full of meaning for their audience' (206).

Sensitive as we should be to contested discourses and the plurality of readings, nevertheless, it is difficult to miss what the preferred meaning was when we look at the image of science and scientists in mass circulation magazines. If this were indeed a reproduction of conventional opinion, then conventional opinion would have it that scientists were the heroes of the modern age. An interview could be as revealing of the journalist's sense of awe as it was of the scientist's domesticity. For one journalist an interview with A.R. Wallace (co-discoverer with Darwin of the theory of evolution through natural selection) was an overwhelming experience.

> When the door opened and I was ushered into the doctor's presence – phew! the inside of my head felt as if it had been stirred up by the tail of a comet, and became like an incandescent floating mass of world material, without form and void. I realised that I was in the presence of a great man.
>
> ('The Whatnot' 1898: 29)

As I have shown elsewhere (Broks 1996), in popular magazines of the 1890s and 1900s there was a stark contrast between the fictional stereotype of the scientist as villain and the non-fiction portrayal of real scientists as heroes. Take, for example, Lord Kelvin, President of the Royal Society, who must have been a household name judging by the amount of press coverage he received. 'A purer and nobler nature than that of Lord Kelvin's I have never known', wrote Donald Macleod, editor of the monthly magazine *Good Words*. Elsewhere we find him described as 'Energetic without being impetuous, quick without any signs of haste, pleased with his own power of cracking philosophical nuts, but never over estimating his own resources, mild and winning in manner, but always decisive'. He was the 'boy prodigy who became a peer', the 'joyful inventor', the 'Napoleon of Natural Philosophy'. We are told he has a 'warm heart and cheerful disposition', 'a smile always ready on his lips' and 'now and again he even perpetrates a joke' (see Broks 1996: 43–5). Nor was Kelvin an exceptional case. Virtuous descriptions of science and scientists were so common they verged on cliché. Scientists were 'courageous', 'patient', 'modest', 'persevering' and, perhaps the most common description, 'indefatigable'. As David Hollinger has argued, the scientist was seen as 'a humble and honest man of steady habits, laboring patiently, diligently, selflessly and without prejudice in the interests of truth' (1984: 142). He was 'the complete Victorian', embodying those virtues thought to be lacking in commercial and political culture, and, as a consequence, provided excellent material for that genre of moralistic literature which the Victorians seemed to value so highly and which is best exemplified in the self-help books of Samuel Smiles.

If scientists were as heroic as the magazines made out then being remote from the public would only serve to enhance the authority of any claims they should make. A feature on the work of the Home Office analytical laboratory, for example, is typical in its appeal to the authority of science. In many criminal cases, it said, science could be prosecutor and defendant, judge and jury:

> . . . in each capacity impartial, dispassionate, unerring; forging the chain of guilt or destroying the links of it one by one; speaking the truth, the whole truth and nothing but the truth, without love and without hate, without fear and without favour.
>
> (Anon. 1906)

As Brian Wynne has written, a public image of neutrality and objectivity was 'part of the social programme of professionalisation under the utilitarian ethos' (1979: 174). Popular magazines were testimony to just how successful that programme was. After the struggles over its status in the early part of the century, by the end of the century 'science' had become a synonym for 'true'. Moreover, as David Hollinger has argued, the scientists' drive for status increased the pressure on the public 'to view scientists as saints. The more detached from their fellow citizens that scientists became, the more necessary it became for the Victorian moralists . . . to trust that scientists were subject to an ethical code intrinsic to their practice' (Hollinger 1984: 147). In other words, being excluded from participating in the scientific enterprise, the lay public were left to trust that scientists did indeed possess the heroic qualities of their magazine stereotypes. One had only to put one's faith in science and submit to the rise of the expert, a situation that was ripe for the caustic humour of Alex M. Thompson writing for the *Clarion* in 1910:

> They will regulate our characters, our feelings, our aspect, and our whole lives with the accuracy and certainty of a mathematical demonstration. They will leave us no appetites, no desires, no passions, no gratifications, no emotions, no worries, and no ailments; we shall just have to live, they will do the rest . . . When we are done with and not wanted any more, they will politely hand us [a] kind of lozenge, and we shall be effectually converted back to the sort of gases they made us from . . . Nothing remains to ordinary mortals but to surrender themselves blindly to the tender care of the scientists, and let them make of us whatsoever they will.
>
> (Thompson 1910: 7)

It was a simple act of faith that was not without some irony. Just a few years before Thompson's humorous piece, A.W. Benn was to write of the 'transfer of authority from religious to naturalistic belief', and with this shift in prestige 'a great part of the reverence once given to priests and to their stories of an unseen universe has been transferred to the astronomer, the geologist, the physician, and the engineer' (cited in Turner 1978: 359). By the turn of the century it was not uncommon to find religious imagery being applied to science, even in religious magazines (Broks 1996: 53). Laboratories were 'temples', a telescope in an observatory was the 'Holy of Holies', Darwin's house was a 'shrine' and Darwin himself was described as one of the 'high priests of inductive science'. Inventors, however, though no less heroic, were more likely to be portrayed with the language of magic. Thomas Alva Edison, for example, was the 'wizard of Menlo Park' and Nikolas Tesla the 'new magician of the west'. (To what extent such differences were significant is something that awaits an enterprising researcher.) As we shall see in the next section, submission to these new priests and wizards did not go unrewarded.

Technological futures

In 1897 Dr Stephen Emmens sold over 600 ounces of gold to the US government – all of it was home-made. Emmens, a British chemist living in New York, had built a steam-driven contraption, which he called a Force Engine, to hammer and freeze Mexican dollars. Apparently, repeated treatment in the Force Engine transformed the silver in the dollars into gold good enough to satisfy the US Assay Office which paid Emmens over $7000 for the stuff. The global economy is probably shaky enough without speculation about how much of the US gold reserves is fake, but the remarkable story of Emmens is a good example of what the Victorians had come to expect. Anything was possible.

Technological miracles were expected on an almost daily basis. Late nineteenth-century magazines give ample evidence of this being a period of commonplace wonders (Broks 1996: 100–6). '[T]he times in which we live may well be called the "age of invention" ', wrote one contributor, 'Never before, it would seem, have men so ardently studied the secrets of nature, and turned the knowledge thus acquired to practical account. We have become so accustomed to hearing of new inventions that nowadays they hardly surprise us.' Even the letters pages bear witness to this age of invention. 'We seem to be so up-to-date nowadays', wrote one correspondent, 'that I don't see that there is really much else to be invented'. Although to modern eyes the technology may look crude or bizarre, it was, by any standards, an impressive achievement. In the closing decades of the nineteenth century the Victorians were to invent or discover much that would help define the twentieth century – wireless broadcasting, the telephone, cinematography, the internal combustion engine, the automobile, X-rays, radiation, and the application of electricity to every imaginable aspect of daily life. Only a few years into the Edwardian period and we would have to add powered flight as well. Just highlighting some of the reports from the popular press gives a sense of the excitement of the age.

- *Radium*
  'The modern philosopher's stone'
  'In the future our homes will be lighted by it, our motor cars driven by it, our food cooked by it'
  'An inexhaustible reservoir of energy'
- *Electricity*
  'The future of electricity is absolutely beyond the realm of imagination'
  'The word "impossible" has been wiped out of the electrician's vocabulary'
- *Liquid air*
  'The force of the future'
  'Another giant caught, imprisoned, and made to work the will of man'
- *Electric telegraphy*
  'By putting the remotest parts of the world in contact with each other, it tends to destroy the barriers of isolation and prejudice, making indifference give place to sympathy and hatred to loving-kindness'.

Scientists were said to be 'a race of men who have conquered time, space, air, fire, water, nature's deepest secrets', and the 'King of the coming age' was to be the engineer.

A sturdy figure, with thoughtful eyes, gazing out at his vast inheritance from under broad heavy brows. His robe of royalty a suit of grease stained overalls, his throne the mechanic's bench, his stool the footplate of the locomotive, his sceptre a piston-rod, his crown a circlet of electric light, his name – the engineer.

As he advances, there advances with him, step by step, civilisation, knowledge, liberty, comfort, and safety.

(Cited in Broks 1996: 105)

Future generations, readers were told, would be able to take an aeroplane to the moon, cross the Atlantic in three days, travel in wagons along pneumatic tubes or on aerial railways, send pictures by telegraphy, make gold, eat pills as food, keep hearts beating with electricity, kill pain with anaesthetics, make the deaf hear, the blind see (1996: 106).

It was, to say the least, a triumphalist vision of the coming century. Nor was it a simple blind faith. One had only to look back over the preceding 100 years to see that technology had impeccable credentials as a guarantor of progress for the next 100 years. Indeed, it was on this basis of past triumphs that many magazines indulged in trying to predict what life would be like 'a hundred years hence', which is naturally of some interest since they are projections forward into our own times. What, then, did they foresee? By the year 2000 all food would be manufactured from chemicals and all power would be generated from the internal heat of the Earth. All labour would be done by machinery and, 'no longer condemned to toil for a coarse livelihood', we would be able to devote our time to intellectual pursuits and pastimes. Diseases would be 'utterly crushed out of existence' and with the perfection of surgery 'death from ordinary injury will barely be possible'. It is a world of cars, trams, airships and aeroplanes; of indoor tropical gardens, air conditioning and entertainment piped into the home; of telephones, electric dishwashers and automatic laundries. It is also a world that is recognizably Victorian with social distinctions of master and servant carefully preserved. It was, in short, their own times writ large (Broks 1996: 106–7).

Visions of the future were not new. The tale of the future can be traced back to the eighteenth century and the associated genre of utopian writing goes back much further. What was new was their proliferation and popular appeal. I.F. Clarke (1979) has done an extensive survey of this form of writing, believing that 'like the alphabet, the tale of the future is a necessary social invention' (51). It had become an established literary form by the 1830s, but it was with the stories of Jules Verne in the 1860s that the form's popularity really took off. The secret of Verne's success probably lies not so much in his ideas (balloon flights, a hollow Earth, lunar travel), all of which had antecedents, but in the detail with which he expressed them and, perhaps even more importantly, the shrewd business acumen of his publisher P.J. Hetzel who was careful to avoid anything that might adversely affect international sales. By the 1870s,

> A new race of journalists and popular writers began to provide complacent stories about the wonders-to-come for the mass of literate citizens in Europe and the United States. They traded in the terrors and delights of technological society with their exciting stories of space travel, future worlds, death rays, demon scientists, imaginary wars, flying machines and the rest of the marvels of science fiction.
>
> (Clarke 1979: 103)

This recognizably modern form of science fiction 'came about through the commercial enterprise of publishers and the specialised writings of professional authors . . . [who] made it their business to understand the requirements of the market' (1979: 118). The result was the mass production of scientific romances in the popular newspapers and illustrated magazines of the 1890s. Although Clarke is careful to separate out the development of science fiction from that of utopian writing, the two were naturally combined in the Victorian belief in progress, a 'pattern of general expectations' that 'at its most simple . . . was no more than the universal agreement that things had changed for the better and would go on changing' (90). As Clarke writes,

> The progressive and rational utopia was the self confident manifestation of the Promethean period in an era of technological progress; and the doctrinal base for these visions of happiness-to-come was the new belief in the immense powers of a technological society – eternal, without measure, self-perpetuating, dominating, and directing the forces of nature to the advantage of mankind.
>
> (Clarke 1979: 118)

Technological progress would bring social utopia, and this could be true even where the utopian vision was not a panegyric to the machine age. William Morris's novel *News from Nowhere* ([1890] 1984) is one of the greatest evocations of a return to mediaevalism, yet even this Arcadian utopia is only made possible through advanced technology. Morris's future landscape is a rural idyll only because industrial centres were broken up by 'the great change in the use of mechanical force', and everyone can take pleasure in crafting goods by hand because 'all work which would be irksome to do by hand is done by immensely improved machinery' ([1890] 1984: 242, 267).

In the quarter century before the First World War, over 100 utopian novels were published in America (Harris 1990: 150) and together with the large number of science fiction epics what many of them had in common was a fascination for technology. Early nineteenth-century American utopianism had largely focused on practical experiments centred on households or villages, but under the impact of urban and manufacturing technologies late nineteenth-century utopianism was more socially comprehensive, emphasizing inter-dependence on a national scale. Not only did technology change the scale of utopian visions, it also created new problems and new solutions. If industrial-ization brought with it squalor and overcrowding, then technology could also highlight the sharp contrast between human potential and the current wretched state of society. Indeed, as Neil Harris argues, this contrast was often central to late nineteenth-century American utopianism: 'Machines raised expectations for physical comfort and social rationality. Their very presence invited dramatic institutional reform. Technology formed more than a footnote to utopian pre-scriptions; it lay at their heart' (1990: 158). Consequently the utopian novels of the period are as revealing of contemporary technological fears as they are of technological hopes.

> Enthusiastic descriptions were coupled with doubts, strange speculations about heaven, mysticism, and timidities. Indeed, despite their technical daring and apparent self-confidence, many of these utopian novels were the products of worried minds and represented a flight from experience, adventure, and confrontation. The technological wonders were surrounded with restrictions and qualifications. Their purpose was to shield utopians from too much direct contact with either the organic world or their fellow human beings. The energies calling forth this literature of marvellous speculation were nourished by dreams of escape . . .
>
> (Harris 1990: 158–9)

These utopian novels can be seen as 'anxious responses to a set of revolutionary changes undergone by this generation of Americans', changes associated with urbanization and industrialization (159). The solutions they proposed were equally characteristic of their generation. They were the solutions of large-scale industry and corporatism: efficiency, social discipline, order and control (see also Segal 1985).

Technological utopianism was not only to be found in magazines and popu-lar novels; it was also, quite literally, on display at the many world fairs and expositions. Starting in London with the Great Exhibition of 1851, the fashion for international exhibitions spread around the world, proclaiming the global victory of capitalism with 'giant new rituals of self-congratulation . . . each encased in a princely monument to wealth and technical progress' (Hobsbawm 1977: 47). The Crystal Palace, built especially to house the London exhibition, was itself a steel and glass marvel of technical ingenuity and attracted as much attention as the thousands of exhibits. Walter Benjamin described these inter-national expositions as 'the sites of pilgrimages to the commodity fetish' and numerous studies reveal the intimate links between science, technology and mass consumption. In the few months that the Great Exhibition was open millions of visitors were to marvel at steam hammers, locomotives, steam turbines, printing machines and cameras as well as such domestic items as clocks, tables and tea sets. The pattern was to be repeated with subsequent exhibitions on an ever larger scale; 14,000 manufacturers exhibited in London in 1851, 50,000 in Paris in 1867. In the United States, between 1876 and 1916 nearly 100 million people were to visit world fairs from Philadelphia to San Francisco, Seattle to New Orleans and many places in between. In addition, millions more would read of the exhibitions in the extensive press coverage. However, for Robert Rydell (1984), who has made a comprehensive study of the US fairs, the importance of the exhibitions is not so much in their scale, but in their ideological power. The fairs were initiated and developed by local and national elites and supported by funds, exhibits and specialists from federal government. What they offered was a 'cohesive explanatory blueprint of social experience'. They were 'triumphs of hegemony', says Rydell, 'because they propagated the ideas and values of the country's political, financial, corporate, and intellectual leaders and offered these ideas as the proper interpretation of social and political authority' (1984: 2, 3). At a time when the US economy was being consolidated into large corporations 'the exposition builders promised that continued growth would result in eventual utopia' and so translated 'an ideology of economic development, labelled "progress", . . . into a utopian statement about the future' (4).

It is widely recognized that the world's fairs were embodiments and legitimations of a new 'culture of abundance', but Rydell exposes another equally significant aspect. On display were not only 'things' but people. Following the example of the Paris Exhibition of 1889, American world's fairs set up 'colonial' villages as living ethnological displays – often located in the amusement section alongside wild animal exhibits. 'Although these villages degraded and exploited the people on display, anthropologists generally testified to the ethnological value of the exhibits' (Rydell 1984: 7). The fairs were 'part of a broader universe of white supremacist entertainments' (e.g. the minstrel show, circus, museum of curiosities, dime novel); 'what distinguished them were their scientific, artistic, and political underpinnings. Whether or not they were the most important source for shaping racial beliefs, they certainly were among the most authoritative' (6). The **Smithsonian Institution**, for example, was the most frequent scientific contributor, providing staff time and collections, regarding the fairs as an important, if inconvenient, means of fulfilling its overall remit, founded as it was 'for the increase and diffusion of knowledge among men'. In an unsettling period of industrialization, cyclical depressions and class warfare, the fairs satisfied a 'search for order' by offering a scientifically validated opportunity 'to reaffirm their collective national identity in an updated synthesis of progress and white supremacy' (4). Scientists provided 'an intellectual scaffolding for the cumulative symbolic universe under construction at the fairs':

> This symbolic construct centred on the interpenetration of Darwinian theories about racial development and utopian dreams about America's material and national progress. Central to the presentation of this constellation of ideas as a valid interpretation of social reality were ethnological exhibits furnished by both reputable anthropologists and well-financed showmen. Anthropological attractions – consisting of cultural artefacts, lay-figure groupings of 'primitive types', and selected nonwhites living in ethnological villages along the midways – charted a course of racial progress toward an image of utopia that was reflected in the main exposition buildings.
>
> (Rydell 1984: 235)

At the Chicago fair in 1893, for example, the clean utopian vision of the exposition's White City was set up in contrast to the dirty pleasures of the Midway Plaisance, the fair's honky-tonk and 'ethnological' sector. 'The Midway made the dream of the future seem all the brighter and the present civilisation all the more progressive', says Rydell, at the same time as providing white Americans 'with a grand opportunity for a subliminal journey into the recesses of their own repressed desires' as they watched half-naked villagers and hootchy-kootchy dancers (1984: 67). Moreover, as contemporary accounts show, visitors were not blind to the 'evolutionary' significance of the fair's layout. A walk along the Midway was experienced as a journey through the evolution of civilization, from African 'savagery' to the glorification of science, technology and American capitalism.

Evolution and progress

Darwin's *Origin of Species*, published in 1859, is rightly regarded as one the greatest books in scientific literature. Most probably it is also the last book in the scientific canon that is easily comprehended by the lay reader, indeed written with a lay reader in mind. The central idea could hardly be simpler – some win, some lose. Add together the fact that *individuals are different from each other*, with *all the pressures that bear on a struggle to stay alive* and you are only a few short steps away from a full-blown theory of evolution by natural selection. Let us put the pieces together.

1   There are variations amongst individuals in a species.

2   There is a struggle for existence.

Putting 1 and 2 together we get:

3   In the struggle for existence some variations will give a slight advantage to some individuals.

The consequence of which is:

4   Those with the slight advantage have a better chance of surviving and reproducing a subsequent generation with that same slight advantage; those who do not are more likely to die without offspring – some win, some lose.

This is the process of 'natural selection', a mechanism as simple as passing soil through a sieve – some bits go through, some do not. With each generation the slight advantage will become more widespread as those without it fail to reproduce at the same rate. Over time, the advantageous variation will become a common feature of the general population. When a population is divided (e.g. by geography) different variations will be advantageous, so modification will take divergent forms and new species emerge. Although it can account for all the fantastic and beautiful diversity of life on earth the whole process is directionless and purposeless – a machine that grinds out species, driven by chance, struggle and death.

'Evolution' is what we see when we view these modifications over long periods of time – like watching a film where each frame is a single snapshot of each generation. What most Victorians saw when they watched this film was a story of progress. Moreover, biological, racial, social and technological progress all seemed to be guaranteed by evolution. The technological utopias of the previous section were thought to be the inevitable outcome of natural law. Sir John Lubbock (prehistorian and X Club member), for example, said precisely that in 1865:

> The future happiness of our race, which poets hardly ventured to hope for, science boldly predicts. Utopia, which we have long looked upon as synonymous with an evident impossibility, which we have ungratefully regarded as 'too good to be true', turns out on the contrary to be the necessary consequence of natural law.
>
> (Cited in Burrow 1966: 275)

However, we must be careful in ascribing this faith in evolution to the impact of Darwin's ideas. It is certainly true that the theory of evolution played a central role in late Victorian thought, and equally true that most Victorians would regard 'evolution' and 'Darwinism' as virtually synonymous, yet it is still possible to claim that the 'Darwinian revolution' was neither Darwinian nor particularly revolutionary. We can do so by pointing out that:

- before Darwin there were already vigorous debates about evolution;
- after Darwin debates were characterized by the persistence of pre-Darwinian ideas;
- the most distinctive feature of Darwin's theory was precisely what was most often left out from the common evolutionary vision.

This is important to remember when considering popular science because it was not simply science being 'distorted' by the public, but rather a range of meanings being constructed by public and scientists alike. I have already touched on pre-Darwinian evolutionary theory in the previous chapter with the discussions of Lamarckism and radical politics, and the debates over Robert Chambers's book *Vestiges*. It is the post-Darwinian situation I want to look at here.

What we need to note first is the nature of the term 'evolution'. Strictly speaking, Darwin did not write about evolution at all but about 'descent with modification'. The term 'evolution' is never mentioned in the *Origin of Species*. As a way of referring to the transmutation of species, 'evolution' never really caught on until after Herbert Spencer started using it that way (Bowler 1975). More significantly, the term was taken from the context of embryological development and was first applied outside that context by anthropologists who adopted a developmental view of cultural evolution (Bowler 1987). We can see at the outset, therefore, not only the way in which evolutionary theory is embedded in a particular cultural perspective, but also how that perspective is framed by the idea of development. Transferring 'evolution' from one context to another, the linear and purposeful development of the embryo provided a conceptual framework for seeing social development along similar pre-circumscribed lines towards a particular final state. None of this owed much to Darwin whose theory was based on random variations and the undirected process of natural selection. However, it did make the idea of 'evolution' much more acceptable to a wide range of publics including scientists. Christian Darwinists, for example, were able to reconcile their theology with their science by seeing evolution as the inevitable unfolding of material, social and spiritual progress; and even T.H. Huxley, who is commonly regarded as 'Darwin's bulldog', at first preferred a non-Darwinian version of evolution that was purposeful and progressive (Moore 1979; Durant 1985; Bowler 1987). What Darwin did provide was scientific credibility and a suitable label. 'Darwin was a name to be invoked as a cliché, to be rejected by the faithful, or embraced by the secularists' (Young 1970: 23). This is clearly the case, for example, if we see how evolutionary theory was used by British socialists. When the socialist magazine the *Clarion* conducted a poll of its readers to find 'Britain's Greatest Benefactor', Darwin was the clear winner, but the reasons given by readers show that when they said 'Darwin' it was Lamarck that they had in mind (Broks 1996: 64–5). As we saw in the previous chapter, early nineteenth-century radicals turned to Lamarckian progressivism as legitimation for their politics and it was this emphasis on environment and evolution that was attractive to late nineteenth-century socialists. The evolutionary socialism found in mechanics' institutes at the end of the century rejected individualism and competition in favour of the more traditional emphasis on environmentalism and cooperation (Laurent 1984).

We can see, therefore, that Darwin's chief contribution to evolutionary debates (his struggle-driven species-machine) is precisely what gets abandoned in favour of pre-Darwinian ideas of purposeful evolution. To a large extent this is true, but we do need to add one important qualification especially when considering the US. By equating evolution with progress it was possible to argue that what applied to one would apply to the other. If evolution was driven by a struggle for existence then a struggle for existence would also bring progress; more particularly, social struggle would bring social progress. This *Social Darwinism* fitted well with an American tradition of rugged individualism and, as a consequence, Darwinism was given 'an unusually quick and sympathetic reception' in the US. 'In some respects the United States during the last three decades of the nineteenth and at the beginning of the twentieth century was *the* Darwinian country' (Hofstadter 1955: 4–5, original emphasis). It also helped that this was an age that was predominantly conservative, since the popularization of Darwinism was able to support conservatism on two counts: first, by emphasizing competition as necessary to enable the best to succeed; and secondly, by showing that improvement came from slow development, not rapid change. The result was a scientifically legitimated defence of the *status quo* and *laissez-faire* politics (something which was attractive on both sides of the Atlantic). Socialist efforts towards the amelioration of humanity's suffering (e.g. protecting the weak through welfare policies) could thus be attacked as unnatural interference into the machinery of progress. Richard Hofstadter (1955) has argued that by the 1890s this individualistic Darwinism was replaced by a more racist and imperialistic strand. However, at a popular level one might question the extent to which the earlier individualism had indeed been dominant over the racism. As we saw with Rydell's study of world fairs in the previous section, the connection between evolutionism and racism goes back further and deeper.

We are all, I imagine, familiar with the classic iconography of evolution, the 'march of progress' – an ape dragging its knuckles on the ground, a series of stooped 'ape-men' and finally the upright posture of 'modern man' leading the procession. Stephen Jay Gould has called it '*the* canonical representation of evolution – the one picture immediately grasped and viscerally understood by all' (Gould 1991: 31, original emphasis). The persistence of the image is testimony to its power, but by retelling the story of evolution as a single epic it is also gloriously wrong. This is evolution as a single linear progression; evolution as that same process of 'development' found unfolding in an embryo but now continuing through adult forms. Nevertheless, it was a conception of evolution that did provide a convenient framework into which could be placed all varieties of humanity, each in its own place along the scale (or its own village along a world fair Midway). The idea of a hierarchy in nature – the Great Chain of Being – had long been a part of western thought. What the theory of evolution did was give this hierarchy a temporal dimension and a new scientific authority (Stepan 1982). Non-whites were now seen not only as inferior but as 'primitive' because they were 'less evolved' than whites.

Nor was it just race that was measured by the evolutionary yardstick. Gender, crime and child development could all be cross-referenced in a single 'web of analogies' that linked difference with pathology (Gilman 1985): women were the 'lower race' of gender, children were naturally criminal, criminals were savages, and the 'savage' was a child. As Nancy Stepan (1986) has argued,

> By analogy with the so-called lower races, women, the sexually deviate, the criminal, the urban poor, and the insane were in one way or another constructed as biological 'races apart' whose differences from the white male, and likenesses to each other, 'explained' their different and lower position in the social hierarchy.
>
> (Stepan 1986: 264)

Deeply held convictions about the 'naturalness' of inequalities surfaced in scientific ideas about 'race'. The 'inferiority' of black races was underlined by their representation as being ape-like, child-like and prehistoric. Their 'natural' role was to serve since they were simple, faithful and gullible. 'The "primitive-as-child" argument', says Gould, 'stood second to none in the arsenal of racist arguments to justify slavery and imperialism' (1977: 126). Nor was this simply the social abuse of scientific knowledge as Brian Street (1975 and 1985) has shown in his examination of Victorian popular fiction. There was a 'unity of consciousness' in the perception of 'primitive man' to be found in science, popular literature and imperial politics. As Street says, 'we find writers using racial characteristics to stereotype whole peoples in ways for which they could claim some justification since the scientists were doing the same thing' (1985: 98). Racial stereotypes were deeply embedded in Victorian culture – in science, popular novels, periodicals, world fairs and elsewhere. For all the diverse meanings attached to evolution by Christians, atheists, socialists and conservatives, it would seem that when it came to the question of 'race', science and the (white) public were united in their prejudices.

Further reading

Broks, P. (1996) *Media Science Before the Great War*. London: Macmillan.

Brooke, J.H. (1991) *Science and Religion: Some Historical Perspectives*. Cambridge: Cambridge University Press.

Bruce, R.V. (1987) *The Launching of Modern American Science, 1846–1876*. New York: Alfred A. Knopf.

Clarke, I.F. (1979) *The Pattern of Expectation, 1644–2001*. London: Jonathan Cape.

Lightman, B. (ed.) (1997) *Victorian Science in Context*. Chicago, IL: University of Chicago Press.

Rydell, R.W. (1984) *All the World's a Fair: Visions of Empire at American International Expositions, 1876–1916*. Chicago, IL: University of Chicago Press.

Turner, F.M. (1980) *Public Science in Britain, 1890–1919*, in *Isis*, 71: 589–608.

3 SCIENCE AND MODERNITY

'. . . so with a kind of madness growing upon me, I flung myself into
futurity'

(The Time Traveller in *The Time Machine* by H.G. Wells)

If H.G. Wells's Time Traveller were to take us back to his own time (1895) we
would find ourselves in a world that was recognizably 'modern'. Plucked from
our own technocentric lifestyles we would be relieved to find telegraphs, telephones, gramophones, petrol-driven engines and electrical gadgets. Soon there
would also be automobiles, cinema, wireless and aeroplanes. We would feel at
home in city centres that were saturated with advertisements, packed with
humanity and congested with traffic (mostly horse-drawn vehicles so mind the
organic pollution underfoot). We could use the London underground or New
York subway to escape to the suburbs where we would find neat lawns and
the usual array of middle-class anxieties (psychoanalysis available in Vienna).
Conversation would reveal worries about keeping up appearances on a small
income, the pace of modern life, the problem of crime, the morals of youth,
and possibly even fears of terrorism (bomb-making 'anarchists' lurked in the
popular imagination even if they were hard to find in the real world). For
relaxation we could go shopping in large department stores, follow the latest
health fads, watch professional sport and find out about our favourite celeb-
rities in the mass media (no television, but the style, tone, content and visual
impact of magazines provided a print equivalent). The popular music may not
be to our taste and we might find the dress sense just a little *too* retro, but those
are details. True, there would be no computers, internet and texting, but at least
their absence gave employment to an army of clerks and messenger boys.

If H.G. Wells's Time Traveller were to stay with us at the start of the twenty-
first century it is easy to imagine how he might marvel at our technology and
express wonder at our general levels of health and hygiene. We might even, in
some respects, measure up to the utopian visions of his contemporaries. Yet he

would probably find it hard to reconcile his Victorian optimism with what we could tell him about the twentieth century. His 'future' and our history would make a sad, even grotesque, mismatch. In his own time, for example, there had been much speculation about the 'next great war', often seeing it as a necessary cleansing process for the new golden age to come. Within fifty years there would be not one but two great wars – the first would kill more people than all other wars from the previous two centuries put together, the second would reach that total every year – and if the scale of war would be difficult to grasp then industrialized mass murder in a Nazi death camp would be completely beyond imagination. Our Time Traveller would no doubt have the same sense of despair as that of his creator who lived through those times. In 1945, in his last published work *Mind at the End of its Tether*, Wells was to write:

> The end of everything we call life is close at hand and cannot be evaded . . . Our universe is not merely bankrupt; there remains no dividend at all; it has not simply liquidated; it is going clean out of existence, leaving not a wrack behind . . . The human story has already come to an end and . . . *Homo sapiens*, as he has been pleased to call himself, is in his present form played out.

> (Wells cited in Kumar 1987: 381)

And this was before Wells had news of the bombs being dropped on Hiroshima and Nagasaki. Furthermore, what our Time Traveller might find most disturbing was the realization that this 'end of humanity' was no simple retreat into barbarism but rather was accompanied by (at times even a consequence of) unprecedented scientific progress. Many of the nineteenth-century visions of the future (social, scientific and technological) were, indeed, to become twentieth-century realities. Though we might smile at the seemingly naïve optimism of the Victorians we do so only because the great tragedy of the twentieth century is the way in which their future became our history.

Being modern

We must begin by first considering what it means to be 'modern'. Taken from the Latin for 'just now', the term 'modern' is intimately bound up with our sense of time and our relationship with past, present and future. The creation of modernity is, in no small part, the history of a shift in vision from looking to the past with a sense of loss to looking to the future not just with a sense of hope but with the confidence that it can be shaped to one's will. Although a key feature of the Renaissance was the confidence to assert that modern culture was equal to that of the classical world of Greek and Roman civilization, the majority of uses of 'modern' before the nineteenth century were unfavourable. Only in the nineteenth, and more particularly in the twentieth century, did 'modern' become virtually synonymous with improved or efficient, and 'modernize' become something that was inherently desirable (Williams 1976). It is, of course, no coincidence that over that same 500-year period since the Renaissance we see the rise of science and capitalism – defining features of what it means to be modern. Marshall Berman (1983), for example, has written of modernity as a mode of experience that has many sources – physical sciences, industrialization, urban growth, mass communication, mass social movements, nation states – all driven by 'an ever-expanding, drastically fluctuating capitalist world market' (16) and, it should be added, a capitalism that is in turn driven by a constant need for modernization, for new markets and new instruments of production. The all too familiar use of 'modernization' as a political slogan has probably numbed us to the full significance of the term. Modernity is the unfinished (and never to be finished) project of a continual process of modernization. It is an inherently unsettling process, a restless now in search of the new, a constant re-newing – so that (with a growing kind of madness) it flings us into futurity. Berman identifies three phases of modernity. The first phase sees the beginnings of modern life in the sixteenth to the late eighteenth century. In a second phase starting with the French Revolution in the 1790s 'a great modern public abruptly comes to life' aware that it is living in a revolutionary age but which can still remember the traditional life of a pre-modern world. In this phase the idea of 'modernization' unfolds until in the twentieth century (phase three) it takes in virtually the whole world (17).

Anthony Giddens (1990) has a similar timescale and trajectory. 'Modernity', he says, 'refers to modes of social life or organisation which emerged in Europe from about the seventeenth century onwards and which subsequently became more or less worldwide in their influence' (1). The features which separate it from traditional society are: the pace of change (most obviously seen with technology), the scope of change (now global), and the unprecedented nature of modern institutions (such as nation states, the dependence upon inanimate power sources, the commodification of products and labour). Of particular interest, however, and picking up the threads of the previous chapter, is what Giddens has to say about how modern social systems are *disembedded*, by which he means 'the "lifting out" of social relations from local contexts of interaction and their restructuring across indefinite spans of time-space' (21). One way in which this is achieved is through the establishment of *expert systems*, 'systems of technical accomplishment or professional expertise that organise large areas of the material and social environments in which we live today' (27). No longer do we consult an expert when needed but instead have to have a continuous faith in their abilities; faith, for example, that tall buildings will not fall down, that cars will be safe to drive, that planes will fly. We rely on a world produced by experts such as engineers even though we may never meet them and in a disembedded system this reliance involves trust. Why do we trust? Giddens uses our trust in scientific expertise as an explanatory example. When we learn about science, he says, we do not just learn the content of technical findings but also 'an aura of respect for technical knowledge of all kinds'. We learn certainty and first principles, not fallibility and contentious issues:

> Science has thus maintained an image of reliable knowledge which spills over into an attitude of respect for most forms of technical specialism. However, at the same time, lay attitudes to science and to technical knowledge generally are typically ambivalent. This is an ambivalence that lies at the core of all trust relations, whether it be trust in abstract systems or in individuals. For trust is only demanded where there is ignorance – either of the knowledge claims of technical experts or of the thoughts and intentions of intimates upon whom a person relies. Yet ignorance always provides grounds for scepticism or at least caution. Popular representations of science and technical expertise typically bracket respect with attitudes of hostility or fear, as in the stereotypes of the 'boffin', a humourless technician with little understanding of ordinary people, or the mad scientist.
>
> (Giddens 1990: 89)

Thus we can see that while science is a central (even definitional) feature of modernity, in return the nature of modernity creates an ambivalent attitude towards science.

Both Berman and Giddens emphasize this ambivalence, presenting modernity as double-edged, as something that offers the greatest opportunities and the greatest dangers. 'To be modern', says Berman, 'is to find ourselves in an environment that promises us adventure, power, joy, growth, transformation of ourselves and the world – and, at the same time, that threatens to destroy everything we have, everything we know, everything we are' (1983: 15). It should be no surprise, therefore, that science, as an integral part of modernity, should take us on the same rollercoaster ride of paradoxes and contradictions. To a large extent the fear and excitement are bound up with questions of control. On the one hand, modernity gives us the power to control nature and ourselves; on the other hand, we seem powerless in the face of modernity's control over us. To understand this duality and how it inflects popular attitudes towards science it will be helpful to pick up the threads of the previous chapter's discussion of progress, evolution and visions of the future.

The great promise of modernity was that the future was not simply something that happened, but that it was something that could be planned and built. As Bauman explains, modernity's faith in progress was an expression of 'the self confidence of the present'. It was through the ability to control the present that one could have the simple faith that the future would be better:

> Modern utopias were never mere prophecies, let alone idle dreams: openly or covertly, they were both declarations of intent and expressions of faith that what was desired could be done and will be done. The future was seen like the rest of the products in that society of producers: something to be thought through, designed and then seen through the process of its production.
>
> (Bauman 2000: 131)

However, a utopia that is planned is inevitably a planners' utopia and 'progress' would thus come to mean life being more and more subject to planning and control. We can see this, for example, in many of the nineteenth-century social utopias such as Edward Bellamy's *Looking Backward* ([1888] 1984), with its population organized along military lines into an industrial army. We can also see it put into practice in Henry Ford's approach to manufacturing which – with its combination of technology and rationalization – can be seen as the symbol and archetype of modernity.

Ford's rejection of the past is famous. 'History is more or less bunk', he told a reporter on the *Chicago Tribune* in 1916. 'We don't want tradition. We want to live in the present and the only history that is worth a tinker's damn is the history we make today' (cited in Bauman 2000: 131). The history that Ford made helped shape the twentieth century. It centred on the production of his Model T motor car but was part of a wider factory revolution between 1880 and 1920. Growing demand for the Model T put pressure on Ford to rationalize the system that made it and to do that he pulled together a range of developments in production when he built a new factory at Highland Park in 1908–10. The principles behind Ford's system were standardization, efficiency and control. The American System of manufacture which used unskilled or semi-skilled labour to assemble products from standardized and interchangeable parts had already been applied to the manufacture of sewing machines and bicycles. Ford now applied the system to the production of motor cars – something which had hitherto only been made by teams of highly skilled craftsmen. As far as possible, standardization and interchangeability were also applied to the workforce. It is not clear to what extent (if at all) Ford or his managers were directly influenced by Frederick W. Taylor's ideas of 'scientific management', but he certainly followed similar principles. Human input (labour) into the production process was treated the same as any other input (materials and energy) and through 'time and motion' analysis a worker's activities would be broken down into its component parts to be examined, improved, speeded up or discarded in an effort to make the worker more efficient, making the workers as much a machine as the machines they operated. As one worker remembered it, the effect was that workers would:

> . . . cease to be human beings as soon as they enter the gates of the shop. They become automatons and cease to think. They move their arms spontaneously to and fro, stopping long enough to eat in order to keep the human machinery in working order for the next four hours of exploitation.
>
> (Cited in Waites 1989: 328)

(Charlie Chaplin captures the experience in the bitter humour of his film *Modern Times* in which he twitches with the rhythm of the factory machinery before being pulled in to be part of it.) It was also to increase efficiency that the layout of the Highland Park factory was based on what was perhaps the most iconic feature of Ford's system: the assembly line – the continuous movement of raw materials and parts using gravity work slides, rollerways and electrically driven conveyors. To speed up production, components were now moved past workers each performing a simple task and, just as important, the speed of the 'line' was determined by centralized management, not the workrate of those on the line.

The effect on efficiency was staggering. Where it had once taken twelve and a half hours to build a chassis it now took only one and a half hours. The effect on the workforce was equally dramatic. 'The workers reacted to these highly regimented, degraded and alienated conditions of labour by leaving the factory in droves: in 1913, the annual labour turnover was 370 per cent; most left voluntarily. Absenteeism and stress-related sickness were chronic problems' (Waites 1989: 328). Nevertheless, there was never any shortage of those willing to work for Ford. To attract a workforce Ford doubled the wage rate to $5 a day and provided his workers with welfare benefits. However, accepting Ford's wages and benefits also meant accepting the extension of management control *outside* the workplace and outside worktime. Included in the $5 a day was a 'profit' element which would be withdrawn if workers failed to meet the required standards of social behaviour in their domestic lives. A Sociological Department was created with teams of investigators to examine the everyday lives of workers to make sure they were sober, prudent, family men – any evidence of gambling, heavy drinking or visiting prostitutes and the 'profit' would be withheld (Hales 1982; Waites 1989). We can see, therefore, that working for Ford gave many people a direct, even visceral, experience of modernity, and a similar direct experience of 'science' through the scientific management of their lives and bodies.

However, we can also see Taylorism and Fordism as only parts of a much broader effort towards the scientific rationalization of the whole of society, and not just in the United States. Across Europe their methods were imitated or home-grown versions developed, even in the newly born and anti-capitalist Soviet Union which, despite ideological differences, shared a commitment to centralized control, technological development and increased productivity. Indeed, for Jürgen Habermas (1970) the twentieth century has seen the 'scientization of politics' and the growing dominance of a 'technocratic consciousness' through which scientific–technical progress is the new basis for political legitimation (with an accompanying depoliticization of the mass of the population). In the early decades of the century, this was to find its clearest expression in the quest for national efficiency in Britain and the politics of Progressivism in the United States (Searle 1971). In both cases the desire for a scientifically managed society ran across party political lines. Of the situation in America, Diane B. Paul has written:

> Progressive reforms involved a vast expansion in governmental authority. Whether Democrat or Republican, the Progressives shared a faith in the virtues of planning and the benevolence of the state. Their bywords were 'organization', 'systematic planning', 'efficiency', and 'social control'.
>
> (1995: 77)

In this respect, Progressives were much like the Fabians in Britain who, while they condemned capitalism, had as their ideal 'a scientifically planned society that would empower experts rather than workers', and 'envisioned a nation managed by people much like themselves: middle-class professionals, such as doctors, scientists, teachers, and social workers' (75).

At this point it is worth recalling the three phases of public science suggested by Turner (see Chapter 2): first, up to the mid-nineteenth century public scientists urged the importance of science as useful knowledge; secondly, from the mid-1840s to the late 1870s public scientists used science to challenge the cultural dominance of the clergy; and finally, from 1875 onwards the public rhetoric of science was directed towards state service. 'After approximately 1875', says Turner, 'the spokesmen for British science shifted their rhetoric and the emphasis of their policy from the values of peace, cosmopolitanism, self-improvement, material comfort, social mobility, and intellectual progress toward the values of collectivism, nationalism, military preparedness, patriotism, political elitism, and social imperialism' (Turner 1980: 592). For example, the interests of the British Association for the Advancement of Science 'between 1880 and 1914 show that many of its supporters believed that the "reform" of British society would at least centrally involve, and perhaps be determined by, science and scientists' (Worboys 1981: 173). Moreover, the British Science Guild, established in 1904, was even more explicit about the need for political involvement. Whereas the British Association had been founded with the aim of promoting science through seeking public and, more particularly, state support, the British Science Guild announced that its purpose was not the promotion of natural knowledge, but rather the use of science 'to further the progress and increase the welfare of the Empire' (cited in Turner 1980: 602). As we have seen in previous chapters, the utility of science has always been part of its public rhetoric, but on this fulcrum of usefulness the balance would appear to have been shifting – from the state promoting science to science promoting the state.

The interests of the state, the rationalization of society, the technocratic drive for efficiency and an attempt to plan the future were all to converge in a programme that would bring modernity into the most intimate aspects of life: the scientific management of breeding – **eugenics**. The idea of trying to breed a better population was not new (it can be found in Plato's Republic); what was new was the position of the professional expert in an emerging welfare state, making it possible to turn a centuries-old idea into a practical programme (Waites 1989; Kevles 1995; Paul 1995). In both the US and in Britain there was a broad spectrum of support for eugenics (even its opponents often supported the idea of the need for some sort of biological improvement), and consequently a great diversity of political opinion could shelter under the eugenic umbrella. Most common was the conservative, capitalist and racist eugenicist, but equally at home were anti-capitalist Marxists trying to fulfil the socialist ideal of planning the future. Not surprisingly, with such diversity eugenicists were divided on most questions – who should be encouraged to breed, who discouraged, who should make the decisions, what the policy should be. 'Eugenicists', says Paul, 'were united only in their enthusiasm for technocratic solutions to social problems' (1995: 21). In Britain eugenicists identified the poor as the problem; the lower orders, it was feared, were breeding faster than the middle class. In the United States, the problem was the influx of immigrants from central and southern Europe. In both cases eugenicist attention became focused on mental deficiency or 'feeblemindedness' and a range of possible solutions were put forward. 'Positive' eugenics sought to encourage the breeding of those deemed to be 'fit' (i.e. from the professional middle classes like the eugenicists themselves) and proposals ranged from maternity benefits to stud farms. 'Negative' eugenics sought to discourage the breeding of those deemed to be 'unfit' (the criminal, the insane, the deviant, the foreign) and proposals ranged from segregation to euthanasia. Thus, 'survival of the fittest' was no longer to be left to the process of evolution but was to be determined by the processes of bureaucracy and the application of professional expertise.

In Britain the eugenics movement only made modest progress in securing legislation, but because it was dominated by influential professionals (doctors, teachers, lawyers, social workers) it was very effective in popularizing a eugenic vocabulary and so helped shape policy in medicine, law and education. It should also be noted that some of the most high-profile popularizers of science

– such as Julian Huxley, J.B.S Haldane and Lancelot Hogben – were eugenicists. In the preface to his *Essays in Popular Science* ([1926] 1937) Huxley wrote:

> Unless the civilised societies of to-day improve their organisation, unless they invent and enforce adequate measures for regulating human reproduction, for controlling the quantity of population, and at least preventing the deterioration of quality of racial stock, they are doomed to decay and to be submerged in some new barbarian flood.
>
> (Huxley [1926] 1937: viii)

It was also Huxley's suggestion that people on unemployment benefit should not be allowed to reproduce, any infringement of which should be met by sending the man to a labour camp – 'and Huxley was considered a very moderate eugenicist' (Paul 1995: 73).

In the United States it was much easier for small groups of activists to be very effective at a state level and, as a consequence, not only did American eugenicists provide biological rationalizations for state laws on marriage and miscegenation, but they also played a dominant role in the introduction of state laws on sterilization (Kevles 1995: 100). Indiana was first (1907), with mandatory sterilization of criminals, idiots and rapists in state institutions when this was recommended by a board of experts. Other states quickly followed suit. By 1912 eight states had sterilization laws and eventually thirty states would have legalized sterilization. In Iowa, inmates of public institutions could be sterilized for a variety of reasons including drug addiction and epilepsy, and sterilization was mandatory for anyone convicted of a felony three times or just a single conviction for involvement in white slavery (Kevles 1995: 100). In Kansas during the 1930s boys and girls in the State Industrial Schools were routinely sterilized as a punishment for misbehaviour (Waites 1989: 351). In all, a total of 60,000 men, women and children were sterilized, over half of them in California.

Popularization

The extent to which experts are 'disembedded' in modernity also highlights the increased importance of communication between experts and the rest of society, to maintain both the authority of the expert and the trust of the public. This is especially true for the relationship between science and the public: firstly, because of the depth to which science is implicated in modernity; and secondly, because of the growing distance between the scientific community and the public that we have seen in previous chapters. Having established its identity by separating itself from the public and consolidating its position against cultural and professional rivals (Chapters 1 and 2), the scientific community was now faced with a widening gap not just between itself and the public, but also – with increased scientific specialization – between its own members. The result was a growing need for some form of mediation to fill these widening gaps and one of the significant features of popular science in the twentieth century is the rise of specialists in science communication. Although one might suppose this would be beneficial to the popularization of science, John Burnham (1987) has argued that it was to have the opposite effect, opening the way for nothing less than a new form of superstition. It is worthwhile, therefore, to take a closer look at what Burnham has to say.

In his book *How Superstition Won and Science Lost* (1987), Burnham argues that changes in the popularization of science and health 'ultimately reduced and frustrated the cultural impact of both science and scientist' (4). The *tour de force* of Victorian popularization 'gradually gave way to the recrudescence of superstition and mysticism in a new guise in the consumer culture' (9). Moreover, it was not so much what was popularized that was the problem, as how it was popularized and by whom. Helpfully, Burnham lists his conclusions:

In the traditional struggle between science and superstition, scientific naturalism and reductionism on the popular level contained a definite negative program against error.

This negative program against error was particularly effective in the last part of the nineteenth century but during the twentieth century became attenuated and derailed.

The reason that superstition was able to win was that the form that it took changed, and hardly anyone recognized it for what it was.

The new form that superstition took appeared as the standards of the world of journalism and advertising or what came to be known as the media.

The media world was nonnaturalistic and like superstition was actively competitive with the traditional world of popularized science.

In the media world the elements of sensationalism and disjointed segmentation of information were exactly the elements of superstition that earlier popularizers of science had attacked with skepticism and naturalism.

So completely did the new obscurantism of sensationalism and isolated fact dominate the media world that magical thinking and even conventional superstition were widely tolerated.

Scientists who believed in science as a calling rather than an occupation tended increasingly to withdraw from popularizing during the twentieth century, leaving the field to media personnel and educators.

In America's specialized society, specialists in popularizing, chiefly journalists, increasingly took over the function of presenting science to lay audiences.

(Burnham 1987: 7)

To understand how he comes to draw these conclusions we need to focus on three key elements in the argument: popularization as a fight against superstition, the retreat of 'men of science' from popularization, and the 'bits-and-pieces' presentation of science.

The history that Burnham presents is very much in line with the account given in Chapters 1 and 2. In the early nineteenth century, popularization can be seen as an attempt to diffuse useful knowledge within a general religious context. In the late nineteenth century, naturalism emerged as a triumphant motif and pious assumptions disappeared to be replaced by an evangelical 'religion of science' that measured 'progress' in terms of how far science had replaced credulity (1987: 23). '[T]he correction of error', says Burnham, 'was fundamental in the process of popularization as it developed in the nineteenth century. People at that time and after advocated learning about science because science furthered thinking in terms of order, rationality, and naturalism, and superstition came to serve the evangels of science in a negative way, to explain what science opposed and replaced' (43–4). The struggle between science and superstition 'was an important determinant of American culture' (6) and '. . . the struggle against superstition was an integral part of the act of popularizing science' (8).

The active campaign against superstition was maintained into the early decades of the twentieth century, even though by that time science could be regarded as the dominant authority with respect to religion. However, in the first half of the twentieth century, while the religion of science persisted, the popularization of science was being transformed:

In the nineteenth century, popular science came to stand for the mission of converting people to the scientific way of life. After 1900, many scientists, teachers, and amateurs continued to evangelize for the unity of nature, reductionism, and explanation. As popularization evolved further, however, what the public heard, instead of translation, condensation, and explanation, was a series of events and products – presented not with an eye to upgrading humanity and society but written in terms of personal interest and payoff for each consumer – or of public relations.

(Burnham 1987: 170)

Burnham argues that in the self-indulgent world of consumer culture the intellectual aspects of popular science did not flourish and 'in the sense that most audiences of the popularizers chose a self-indulgent approach to the world, Americans willingly capitulated to the new superstition' (8). As with old forms of superstition, blind faith and appeals to authority compensated for a lack of understanding, but with the new superstition such faith and appeals were directed towards science. The 'correction of error' that had been so important in the nineteenth century was no longer a significant part of popularization. Indeed, for Burnham, in the twentieth century the new forms of popularization were themselves sources of error.

What distinguished twentieth-century popular science from its predecessors was not its content but who did the popularizing. For the nineteenth-century 'men of science' popularization was regarded as a duty and with the cultural ascendancy of the scientific community in the second half of the century 'they became aggressive in defending science not only from superstition but from poorly qualified writers and speakers and ill-informed journalists' (1987: 152). By the end of the nineteenth century, says Burnham, popularization was developing into a 'two-tiered' activity: one part engendered by the 'men of science' saw popular science as a medium for enlightenment and education; and the other typically more commercial 'newspaper science' was driven by a demand for news and entertainment. As scientists increasingly devoted themselves to pure research the task of popularization was more and more left to the communication specialists. 'Whereas in the late nineteenth century, scientists – and often leading scientists – themselves translated and explained science to the lay audiences, increasingly in the twentieth century the scientists turned the job over to someone else' (207). There were some exceptions, says Burnham, but 'the overwhelming momentum continued in the direction of letting nonscientists do the work' (207). The 'triumph of superstition', says Burnham, was 'signalled by the retreat of broad, well-educated missionaries of science from the field of popularization and their replacement by those who were influenced by the mass media or actually worked in journalism, public relations, and advertising' (4).

However, some scientists were just as eager to play the new game and the upsurge in popularization in the 1920s was in part due to an overt public relations campaign to improve the image of science, which had been tarnished by its association with the technologies of mass destruction in the First World War. As Marcel LaFollette has written, despite some opposition within the scientific community who regarded popularization as an unnecessary diversion away from research:

. . . a small group of scientific leaders remained convinced that to attract public sympathy, research must be seen as an *American* activity. Projecting messages about scientific solidarity, about science's usefulness, and about science's importance to the *national* interest, they believed, would improve science's overall public image as well as increase scientists' own sense of community.

(LaFollette 1990: 10)

In 1921, for example, a collaboration between the National Research Council and the **American Association for the Advancement of Science** established the Science Service as a national news agency. Although the agency may have been successful in promoting a more positive image of science, by supplying dramatic copy to newspapers, magazines and radio it would also contribute to the growing differentiation between the popularization of science and science news. A similar concern for popularization of science as public relations can be seen in the activities of the British Association for the Advancement of Science in the 1920s and 1930s (Collins 1981).

Burnham has very little that is positive to say about the impact of news culture upon the popularization of science. In the twentieth century, he says, 'the news standard . . . overwhelmed all popularizing' (1987: 234), and the influence of journalists 'was altogether corrupting, turning high culture into trivial news items and reducing men of science to purveyors of bits and pieces of information' (249). The influence of journalism had changed popular science from a coherent view of nature 'into choppy, unconnected "facts" ' (5) and this emphasis on 'facts' rather than context was 'the first step in destroying the classic uplift popularization of science' (229). With the information stripped of its context, readers were left to supply their own meaning:

But the subversive element in bits-and-pieces, contextless popularization of science and health was the circumstance that the reader, or 'consumer', was left to make his or her own sense of it.

(232)

Clearly, for Burnham, this is a lamentable state of affairs – scientific information should be understood in its proper scientific context – but should we expect it to be otherwise? As we saw in Chapter 1 (particularly with Secord's work on the plurality of readings for *Vestiges*), making one's own sense of a text is precisely what a reader does in any case, whether it is 'bits-and-pieces' popularization or the 'classic uplifting' sort. We shall return to this idea of making sense of science in Chapters 5 and 6 when we look at models of communication and the importance of context in the construction of meaning. Moreover, as we shall see below, in the 1930s there was a trend to contextualize science, but by highlighting the social relevance of science this was more a social context than a scientific one.

There are other questions prompted by Burnham's study, which need to be considered if we are to understand popular science. For example, his separation of popular science into 'two tiers' of activity seems to be not so much the beginnings of a taxonomic system as more a value-driven attempt to sort the 'good' from the 'bad'. Uplifting, enlightening, educational popular science (increasingly confined to communication between scientists) is taken as good; journalistic, entertaining, decontextualized popular science (usually for the 'public') is taken as bad. This naturally leads to a second set of questions. What *is* popular science and what is it for? In previous chapters we saw how popular science came to be redefined as the science which is popularized; now it would seem we might need to redefine popularization. For Burnham, the diffusion of accurate and contextualized information is acceptable as 'popularisation': the presentation of contextless, bits-and-pieces of information is dismissed as 'science news'. To what extent, therefore, do we need to distinguish between popularization, diffusion, communication, journalism, news? Moreover, how we answer that question is likely to depend on what we think popular science is for (e.g. education, enlightenment, entertainment), which in turn will shape the questions we ask about it (e.g. whether it is good/bad, helpful, relevant or trivial and whether it needs to be learnt, used, enjoyed or understood). As we have seen in previous chapters, such considerations are not without political significance and these issues will resurface when we come to examine what is meant by the 'Public Understanding of Science' and 'scientific literacy' (Chapters 5 and 6).

The popularization of scientific values

One notable trend of popular science in the interwar period was the placing of science within a social context, often with explicit reference to its political significance. This was especially true of Britain in the 1930s. In their social history of interwar Britain, written just as the period ended, Graves and Hodge (1941) were to write, 'Scientists towards the close of the Thirties were less occupied with the theoretical implications of their work, or with trying to give it religious and philosophical significance, than with asking themselves what was the place of science in the social system. They were beginning at last to have a social conscience' (393). One of the most popular books on science at the time, for example, was Lancelot Hogben's *Science for the Citizen* (1938). In an 'Author's Confession' which acts as a preface to the first edition, he wrote that the book was:

> . . . partly written for the large and growing number of intelligent adults who realize that the *Impact of Science on Society* is now the focus of genuinely constructive social effort. It is also written for the large and

growing number of adolescents, who realize that they will be the first victims of the new destructive powers of science misapplied.

(Hogben 1938: 9, original emphasis)

The idea that the scientific worker has no time to be socially responsible, he said, was 'nonsense' and ready to be 'debunked'. As the title of the book implied, the key to such social responsibilities was the idea of citizenship, both in the sense of scientists becoming active citizens and of the public needing science to exercise their citizenship. The book ends with a discussion of whether the bulk of mankind will benefit from scientific progress and concludes that 'the further progress of science depends on how far the scientific worker and his fellow citizens co-operate with one another in applying scientific knowledge to the satisfaction of the common needs of mankind' (1938: 1077). Capitalism, he said, had 'lost the initiative of its youth' and scientists in democratic countries were 'awakening to a new sense of responsibility'. Science needed public support and the focus of politics upon property and ownership was misguided. 'The primary task of constructive democratic statesmanship is not to transfer property rights in existing industry from private to public ownership. It is to devise the machinery of social ownership to exploit new technical resources made available by State subsidized research' (1082–3). As Gary Werskey (1988) has shown, such ideas about the social responsibilities of science were not uncommon and were often mixed with radical left-wing politics. Hogben, J.D. Bernal, J.B.S. Haldane, Joseph Needham and Hyman Levy were all prominent popularizers and by the early 1920s all of them had 'in their own distinctive ways, conjoined the causes of science and socialism' (Werskey 1988: 76). Popularizing science went hand in hand with campaigning for socialism. As Haldane was to write in one of his frequent articles for the communist newspaper the *Daily Worker*, 'a knowledge of science should be spread among socialists, and a knowledge of socialism should be spread among scientists' (cited in Gregory and Miller 1998: 32).

Although Hogben's book is filled with detailed scientific information, what was more important to these popularizers of social responsibility was the spread of a more general scientific way of thinking. This was made clear in a number of books published as cheap paperbacks under the Pelican imprint. As part of Penguin books (established by Allen Lane in 1934), Pelicans were soon to show an interest in both science and left-of-centre politics. Julian Huxley's *Essays in Popular Science*, for example, was reprinted as a Pelican in 1937 and argued that 'in these days of manifolded information and broadcast amusement' there was a danger 'the world will become divided into those who have to think for their living and those who never think at all' (v). There would be a 'lamentable divorce' between science and general thought if scientists were too lazy and proud to make themselves understood or if the public were too stupid and prejudiced to understand. If this were to happen then 'it will not be merely the results of science which will not be assimilated, but science herself and the spirit of science will not be understood; and scientists will become an isolated caste in a half-hostile environment' (vi). It was, therefore, the duty of the scientist 'to make available to the lay public the facts and theories of their science, and especially to try to re-create something of the mental background that is engendered by those facts and those theories' (v). Another Pelican author, A.P. Rossiter, expressed a similar sentiment in 1939 when he argued that there was a need and, he believed, a demand for more than just facts. With a final comment sounding very much like one of Burnham's criticisms, he wrote:

> There is an increasing public for books on science which make an attempt to be something better than surprising: those which give some idea of the processes of argument by which theories come into being, and the effects of those theories on beliefs and behaviours – something better than improbable 'facts' of the headline and advertisement sort.
>
> (Rossiter [1939] 1945: 5)

For C.H. Waddington (also a Pelican author), science not only solved technical problems but had also 'developed an attitude to the world which makes some things seem valuable and others not' ([1941] 1948: ix). We might need science for the day-to-day workings of democracy but its true influence was 'an attitude of mind, a general method of thinking about and investigating problems' (viii). In Waddington's view, the old system of private profit and supply and demand were to be replaced by a new system 'centralised and totalitarian in the sense that all the major aspects of the economic development of large regions are consciously planned as an integrated whole' (171). This 'application of conscious control', he thought, was 'actually a step along the path of man's evolutionary advance' (171).

To many people these ideas of a scientifically planned future would be most associated with H.G. Wells. A prolific writer of social novels, science fiction and popular science, Wells moved freely between literature and journalism. He first caught the public's imagination in the 1890s with his 'scientific romances' (*The Time Machine, War of the Worlds, The Island of Dr Moreau, The Invisible Man*) and soon established himself in the public's mind as the leading authority on what the future would be like – as Patrick Parrinder says, his forecasts 'were treated more as news than as subjects for critical judgement' (1972: 2). Wells once explained that 'I am strongly of opinion that we ought to consider the possibilities of the future much more than we do . . . At present we are almost helpless in the grip of circumstances, and I think we ought to strive to shape our destinies' (quoted in Broks 1996: 98). In the early years of the twentieth century

Wells devoted much of his creative energy to describing the utopian future for which man would and should strive. His complete faith in the idea of progress meant that in Wells's vision of the future the possible and the desirable were largely interchangeable, conflating what 'will' be with what 'ought' to be. What he first predicts in *Anticipations* has much in common with what he prescribes in his later, more propagandist book, *A Modern Utopia* – the mechanization of labour, eugenics, the world-state, and the governing of the 'New Republic' by a technocratic elite whether they are described as 'the Efficients' or the 'Samurai'.

Wells's most extensive examination of the future is to be found in his book *The Shape of Things to Come*, published in 1933 and soon turned into a popular film (produced by Alexander Korda as *Things to Come*). The film is probably better remembered than the book, becoming a science fiction classic with its stirring visual imagery and its heroic depiction of technocrats building a better world. By contrast the book can be incredibly dull with its heavily detailed account of changes to economic and political systems. Both show events leading to the development of the World State (after an eerily prescient description of world war breaking out in 1940), but where the film has simple appeals to 'technology', 'science' and 'progress', the book looks in detail at the foundations upon which the World State is built – the transformation of every-day life. Through the book, therefore, we can see Wells's belief that it is not just advanced technology that will bring the future utopia but, more importantly, the spread of scientific values into the social realm.

Presented as a history written in the year 2106, the book describes how a conference of scientific and technical workers formulate the idea of air transport as the 'combining and directive force' upon which the world state could be based (291). Later, this New World State is imposed on the rest of the world under the 'Air Dictatorship' which carries out a ruthless 'disentanglement of tradition', quickly suppressing all religions and setting up the New World State as global government, new social order and universal faith (401). Under this 'Puritan Tyranny' eugenics is used to help 'tidy up' the world: 'the painless destruction of monsters and the more dreadful and pitiful sorts of defective was legalised, and also the sterilisation of various types that would otherwise have transmitted tendencies that were plainly undesirable' (408). By the year 2059 this 'intolerant militant stage of the World State' (380) is over, its job complete. The World Council dissolves itself (since there is no longer any need for a world government) and is superseded by Educational Control which is, in effect, rule by social psychologists. Thus, the Modern State was to be founded on social control through education, the purpose of which was propaganda seeking 'to establish a new complete ideology and a new spirit which would induce the individual to devote himself and to shape all his activities to one definite pur-pose, to the attainment and maintenance of a progressive world-socialism'

(413). Through the book, Wells dismisses the revolutionary movement of the nineteenth century as 'a tiresomeness of slacking workers, aided and abetted by critics like Ruskin, artists like William Morris, playwrights like Bernard Shaw and suchlike impracticable and unconvincing people'. By the 1930s, however (i.e. the immediate future for Wells's book), 'two-thirds of the technicians, scientific workers and able business organisers were talking active revolution. It was no longer to be class insurrection of hands; it was to be a revolt of the competent' (274). Reverting to the voice of its present-day editor, the book concludes that the world is heading for disaster until a comprehensive faith in a modernized World State takes hold of the human imagination, 'and it must needs be the work, first of all, of an aggressive order of religiously devoted men and women who will try out and establish and impose a new pattern of living upon our race' (446). Picking up the theme of the previous chapter, what was needed, in short, was nothing less than the dictatorship of the expert.

The popularization of science as the popularization of scientific values was also to be seen in century-of-progress expositions in the United States, but here the technocratic faith was to be mediated through consumerism rather than socialism. The participation of scientists in the expositions, says Robert Rydell, 'was part of the persistent effort by American scientists after World War I to popularize science, mold a "true" American culture with scientific values, and affirm the hegemony of the corporate state' (1993: 93). At Chicago (1933) and New York (1939), for example, scientists tried to do more than simply convey scientific information, but instead 'regarded the expositions as unsurpassed opportunities for embarking on a "cultural" offensive that would create a scientific culture with pragmatic values and thus provide Americans with faith in corporate leadership and in scientific expertise' (1993: 113). The expositions were major public relations exercises for both the corporations who staged them and the scientists who lent them their authority. As such they 'presented Americans with blueprints for modernizing the United States' whereby future progress was defined in terms of material growth and science and technology were integrated into American cultural life through consumerism (213–14). 'Visitors to science exhibits at the fairs were not expected to enter intellectually into science', says Rydell, 'but to become consumers of science through mass production' (215). This was a crucial shift from the previous World Fairs (see Chapter 2). Like their predecessors, they displayed a positivist faith in technology flawed by racism, but where they differed was in the growing emphasis on entertainment and leisure as central to the modernizing strategies. Moreover, in the Victorian fairs the scientists involved were usually anthropologists who constructed and displayed ideas about race and evolution, and were not tied to the corporate elites who organized the exposition. In the century-of-progress expositions scientists were more likely to be from the 'hard' sciences linked to corporate research laboratories or corporate sponsored research programmes. Rydell argues that from their positions within or closely allied to corporations, scientists not only 'helped rationalize the machine-age ethos on display at the expositions' but also, and he suggests perhaps more importantly, 'lent legitimacy to claims by corporation managers that they could be entrusted with planning the future course of American society' (215).

The public image of science

So far in this chapter we have seen how science is implicated in modernity and have drawn out some of the ideological affinities between science, the state and mass production. Moreover, we could also say that the popularization of science in this period with its emphasis on modernization, planning, rationalization and efficiency was, in effect, the popularization of modernity (the consequences of this will be returned to in the next chapter). However, what we still need to do is to find out what the public thought of all this. The work of Marcel LaFollette (1990) helps us to get a picture of what the situation was like in the United States. She starts her study by saying that:

> . . . the half-century from the 1910s through the 1950s represented a time of exciting rearrangement for the scientific research enterprise in the United States, a period during which its political and social power strengthened and scientists began to pay attention to their public image.
>
> (LaFollette 1990: 1)

Prior to the First World War scientific research was modestly funded, centred on the individual researcher and regarded as culturally important rather than relevant to national politics. After the Second World War US science was increasingly done in large teams supported by massive research budgets from federal support. However, despite the dramatic transformation of science in this period the public image of science remained remarkably consistent. From a survey of nationally circulated magazines she found that 'in the 1950s, authors (nonscientists and scientists alike) used the same descriptive phrases as had authors in 1910' (6). This consistency was to be found across different types of magazine, different media and different periods (for example, compared with TV in the 1970s and 1980s) and leads LaFollette to believe that 'the images must have had deep roots in American culture' reflecting the 'aggregated, collective, undifferentiated ideas that general audiences shared about science' (5 and 20). Now, while we might wish to raise the possibility of a plurality of readings and meanings (as seen in previous chapters and to be discussed later), such consistency must also be taken into account and it is difficult to get away from the sense that it must be indicative of something. For LaFollette, the images 'are just as much products of American culture as of American science. The face of science shown here was not only the face that scientists wanted presented but also the one that Americans wanted to see as their own' (viii).

LaFollette's study is based upon a survey of eleven mass circulation magazines like *The Saturday Evening Post* and *Cosmopolitan* which tried to combine information with entertainment. In these magazines the term 'science' was used interchangeably to refer to science as a research process, a body of knowledge and as a professional community. 'Science' became anthropomorphized into 'a living, growing thing that could "do" things, could "act", could even "assert" ', implying that there was 'some powerful entity called *science* – with a mysterious and unstoppable life of its own' (6). By contrast, as science became anthropomorphized, scientists themselves became dehumanized with stereotypical 'scientists' possessing many characteristics more appropriately applied to machines and, as a group, acquiring a 'mysterious uniformity' (6). However, science was also presented as an integral part of modern life with science coverage not limited to straightforward accounts of research findings but also addressing science's political and social context as well. (It would seem that the public has long thought of science as social – something worth remembering when we discuss scientific literacy in Chapters 5 and 6.) In that social (and cultural context) the 'belief in progress became a central article of "the dominant American faith" ', and science would be on hand to speed up the process (9):

> None of these publications presented an unqualified negative image of science ... Instead, the popular magazines consistently approached science as a pragmatic and progressive national force, held up scientists as reliable authorities, and pointed to scientific knowledge as useful even when it seemed incomprehensible ... The consistency in these ideas across seemingly different publications owned by different publishers lend them credibility as being representative not only of what was offered to the audience, but also of what millions of Americans agreed with, approved of, and found appropriate and correct.
>
> (LaFollette 1990: 44)

Amidst the radical changes that incorporated science into the US political framework, 'the public images of science exhibited strong continuity of interpretation, consolidating oft-repeated subthemes of authority, usefulness, complexity, and bounty' (174).

Does the consistency and continuity that LaFollette finds – a consistency which stretches across magazines, publishers and periods – also extend across the Atlantic? My own study of British magazines might provide an opportunity to see if this is the case (1988, 1996). In many ways the two studies are comparable. Both studies analysed the content of thousands of magazines statistically and textually. Both studies sampled magazines which included high-quality non-fiction, were directed at general audiences, and tried to combine information with entertainment. Both studies found a language of heroic perseverance associated with scientific practice. Both studies found fluctuations in the amount of science coverage which could be related to wider social and cultural contexts. With so much in common the differences become more striking. In American magazines between 1910 and 1955, LaFollette found that 4 per cent of all non-fiction articles were devoted to science. This is the same as the amount of non-fiction editorial space found in downmarket British weekly magazines, but is a good deal less than the 10 per cent of non-fiction editorial space to be found in the more upmarket monthly magazines (Broks 1988). Should we see the American magazines as more downmarket than their British counterparts? Do the differences reflect the different cultures (US and British) or the different periods (1890–1914 and 1910–55)? Or are the differences simply products of different sampling techniques and statistical procedures?

The most striking difference, however, comes when we consider the magazines' fiction. LaFollette did not analyse fiction but a brief analysis of magazine short stories did not convince her that 'fiction content necessarily contained images of scientists different from those in the nonfiction' (25). This is in stark contrast to the British magazines with their representation of fictional scientists as villains and real scientists as heroes (Broks 1996: 41–52). Again we are left to wonder whether we should look for explanations in differences of time or place. In the work of Haynes (1994) there is a suggestion that it might be the former. While showing that images of science from the middle ages to the present day draw on six recurring stereotypes, she does note that in the late nineteenth century there were 'sporadic protests against the cult of efficiency and uniformity engendered by the machine age' (143). These sceptical treatments, she says, were 'little more than a thoughtful pause between the unthinking exuberance of Verne's adventurer-scientists and the frank glorification, in the first decades of the twentieth century, of the new scientist hero, either as inventor or as leader-elect of a future utopia' (161). Unfortunately, this idea of a late nineteenth-century 'thoughtful pause' runs counter to both my own and LaFollete's findings. LaFollette has noted that in the 1930s and 1940s there was a growing realization that each new advance of science carried the potential for both benefit and harm (12–13), and my own work has shown that this undercurrent of ambiguity was developing before the First World War. Taking all three studies together we would seem to have a pause for thought stretching from the late nineteenth through to the mid-twentieth century (the idea of sporadic protests against the machine-age will be returned to in the next chapter). However, it might also be the case that although comparisons between different studies are tantalizingly suggestive, ultimately they simply indicate just how much more work still needs to be done.

However, we do get a fascinating glimpse into the public's feelings about science through the contemporary reports and files of Mass Observation. Set up in Britain in 1937, Mass Observation was a social research organization which aimed to study the everyday lives of ordinary people. Not only did it pay investigators to record conversations and behaviour at work, in the street and at public events, but it also employed hundreds of untrained observers to keep diaries and respond to open-ended questionnaires. In 1940 it produced a file on 'Treatments of Science', a report put together from a random sampling of newspapers and wireless broadcasts to give 'the layman's picture of scientific method and purpose' (File 432). It reported that 'even the most superficial reading of popular dope on science shows that there is no understanding at all of scientific mentality, method or research. Only the *products* are recognised' (original emphasis). Amongst the 'popular dope' sampled were the strip cartoon *Buck Rogers*, the latest novel from Hammond Innes which included a Jewish refugee inventor, a diatribe against the theory of evolution in the weekly magazine *Everybody's*, and the abuse of the term 'scientific' in adverts. As a summary of popular attitudes its conclusions are worth quoting at length:

> This exploitation of the word 'scientific' to give prestige all helps to increase the magic of science, 'something difficult to understand but sure to be correct'. And this often actually hinders any propaganda for science, by making laymen believe, but also believe that they cannot understand how the marvellous clever scientists did it . . . In general, there is an enormous popular misconception about science, coupled with a considerable admiration for science as a whole and a semi-humorous, semi-reverant attitude to scientists as people . . . It may be gratifying to the scientist to be regarded as an erratic supernatural, but the other implications of this attitude are opposed to any understanding of science. At the same time, some of the voodoo which surrounds science can easily be exploited in developing a more informative and intelligent propaganda for science. In fact little can be done unless propaganda for science recognises the situation as it exists, and as we have attempted to describe it above. This brief survey indicates the abundance of material about science which flows through the channels of publicity BUT DOES NOT FLOW *FROM* SCIENCE.
>
> (Mass Observation 1940: file 432, original emphasis)

These problems of the 'propaganda for science' will be returned to in later chapters.

A second report in the Mass Observation files gives us a much more direct look at public opinion. In 1941 volunteer observers were asked what their 'normal everyday attitudes to science' were. Built on observers' responses, the report found that 'though there are many subsidiary feelings about science and scientists there is one overwhelmingly prominent attitude . . . *People feel that science has got out of control*' (file 951, original emphasis). However, in the majority of cases this was not considered to be the fault of scientists but rather the misapplication of their discoveries was 'the fault of unscrupulous people, or of the whole community'. Understandably in the middle of the war, most apprehension was felt about the application of science to warfare, but blame for the misuse of science was seldom placed on the scientists' shoulders. However, what is especially fascinating about this second report is that we finally get to hear the voice of the public – even if it might be a deeply mediated, unrepresentative whisper. I shall leave the final word to a 'young housewife' who thought that science was 'horribly abused':

> If only it could be used to constructive ends instead of destructive, the world would be a marvellous place in no time. I have a colossal faith in science properly applied, that it could cure almost all ills and put all our troubles right. Instead of the scientists' energy being diverted to war, if only they would find out means of doing the dirty jobs of the world quickly and economically, so that nobody had to bother about doing them, and we could spend time doing the things we liked.
>
> (Mass Observation 1941: file 951)

Further reading

Bauman, Z. (2000) *Liquid Modernity*. Cambridge: Polity Press.

Berman, M. (1983) *All That is Solid Melts into Air: The Experience of Modernity*. London: Verso.

Burnham, J.C. (1987) *How Superstition Won and Science Lost: Popularizing Science and Health in the United States*. New Brunswick, NJ: Rutgers University Press.

Haynes, R.D. (1994) *From Faust to Strangelove: Representations of the Scientist in Western Literature*. Baltimore, MD: Johns Hopkins University Press.

LaFollette, M. (1990) *Making Science Our Own: Public Images of Science 1910–1955*. Chicago, IL: University of Chicago Press.

Rydell, R.W. (1993) *World of Fairs: The Century of Progress Expositions*. Chicago, IL: University of Chicago Press.

Werskey, G. (1988) *The Visible College: A Collective Biography of British Scientists and Socialists of the 1930s*. London: Free Association Books.

CONSUMING DOUBTS

4

Towards the end of 1945 the slogan 'shoot all scientists' was being chalked on walls in London. The timing, perhaps, reveals all. Late 1945 is immediately after the dropping of atomic bombs on the Japanese cities of Hiroshima and Nagasaki. It would be easy, therefore, to see the first use of nuclear weapons as marking a major turning point in the relationship between science and the public – a convenient punctum (8.15 a.m. local time, 6 August 1945) with a distinct before and after. Indeed, there are few images from the twentieth century that are as iconic as the mushroom cloud that rises above a nuclear explosion; it might even be thought of as the defining image for the century. It marked the beginning of the 'atomic age' and the first product of that new age was a weapon. In the years to come, although thousands of nuclear warheads were made, it quickly became known simply as *the* bomb. Nevertheless, we must be careful about adopting such easy formulations. The post-war world was deeply contradictory in its attitudes towards science. It was clear that science had played a key role in winning the war, but with it came a new atomic nightmare. Fear was the price of peace. After the war, the public seems to have had a genuine thirst for knowledge about science, yet there was growing concern amongst scientists and governments about public ignorance. Within two decades the public were enjoying a technology-based consumer boom, and at the same time voicing concerns about the role of science in society. In 1961 John F. Kennedy inspired technological dreams in declaring his country's intention to put a man on the moon: in 1962 Rachel Carson's *Silent Spring* stirred environmental consciences with a coruscating attack on the damage being done to our home planet. Clearly, the cultural meaning of science was openly contested. This chapter will explore those contested meanings to see how fears of an 'anti-science' movement could coincide with a boom in popular science.

Nuclear reactions?

Opinion surveys of the time regularly showed that the great majority of the US public welcomed the bomb as a way to bring a swift end to the war and so save the lives of allied soldiers. Media coverage was equally supportive and any voices of dissent (even if only on the letters pages of a newspaper) 'often engendered extraordinarily hostile reactions' (Allan 2006: 94). This may have been, at least in part, due to media management by the military. When news of the bombing of Hiroshima first appeared no details of the bomb's effects were given. Instead, the report focused on the test explosion at Alamogordo three weeks earlier to describe the new weapon. In the days that followed – even with the dropping of a second bomb on Nagasaki – press attention quickly waned and typically focused on how the bomb was made, biographies of those involved, and the potential for industrial applications of nuclear power. In an attempt to maintain control of the coverage, an authorized delegation of US reporters (with an accompanying official censor) was flown to Hiroshima in early September. All the journalists were carefully screened to ensure that they would reproduce the official perspective. The 'official line' from Washington, says Stuart Allan, 'revolved around the perceived necessity of restricting reportage to the technological achievement of the atomic bomb itself, especially with regard to its tremendous destructive power on the urban infrastructure' (86;). The effects of radiation were explicitly denied. Thus, as Allan argues, 'the broad parameters marking the normative limits of public debate' were soon established as a 'remarkably consistent narrative frame' for nuclearist discourses quickly emerged. Invoked as self-evidently 'common-sense', the narrative was rarely questioned and established a consensus around the reluctant, but justified, use of the bomb.

However, Stuart Allan has also shown how these nuclearist assumptions were profoundly challenged by the reportage of Wilfred Burchett for the London *Daily Express*, and John Hersey for the *New Yorker* magazine. Of particular importance, says Allan:

> . . . was the extent to which their reports helped to give voice to the experiences of the *hibakusha* (literally, 'explosion-affected persons') still alive in the shattered city of Hiroshima. In attempting to draw the world's attention to their plight, both Burchett and Hersey endeavoured to place a human face on official statistics regarding the atomic obliteration of the

city's inhabitants. In so doing, their writings contributed to the eventual emergence of a counter-narrative over the years, namely one which sought to redefine the atomic bombings as horrific acts of political violence.

(Allan 2006: 84)

Hersey's account, for example, which took up an entire issue of the *New Yorker* magazine, was built upon interviews with six survivors of the Hiroshima bomb. It provides a stark illustration of how an appeal to lived experience can help provide a counter-narrative to officially sanctioned truth claims – a point that we shall return to in later chapters.

Challenges to simple nuclearist discourses are also to be found in the mixed reactions of the British public. In August 1945, within days of the bombs being dropped, the Mass Observation volunteers were asked to 'describe in detail their own feelings and views about the atomic bomb, and those of the people they met' (File 2277). The report compiled from the volunteers' responses recorded that in most cases the initial reaction was one of horror.

'When the news came over the radio I was just horrified. I felt sick at heart that a civilised nation could use such a weapon. My sister and I heard it while at breakfast, we looked at each other. I could see her face quite white.'

'I personally feel very depressed about the atomic bomb, and I fear that "the powers that be" will not be able to use it solely for the benefit of humanity. One has an unpleasant feeling that not many years will elapse before it will be used as the major weapon in another war.'

'Too horrified to want to think or speak about it and yet it is seldom out of my mind. It casts a gloom over everything and its terrifying possibilities make nothing worthwhile doing.'

(Mass Observation 1945: file 2277)

However, despite these expressions of horror, few had doubts that its use was justified, often on the grounds that it helped end the war. Even so, from a moral point of view, although some thought it no worse than other weapons, more people were definite about it being wrong – in particular because it highlighted the hypocrisy of the allies in their claims about not bombing civilians.

From reading the Mass Observation files we can see that misgivings about science were to take root in the early post-war years. A later report (1947) attributed the growing sense of unease directly to 'the shock of the bomb'. Since Hiroshima, it said, 'there has been an increasingly strong, if vague, feeling that science is getting out of control' (file 2489). The atom bomb was a turning point because it emphasized the need to consider the moral aspects of science:

Up to then science had existed for the majority in a moral vacuum. For many people it had become Science and had replaced God, but it did not take over all his functions. Science did things: it made it easy for us to travel long distances, it warmed our houses, it turned out domestic utensils at great speed and low price, it brought music to the fireside but it was not concerned with moral problems. Now the lack was beginning to be regretted. Man was lagging behind his own monster.

(Mass Observation 1947: file 2489)

As a result of the bomb there had been 'an astonishing mental adjustment over a very short period', talk of 'ultimate destruction' was no longer considered alarmist, and when asked to think of science 'most people . . . think of the bomb'. There was still an awareness of the benefits of science, but this was now balanced by a more critical outlook which, the report said, was an indication of a new distrust: 'There is a feeling that we have been cheated. The great panacea simply hasn't worked.'

From the work of Marcel LaFollette (1990) we can see that this sense of disappointment is also to be found in American attitudes to science. Through the century there had been a growing tension in the relationship between science and society. The origins of this tension, LaFollette explains, lie in the widely shared images of science and, more particularly, in 'the significant discrepancy between what the public expected from science and what science delivered' (1–2). In turn, this tension helps to explain the problems that present-day science faces in trying to elicit public support:

No single negative image led to the current political reassessments of science. Citizens and politicians alike have simply reacted, with characteristic American pragmatism, to decades of mismatch between positive images and negative effects, between an idealized expectation of benefit and the reality of unpredicted harm, between the scientists' endless promises and the public's unfulfilled desires.

(LaFollette 1990: 17)

One might say that this had always been the case, that the history of popular science is a history of the public's unfulfilled expectations. Even before the First World War we can detect a creeping sense of disillusion (Broks 1993, 1996). In 1909 C.F.G. Masterman, writer and politician, wrote that:

The large hopes and dreams of the Early Victorian time have vanished: never, at least in the immediate future, to return. The science which was to allay all diseases, the commerce which was to abolish war, and weave all nations into one human family, the research which was to establish ethics and religion on a secure and positive foundation, the invention which was to enable all humanity, with a few hours of not disagreeable work every day, to live for the remainder of their time in ease and sunshine – all these have been recognised as remote and fairy visions.

(Masterman cited in Hynes 1968: 132)

That same year George Bernard Shaw told the Medico-Legal Society: 'At the present moment we are passing through a phase of disillusion. Science has not lived up to the hopes we formed of it in the 1860s' (cited in Hynes 1968: 133–4).

We should be careful, therefore, of assigning too much significance to a single event in shaping public attitudes (i.e. pre-bomb pro-science: post-bomb anti-science). We should also note that feelings of disillusion and disappointment do not necessarily translate into downright hostility. Nevertheless, we still might want to see the war as accelerating existing trends and, more importantly, see those trends not simply as a general move against science but rather as a progressive questioning of the relationship that science has with society.

We can see something of the shifting relationship if we turn to the proposals put forward by Vannevar Bush, principal science adviser to the president. During the war Bush was director of the Office of Scientific and Research Development (which he helped establish) and played a prominent role in setting up the Manhattan Project to build the atom bomb. In November 1944 President Roosevelt asked Bush how the experience of coordination of scientific efforts, which had been so successful in wartime, might be continued when the war was over. Bush's response (to Truman following Roosevelt's death) was delivered in July 1945. Picking up on a reference to the need to pioneer 'new frontiers of the mind' that was in Roosevelt's original letter, he called his report *Science – The Endless Frontier*. The key to Bush's vision was that government should accept responsibility for promoting new scientific knowledge and developing new scientific talent – much as previous US governments had fostered the opening of new frontiers by giving land to pioneers. As Bush explained: 'It is in keeping with the American tradition – one which has made the United States great – that new frontiers shall be made accessible for development by all American citizens.' Moreover, scientific progress was vital to the national interest for without it national health would deteriorate, the standard of living would decline, unemployment would increase and 'we could not have maintained our liberties against tyranny'. There was much in his report that was reminiscent of the appeals to the public utility of science which we saw in previous chapters, and will see again in the more recent concerns for scientific literacy and the Public Understanding of Science (Chapters 5 and 6). Bush, however, was probably more successful than most in translating the vision into reality.

By persuading the military that weapons research should be contracted out to academics at elite institutions he can be credited with helping to establish the military–industrial–university complex that persists through to today.

For present purposes, however, what is most relevant about the Bush report is what it proposed for the relationship between scientists and government. Bush asked that the government provide substantial funds for medical research, military research and for the training of scientists to help stimulate industrial growth. In addition there would have to be stability to such funding in order to support long-range programmes and presumably, since this was an 'endless' frontier, such stable funding might have to be provided for a very long time indeed. However, even though the government was expected to provide the funds it was 'of the utmost importance' that the scientist should be independent of any government interference. The government, said Bush, 'should recognise that freedom of inquiry must be preserved and should leave internal control of policy, personnel, and the method and scope of research to the institution in which it is carried on'. For Bush the key to scientific progress was 'the free play of free intellects, working on subjects of their own choice, in the manner dictated by their curiosity for the explanation of the unknown'. In short, what Bush wanted was for scientists to have large sums of public money *and* freedom from public control over how it should be spent.

Not surprisingly, Bush's proposals faced strong opposition – after all, they did run counter to the traditional American political principle of public accountability. Opponents accepted the idea of federal support for science but wanted more bureaucratic control over the money. In the end the Bush model of scientific independence prevailed, says LaFollette, because 'it embodied the prevalent cultural images of science':

> The images underpinning the political justifications for the Bush model represented entirely natural choices, common views at the time. Bush employed metaphors and ideas that epitomized Americans' trust in and expectations of science and scientists, while [opposing] forces drew on suspicions and uneasiness that represented at that time only a minority view.
> (LaFollette 1990: 15)

It might be seen as the high-water mark of scientific freedom without responsibility (indeed, of public-funded freedom without responsibility), but the tide was about to turn. If we can understand the success of the Bush model, as LaFollette suggests, through the 'prevalent cultural images' and 'common views' of Americans then we might also understand its decline in the same way. Although the military–industrial–university complex remains as part of the Bush legacy, science now operates within a much stricter regulatory environment. It is not that the public have turned against science, but rather that the trust which Bush could assume and rely on is no longer there. As an explanation of post-war trends, it is worth presenting LaFollette's analysis at length:

> Opinion polls and other cultural barometers do not reveal widespread antiscience feelings among the majority of the American people. People admire famous scientists. They support funding for research. They flock to science museums in ever growing numbers. They may even like science. The wholesale rejection of science predicted by some analysts in the 1970s has simply not materialized. Nevertheless, as demonstrated by the extent of regulation, the American public also does not fully trust either scientists or scientific institutions, especially in regard to how research should be conducted.
>
> Examining these seeming contradictions in the light of the popular image of science since 1900 helps to explain what happened. The popular image early in the century was strong and self-assured but less entwined with national interests. When other oracles, such as religion or political ideology, failed to supply sufficient hope of better times, science could be (and was) substituted as an instrument of faith. Science's record of positive achievement throughout the century and scientists' incessant promises of infinite progress reinforced its social authority. When journalists hailed each new discovery as a 'whisper of salvation', the public naturally expected more. These expectations – unquestioning and ill-informed – dressed scientists in a mantle of mystery and endowed them with almost supernatural attributes. The overall image was not negative, and the level of concern low.
>
> The images of science present in the Bush report and similar policy statements represented an inaccurate, idealistic view of science, however – a view that could not be sustained. The view ignored how science was really done, it exaggerated what scientists could really accomplish, and it miscommunicated what scientists were really like. It proposed an impractical, improbable array of promises; it made assumptions of good behavior that were simply incompatible with human nature; and it advocated programs that flew in the face of basic democratic ideas about whose interests should govern – those of the special interest group or those of the public.
>
> (LaFollette 1990: 15–16)

The Bush model of independence and freedom was accepted because the public image of science was so glowing, but its inconsistencies meant that it was politically unstable. The public maintained its faith in science and so the government maintained funding, but as trust diminished so regulation increased.

'Americans needed science', says LaFollette, 'they continued to admire experts but began to remove science's special political privileges' (16).

To raise the issue of trust is to return to Giddens's idea of disembedded expertise that was introduced in the previous chapter. A disembedded social system, it will be recalled, relies on trust. Scientists had distanced themselves from the public as part of the process of self-definition, a necessary separation to establish their own realm of professional expertise (see Chapters 1 and 2). Now such distancing became a convenient tactic for avoiding accountability by separating the 'pure' practice of science (done by scientists) from the 'abuse' done to it by others, but such a separation could only be maintained so long as the bond of trust could be maintained with it. Although many prominent scientists might insist that they should not be held responsible for how their research was used, the Manhattan Project gave the public a different impression:

> The realisation that for years scientists had been cooly [sic] working on this project, clearly knowing the effects, became all the more amazing. The futile pleas of these men that they would much have preferred to have used the energy for peaceful means showed a guilty conscience, but not one sufficiently stirred to make them feel impelled to do something drastic in the matter. We have no knowledge of a scientist who had the courage to refuse to undertake the work.
>
> (Mass Observation 1945: file 2277)

In the post-war period, even though some scientists might assume 'modest' responsibility for the harmful impacts of science, fewer and fewer journalists were to accept this and 'began to assess society's stake in the practice of science more openly. Scientists enthusiastically took credit for the advances of beneficial technologies, but the mass media began quietly to hold them accountable for any harmful effects' (LaFollette 1990: 13).

In this way, if we wish to see the war (and the bomb) as a turning point then it may be best not to see it simply in terms of a swing in public attitudes against science, but perhaps as a point of departure for new concerns about accountability and control. In the relationship between science and the public the crucial issue was not support but responsibility. Before the war, for example, scientists such as Hogben, Haldane and Bernal had expressed their sense of social responsibility through popularization and their attempts to spread scientific values throughout society (see Chapter 3). After the war, the public increasingly took social responsibility to mean the injection of social values into science. We should not be surprised, therefore, that there should be so much concern over and demand for popular science in the post-war period, nor that it should eventually become such a fiercely contested area. On the one hand we would appear to have a scientific community wanting it to be known that to understand science is to appreciate that it cannot be held responsible for any misuse of that science; and on the other, a public that was coming to feel that it understood science only too well and wanted to hold it to account. It is, of course, in the interests of scientists that our attention be focused on whether the public are for or against science, rather than focused on questions of responsibility and accountability – questions about support interrogate the public: questions of responsibility interrogate the scientist. (It is worth remembering this in the next chapter when we look at the fears about the public being 'anti-science'.) As is so often the case in studying popular science, it is not the answers that are so important as the questions we decide to ask in the first place.

Cultural challenges

Even if we accept the simple framing of attitudes into whether the public is 'for' or 'against', we still need to examine what this opposition meant. Early images of radiation and radium, for example, were generally optimistic in their references to transmutation and alchemy. H.G. Wells might give a frightening vision of the power of an atom bomb in his story of *The World Set Free* (a story which inspired physicist Leo Szilard to help make one for real), but on the whole the popular pre-war presentation of nuclear physics was in positive terms of medical uses and potential energy sources. After the bomb nuclear anxieties became more prominent but, as Jon Turney (1998) points out, it was often the possible biological effects that became the focus for people's fears and not the prospect of apocalyptic physical destruction. Countless B-movies of the 1950s are testament to this pervasive fear of radiation – a threat as invisible and insidious as the communism against which so many of the films were thinly disguised warnings. One consequence, says Turney, was that the meaning of 'mutation' became 'irrevocably skewed'. Increasingly it came to mean not just change, but bad change: a sense which has persisted to today and which 'colours every lay reading of accounts of molecular biology, every genetic counsellor's consultation. Mutation means monstrosity' (Turney 1998: 128). What this shows is that if we are to see nuclear anxieties as evidence of post-war anti-science sentiment, then we also need to examine common images and cultural references to see what meanings those fears were based on.

Similarly, if we see anti-science as being oppositional we need to ask the question: opposition to what? Science has never enjoyed complete unequivocal support from the society of which it is part, but the grounds for reaction against it will be as diverse as the meanings attached to it. As we have seen from previous chapters, opponents might be able to attack it on grounds of being too religious, not religious enough, too radical, too conservative, pro-socialist, pro-capitalist, and so on. Moreover, can we always be sure that science is the target? Are attacks on science better understood as attacks on the products of science, on applied science and technology, or even – if we accept the diversionary tactics of scientists mentioned above – on the *abuse* of science or the *abuse* of technology? In the previous chapter it was suggested that the popularization of science was, in effect, the popularization of modernity; to what extent, therefore, might we also (perhaps mistakenly) see opponents of modernity as opponents of science and vice versa? Once again it is the circulation of meanings that demands our attention and not simply the totting up of attitudes for and against.

By way of example, let us look at a novel which is one of the great science fiction dystopias of the twentieth century and as such might be seen as part of the anti-science canon: Aldous Huxley's *Brave New World*. Published in 1932 at a time of enthusiasm for eugenics, it has since become a convenient shorthand for present-day fears about cloning and genetic engineering. The novel's principal idea of biological engineering, however, was not new to imaginative fiction. In H.G. Wells's novel *The First Men in the Moon*, the scientist Cavor marvels at how the Selenites who live on the moon are grown to suit their intended function in Selenite society; and in Karel Kapek's play *R.U.R.* from the 1920s the 'robots' are made from organic material on a production line (Turney 1998). In *Brave New World* it is the growth of identical people from a single egg (the 'Bokanovsky Process') which ensures that there are the correct numbers of workers appropriate for each particular job: from the exceptional Alphas doing the most intellectual work through to the mass-produced Epsilons doing the most menial. Chemical and physical conditioning before embryos are 'decanted' together with psychological conditioning as babies ensures that children are successfully 'predestinated' into their allotted place in society.

What makes *Brave New World* so powerful, though, is not the imagined technology but its social critique. In a foreword to the novel in 1946 Huxley explained that 'The theme of Brave New World is not the advancement of science as such; it is the advancement of science as it affects human individuals' (Huxley [1932] 1977: 9). It is the future of humanity that Huxley wants to examine, not the future of science. Indeed, in this New World science has been reduced to 'just a cookery book, with an orthodox theory of cooking that nobody is allowed to question . . . "real science", inquisitive science is unorthodox and illicit' (181). As Mustapha Mond the Resident World Controller for Western Europe explains, 'Science is dangerous; we have to keep it most carefully chained and muzzled' (181). With its potential to introduce an element of change into society, science is seen as a threat to the social stability which is the primary goal of this New World. Stability is achieved through the simple expedient of ensuring that everybody is happy. Biological engineering and psychological conditioning create the foundations for a happy population; state-sponsored pleasure (drugs and promiscuous sex) does the rest. Mond rejects the idea that the lower castes find their work awful:

> Awful? *They* don't find it so. On the contrary, they like it. It's light, it's childishly simple. No strain on the mind or the muscles. Seven and a half hours of mild, unexhausting labour, and then the *soma* ration and games and unrestricted copulation and the feelies. What more can they ask for?
>
> (Huxley [1932] 1977: 180)

As Huxley explained in his foreword, 'A really efficient totalitarian state would be one in which the all-powerful executive of political bosses and their army of managers control a population of slaves who do not have to be coerced, because they love their servitude' (12). This is, perhaps, the most chilling aspect of the novel: the way that Huxley shows how Utopia can be so horrific.

But whose Utopia would it be? Constant references to 'Our Ford' (as in Henry Ford) and the replacement of the Christian crucifix with the sign of the T (as in Model T) show that the New World has elevated the belief in mass production to the heights of a religion. In the 'time of our Ford' there had been a belief in never-ending scientific progress, but since then there had been a shift from the pursuit of truth to the pursuit of happiness:

> Knowledge was the highest good, truth the supreme value; all the rest was secondary and subordinate. True, ideas were beginning to change even then. Our Ford himself did a great deal to shift the emphasis from truth and beauty to comfort and happiness. Mass production demanded the shift. Universal happiness keeps the wheels steadily turning; truth and beauty can't.
>
> (Huxley [1932] 1977: 183)

In turn, universal happiness is dependent on mass consumption, and mass consumption creates the demand for mass production – so the wheels go round:

> . . . industrial civilisation is only possible when there's no self-denial. Self-indulgence up to the very limits imposed by hygiene and economics. Otherwise the wheels stop turning.
>
> (190)

In such a hedonistic technocracy the role of science is reduced to the hand-maiden of technology; and the role of technology is reduced to ensuring a constant supply of new products and the (literal and metaphorical) mass production of consumers. Consequently, the 'science' in Huxley's science fiction is merely an enabling device allowing him to extrapolate from existing trends – mass production, consumerism, self-indulgence, advertising, planning, the search for efficiency – to show how people are the willing victims of capitalism and modernity.

Whereas in the 1930s Wells had dreamed of a future technocratic society and Huxley had warned against it, for rebellious youth of the 1960s it was a nightmare that had already arrived. The revolt against technocracy was recorded (and applauded) by Theodore Roszak in his popular book *The Making of a Counter Culture*, published in 1968. For Roszak what was distinctive about 1960s counter culture was that the revolt was youth-based not class-based and, unlike previous generations of radicals, it had rejected the idea of science as a social good. Drawing heavily on the ideas of Marcuse, he argues how the leading figures in the counter culture have 'called into question the validity of the scientific world view, and in so doing have set about undermining the foundations of the technocracy' (Roszak [1968] 1970: 205). By technocracy he means 'that social form in which an industrial society reaches the peak of its organizational integration. It is the ideal men usually have in mind when they speak of modernizing, up-dating, rationalizing, planning' (5). In short, it is the realization of that vision of modernity we saw in the previous chapter, where the demand for efficiency (an 'unquestionable imperative' says Roszak) and the scale of organization create a dependency upon specially trained experts. It is a dependency that pervades the society:

> Further, around this central core of experts who deal with large-scale public necessities, there grows up a circle of subsidiary experts who, battening on the general social prestige of technical skill in the technocracy, assume authoritative influence over even the most seemingly personal aspects of life: sexual behavior, child-rearing, mental health, recreation etc. In the technocracy everything aspires to become purely technical, the subject of professional attention. The technocracy is therefore the regime of experts – or those who can employ experts.
>
> (Roszak [1968] 1970: 7)

Behind the experts lies the 'scientific world view' since 'those who govern justify themselves by appeal to technical experts who, in turn, justify themselves by appeal to scientific forms of knowledge. And beyond the authority of science, there is no appeal' (8). Indeed, it would be a 'violation of reason' not to defer to those who know better. Consequently the technocracy 'eludes all traditional political categories' and can 'render itself ideologically invisible', holding the place 'of a grand cultural imperative which is beyond question, beyond discussion' (8 and 9). So all-encompassing is this technocratic imperative that by exerting its authority over the whole of life it is, says Roszak, a form of totalitarianism. However, as with Huxley's *Brave New World*, it is a non-violent totalitarianism, all the more perfect 'because its techniques become progressively more subliminal':

> The distinctive feature of the regime of experts lies in the fact that, while possessing ample power to coerce, it prefers to charm conformity from us by exploiting our deep-seated commitment to the scientific world-view and by manipulating the securities and creature comforts of the industrial affluence which science gives us.
>
> (Roszak [1968] 1970: 9)

The great secret of technocracy, says Roszak, lies in being able to convince us that our vital needs are indeed purely technical in character, that all problems have technical solutions and that the experts really do know what they are talking about (10–11). The question, of course, is: who are the experts? Technocracy is legitimized because it has the approval of the experts, and the experts are legitimized because without them there would be no technocracy. To break out of this circular argument, says Roszak, experts have to claim that their knowledge is scientifically sound, which in turn means an appeal to the objectivity that characterizes scientific knowledge. On this basis, an expert is an expert because he or she cultivates an 'objective consciousness' and it is the 'myth of objective consciousness' that maintains the power of the technocracy over us. 'What flows from this state of consciousness qualifies as knowledge, and nothing else does. This is the bedrock on which the natural sciences have built; and under their spell all fields of knowledge strive to become scientific' (208–9). Objectivity, argues Roszak, has become 'the one most authoritative way of regarding the self, others, and the whole of our enveloping reality'; so much so that 'the mentality of the ideal scientist becomes the very soul of the society' (216). It is this mentality that needs our critical attention, not the epistemology of science. It is an alienating and dehumanizing mentality that diminishes our lives, he argues, and what we need instead is for our lives to be as expansive and as open as possible. Objective consciousness is '. . . an arbitrary construct in which a given society in a given historical situation has invested its sense of meaningfulness and value' (215). In response the counter culture looks for meaningfulness and value elsewhere, to the realm of non-intellective personal experience where there are no experts. The test is not whether something 'squares with objectively demonstrable knowledge', but rather 'the degree to which it enlarges our capacity to experience: to know ourselves more deeply, to feel more fully the awesomeness of our environment' (236–7). The result was a search for alternative lifestyles based on unorthodox psychologies, hallucinogenic drugs, Eastern philosophy and rock music. It is, perhaps, a great irony that in the pursuit of pleasure through drugs and promiscuous sex, the form of revolt in the 'swinging sixties' often resembled the form of control in Huxley's *Brave New World*.

Even as the quest for personal authenticity in the 1960s was degenerating into the rampant individualism of the 1970s, so a fresh challenge to modernity was emerging and with it a renewed questioning of the status of science. For those who wish their historical periods to be well defined by specific dates, the oil crisis that followed the Yom Kippur war of 1973 is often taken as the start of that insecurity that characterizes the closing decades of the twentieth century. The world economy was changing before that (as early as 1967 J.K. Galbraith was writing of *The New Industrial State*), but it does give a convenient marker. In the twenty years that followed, according to Hobsbawm, the world 'lost its bearings and slid into instability and crisis' (Hobsbawm 1994: 403). It was not simply that much of the world's economy was in recession (which was true), nor that the inequalities between rich and poor had grown (which was also true), but that the operations of the capitalist economy had become uncontrollable (404–8). Planning the future – a central part of modernity's promise – no longer seemed a practicable proposition. Commentators began to talk of 'post-industrial society', of 'post-Fordism' and of 'post-modernity'.

If the essence of modernity was order, planning and control, then post-modernity might best be characterized by fragmentation, uncertainty and instability – hence the postmodern fascination for **fractal geometry, quantum physics** and **chaos theory**. In the previous chapter we saw how the drive for change made modernity an unsettling experience, and in some respects post-modernity might be regarded as modernity pushed to the extremes. Giddens, for example, sees it as a period 'in which the consequences of modernity are becoming more radicalised and universalised than before' (Giddens 1990: 3) and Bauman writes of it as 'fully developed modernity' (Bauman 1992: 187). However, postmodernity is different in at least two respects. The first is the sense of purpose, or rather, the lack of it. 'The postmodern condition is a site of constant mobility and change', says Bauman, 'but no clear direction of development' (189). In short, unlike the utopian, and often evolutionary, visions of modernity, there is no sense of change towards anything, no sense of progress. Any patterns that emerge are temporary and random. All order that can be found is local, emergent, transitory. The second respect is that whereas modernity might be equally unsettling, postmodernity is *intentionally* unsettling. It actively searches for and celebrates that which is ambivalent and unstable. The pluralism, variety and contingency which were seen as signs of failure in modernity are seized upon to dissolve the boundaries which had once seemed natural. Indeed, the very definition of postmodernity is undecided and contested, an example of the very fluidity which it is trying to describe (see also Sarup 1993 and Smart 1993).

This fragmentation and fluidity has important consequences for the public's relationship with science. We can see this most clearly in the work of Jean-Francois Lyotard ([1979] 1984). For Lyotard the defining feature of the post-modern condition is an 'incredulity towards metanarratives' (25). It is no longer possible, he argues, to legitimate knowledge through an appeal to a grand narrative or metadiscourse such as the dialectics of spirit, the emancipation of the working class, or the Enlightenment belief in Progress. Postmodernity's anti-universalism is a war on all totalizing discourses (e.g. Christianity, Marxism or Imperialism) and its anti-foundationalism is a constant challenge to institutional authority. Indeed, there are no authorities. There is no final court of appeal to which we can refer (or defer). Instead, according to Lyotard, we are to play 'games' of move and counter move trying to increase the space for our own 'little narratives'. This is no simple reaction against science which, as we have seen, has a history that predates Lyotard's 'Report on Knowledge'. Hiroshima and Nagasaki had already marked a loss of innocence, and attacks on the one-dimensional thinking of reductionist science were already part of a youth counter-culture. The challenge from postmodernism, however, is more funda-mental because it challenges not only what science *does*, but what science *is*. The cultural position of science is undermined not just because of any abuse of science, but because it can no longer claim to have privileged access to nature. What it tells us is no longer a single, unmediated, transcendental truth, but a historically contingent collection of stories in an anthology of little narratives. Its epistemological authority is shattered into a thousand pieces, a thousand local knowledges.

It has become a commonplace to see science as a new form of religion with its own rites and rituals, its own initiation practices, its own esoteric language, its own priesthood and martyrs. We might now add a further analogy and see the authority of science facing the same challenges as those faced by the Catholic Church at the time of the Reformation (Broks 2003). In this way we can see the fragmentation of belief in the sixteenth century being replayed as a fragmentation of knowledge in the twenty-first. Just as the spiritual authority of the Catholic Church was challenged by the Reformation, so too the epistemological authority of science is now challenged by postmodernity. In the fragmentation and uncertainties of the *Postmodern* Reformation, truth is now to be found in subjective lived experience and one's own readings of the sacred texts, not in expert proclamations. As the Reformation dissolved boundaries between clergy and laity, so too the 'Postmodern Reformation' dissolves the boundaries between lay and expert thinking. Luther's priesthood of all believers has become a priesthood of all knowers – we are all experts now, experts in our own lives and experiences. Not surprisingly, the reaction from some scientists has been fierce (one might even say Jesuitical), but the undermining of authority exposes a real dilemma for the conscientious scientist: how to release science into the public arena and at the same time control what the public does with it. The more science is made public, the less scientists have control over what it means. It should not be surprising then that the more the 'church scientific' is opened to the new priesthood of all knowers, the more protest-ant we are likely to find the congregation.

The popular science boom

So far in this chapter we have seen how we must be careful in any comments we might make about there being a post-war popular reaction against science triggered by the explosion of atomic bombs. If a new critical tone began to emerge, it pays to look more closely at what exactly was being questioned. Even a simple reference to the 'abuse' of science might hide more subtle issues about trust, responsibility and accountability; and if we do find opposition to science, closer inspection might show that it is better understood as opposition to mod- ernity and capitalism (as with Huxley), opposition to a technocratic mentality (as with Roszak) or opposition to the authority of science (as with postmoder- nity). There is, however, one other factor which needs to be taken into account when considering any post-war reaction – popular science had never been so popular.

Gregory and Miller (1998) have called it the 'post-war bonanza'. There was an outpouring of popularizations in all forms, an increased concern that the public should be made more aware of science and maybe even increased demand from the public to know more. Specialist communicators of science, who had emerged as a profession before the war, were now a much more visible and organized presence, and for Gregory and Miller 'the post-war period in popular science is perhaps characterized by the rise and rise of the science journalist' (380). In the UK before the war there had been only three or four specialist science writers; by 1947 there were enough to form the Association of British Science Writers. In the US the National Association of Science Writers, which had been founded in the 1930s, had over 100 members by 1950 and over 400 by 1960. In addition to the print media the development of television meant that key popularizers were now likely to be broadcasters. Viewing figures for science programmes would be measured in the millions and broadcasters such as Jacob Bronowski, Jacques Cousteau, Patrick Moore and David Attenborough were to become (in some cases still are) household names. *Science Review*, broadcast in 1952, was the first full-length science documentary; *Zoo Quest*

(1954), which recorded expeditions to capture animals for British zoos, shows the early appeal of natural history on TV; and *Your Life in their Hands* (1958), a documentary about the work of doctors and surgeons, is indicative of the perennial human interest value of medical stories. The extent to which science was able to establish itself on UK television can be seen in the longevity of the major programmes: *The Sky at Night*, first broadcast in 1957 is still presented by Patrick Moore and is the longest-running programme on British Television; *Horizon*, first broadcast in 1964, is still going strong; and *Tomorrow's World* would hold a prime-time slot from 1965 to 2002 with weekly viewing figures of over 10 million in the 1970s and 1980s. High-quality series such as Jacob Bronowski's *Ascent of Man* (1973) and David Attenborough's *Life on Earth* (1979) were landmarks not just in the popular science landscape, but in television history as a whole. Inspired by the Bronowski series, Carl Sagan's *Cosmos* (1980) would reach an estimated worldwide audience of 140 million within three years, or, as Sagan put it, '3 per cent of the human population of planet Earth' (Sagan 1983: 14) – a biography of Sagan on the NASA website puts the eventual figure at 500 million.

By the 1980s there was talk of a popular science 'boom'. Stephen Hawking's *A Brief History of Time* (1988), for example, was a phenomenal success, staying in the bestseller lists for four and a half years and selling over nine million copies and translated into thirty languages in eight years. It was soon followed by a film version, an illustrated and expanded edition, documentaries and public lectures that filled the Albert Hall. For Hawking it also brought an audience with the Pope and appearances in television commercials, *Star Trek: The Next Generation*, and (the greatest marker of cultural esteem) *The Simpsons*. It is quite likely that the book was bought more than it was read, though this in itself is an indication of its 'must have' status. It is not an easy read (as much for its writing style as for its science content). A beginner's guide was published in 1995 and, with the editorial guidance of Leonard Mlodinow, Hawking brought out his own 'more accessible' version in 2005 – a rare instance of a work of popular science needing further 'popularisation' (White and Gribbin 1992; Rodgers 1992; McEvoy and Zarate 1995; Hawking 1996; Hawking and Mlodinow 2005). However, even away from the superstars like Hawking, Sagan and Bronowski, there are other indicators of a cultural shift beginning around the late 1970s and early 1980s. Popular science was one of the greatest growth areas in publishing at the end of the twentieth century, with many bookstores creating new sections to accommodate all the books. Waterstone's bookstores even published its own *Guide to Popular Science Books*, in the introduction to which Igor Aleksander wrote:

The world of science literature has seen an astonishing sea change over the last fifteen or so years. Many more high quality books are being published which have literary merit as well as informative content. The major reason for this is that readers who are not experts in science have developed an appetite for joining in the debates that rage as thunderously in science as they do in politics or economics.

(Aleksander in Rennison 2000: 3)

In the first thirty years after the Second World War only two science-oriented books won Pulitzer prizes. In the following twenty years there were ten. Before the late 1970s it was very rare for there to be as many as ten science-oriented books added to the New York Times Bestsellers list in any one year. From the late 1970s it was very rare for there to be fewer than ten (Lewenstein 2002).

As we shall see in the next chapter, the popular science boom of the 1980s was accompanied by fresh concerns over the 'public understanding of science'. Why should there be increased anxiety about the public communication of science when there had never been so much of it before?

Immediately after the war, although scientists were increasingly removed further from the public as more and more journalists took up the role of science communicators, the expanding field of science writers would still ensure that science had a good press. Indeed, as Bruce Lewenstein (1992a) has argued, in the generation after the Second World War science journalists often saw themselves as 'advocates of science'. There was, says Lewenstein, no clear indication that there actually was a demand for science, but a moral certainty about the importance of science among a network of organizations and journalists meant that there was a broad interest in the supply of science. Commercial publishers, scientific associations, science writers and government agencies all responded to the new opportunities offered by the immediate post-war period with efforts to promote science. Each group may have had its own agenda and worked with different rationales and approaches, but they were united in a common purpose: 'Though much of the rhetoric of these groups talked about improving the public's *understanding* of the relationships between science and society, in practice they meant improving the public's *appreciation* of the benefits that society received from science.' The 1960s, however, were to bring a more critical attitude: 'With the rise of a new, politically-oriented environmental journalism, the close ties between science journalism and mainstream scientific institutions began to break down' (Lewenstein 1992a: 62).

At the forefront of the new critical writing was Rachel Carson's *Silent Spring*, serialized in the *New Yorker* and published as a book in 1962. Trained as a biologist, Carson presented a shocking account of the damage being done to the environment by the widespread use of pesticides such as DDT. Since the mid-1940s, she said, over 200 chemicals had been created to kill insects, weeds and rodents and were almost universally used on farms, in gardens and in homes. Drawing on existing scientific literature and the knowledge of her colleagues, she showed the toxic effects of these chemicals not only on the wildlife which they killed indiscriminately but on humans as well. Her accumulated evidence was a searing indictment of the greed of chemical companies and the inadequacy of government regulation and industry guidelines. In an afterword to a later reprint of the book, Carson's biographer Linda Lear writes:

> She was one of the first to convince a complacent and increasingly affluent post-war generation that the government could not be trusted to take care of them . . . The hostile reaction of the establishment to Carson and her book was evidence that many government and industry officials recognised that Carson had not only challenged the conclusions of scientists regarding the benefits of the new pesticides, but that she had undermined their moral integrity and leadership. She had toppled America's blind faith in science and, more damaging still, she had initiated public debate over the direction of technological progress.
>
> (Lear in Carson [1962] 1999: 259)

The book sold nearly a million copies before Carson's death in 1964 and has remained a classic ever since. By the end of the 1960s the critical attitude would expand from environmental concerns to encompass such worries as biological manipulation and the pace of technological change, both of which were the subjects of bestsellers. Gordon Rattray Taylor's *Biological Time-Bomb* (1968), which was seen as a landmark in public debate at the time, took its rhetoric from environmentalism in highlighting the social, ethical and legal problems arising from reproductive physiology, transplant surgery, neurochemistry and genetic engineering (see Turney 1998: 157). Alvin Toffler's *Future Shock* (1970) describes an emerging new 'super-industrialism' that in many respects is postmodern society in all but name – fractured, diverse, transient, nomadic, and whose chief characteristic is uncontrollable, accelerated change. 'Change is avalanching upon our heads and most people are grotesquely unprepared to cope with it', says Toffler. 'Future shock is the dizzying disorientation brought on by the premature arrival of the future' (12 and 11). How different from the planned utopias of modernity.

Moreover, together with the new critical voice some popular science books began to reflect the emerging postmodern culture. This is especially seen in the work of Fritjof Capra, whose *Tao of Physics* ([1975], second edition 1983) was one of the best-selling books on science and also became one of the canonical texts of the New Age movement. The book was an exploration of the parallels between Eastern philosophy (principally Hinduism, Buddhism, Taoism and

Zen) and the 'new physics' of quantum theory and particle physics. The aim was not a rigorous demonstration but rather to give the reader an opportunity to relive Capra's own experience 'that the principal theories and models of modern physics lead to a view of the world which is internally consistent and in perfect harmony with the views of Eastern mysticism' (336). This appeal to experience rather than rationality was an essential part of the case that Capra presented. Indeed, the book opened with a 'beautiful experience' Capra had on a beach watching the waves rolling in and feeling the rhythm of his breathing:

> . . . I suddenly became aware of my whole environment as being engaged in a gigantic cosmic dance . . . I 'saw' cascades of energy coming down from outer space, in which particles were created and destroyed in rhythmic pulses; I 'saw' the atoms of the elements and those of my body participating in this cosmic dance of energy; I felt its rhythm and I 'heard' its sound, and at that moment I *knew* that this was the Dance of Shiva, the Lord of Dancers worshipped by the Hindus.
>
> (Capra [1975] 1983: 11, original emphasis)

In the preface to the second edition, Capra was quite explicit about the counter-cultural origins of the book:

> The 1960s and 1970s have generated a whole series of social movements which all seem to go in the same direction. The rising concern with ecology, the strong interest in mysticism, the growing feminist awareness, and the rediscovery of holistic approaches to health and healing are all manifestations of the same evolutionary trend. They all counteract the overemphasis of rational, masculine attitudes and values, and attempt to regain a balance between the masculine and feminine sides of human nature.
>
> (Capra [1975] 1983: 15)

With the hindsight afforded by the second edition, Capra was able to see that the parallel he presented '. . . now appears as an integral part of a much larger cultural transformation' (16).

It was a theme he explained more fully in *The Turning Point* (1982), where he argued that a range of current crises including inflation, unemployment, pollution, environmental disasters, violence and crime are all facets of the same crisis, a crisis of perception. The old 'mechanistic world view of Cartesian–Newtonian science', he said, was no longer appropriate to understand the globally interconnected world we live in '. . . in which biological, psychological, social, and environmental phenomena are all interdependent' (xviii). What was needed was a new '**paradigm**', a new way of looking at the world, and the purpose of the book was 'to provide a coherent conceptual framework' for the holistic conception of reality found in the social movements of the 1960s and 1970s (xviii). The shift from a reductionist to holistic perspective entailed a shift in thinking from parts to wholes, to connectedness, relationships and contexts. It was a perspective with very postmodern characteristics. In *The Web of Life* (1997), Capra explained that seeing nature as an interconnected web meant that no part of science was any more fundamental than any other part; physics was no more fundamental than biology; there were no fundamental laws, constants or equations. 'As we perceive reality as a network of relationships, our descriptions, too, form an interconnected network of concepts and models in which there are no foundations' (39).

Capra's books were not the only examples. There was a fashion for books that made links between science and spirituality or religion. Gary Zukav's *Dancing Wu Li Masters* (1979), for example, began with an explicit denial that the book was about physics and eastern philosophy, but still ended with a section on 'Enlightenment' and took the Chinese phrase Wu Li meaning 'patterns of organic energy' (and, *inter alia*, also 'nonsense') as a 'poetic framework' for understanding quantum theory. Zukav's interest in spiritual evolution was made explicit in his second book *The Seat of the Soul* (1990). Stephen Hawking famously ended his *Brief History of Time* with the belief that through a unified theory of the universe 'we would know the mind of God', a theme (and phrase) taken up by Paul Davies in his book *The Mind of God* (1992). Davies would later be awarded the Templeton prize for 'Progress toward research or discoveries about spiritual realities', a prize that is worth more than a Nobel and which had previously been won by Mother Teresa and evangelist Billy Graham[1]. Even physicist Leon Lederman – who once complained in a TV documentary that 'the crazies are rampant' – was persuaded to call his book on the Higgs boson, *The God Particle* (Lederman 1993; Channel 4 1995). Not surprisingly, perhaps, a front page of *Newsweek* in 1998 proclaimed 'Science Finds God' (Begley 1998).

Of course, science and religion have a long, if sometimes troubled, relationship and popularizations of the religious significance of science were not new. William Paley's *Natural Theology* can be seen as an early nineteenth-century example (see Chapter 1). Likewise, in the 1920s and 1930s the books of James Jeans and Sir Arthur Eddington have such a strong metaphysical flavour that one contemporary critic complained that they presented their views in such an 'emotional fog' that it reduced them to the 'level of revivalist preachers' (Stebbing [1937] 1944: 13; see also Bowler 2001). What was different at the end of the twentieth century was that many of the books, such as those by Capra, were self-consciously part of, and advocates for, a broader cultural transformation. In postmodern culture what was being popularized was 'postmodern science'. It was not simply that ideas from science were being 'distorted' or 'appropriated' by the wider popular culture, but rather that new meanings were being created around them. The centrality of disorder and uncertainty to be found in ideas about entropy, chaos theory and quantum physics, for example, meant that these could be seen as instances of postmodern science even though the mathematics and physics on which they were based were much older (Best 1991; Hayles 1991; Smith and Higgins 2003). It was suggested in the previous chapter that in the first half of the twentieth century the popularization of science was in effect the popularization of modernity. Now, at the end of the twentieth century, in some quarters at least, we might see it as the popularization of postmodernity, and it was a development that not everyone in the science community felt comfortable with. It would be all too easy to equate theories of postmodernity with earlier critiques of science and see it as opening the door to all manner of hippy-dippy, jingle-jangly, counter-cultural nonsense. The fact that it was popular science which was helping to do that could only make matters worse.

There is, therefore, no contradiction in having a popular science boom at the same time as rising fears of 'anti-science'. It was not so much that there was opposition to science as a struggle over its meaning. It was not simply a matter of weighing in the balance those who were for and those against, or even examining whether science had been used or abused, but rather considering more subtle questions of trust and accountability. Moreover, on closer inspection, critiques of science might turn out to be better understood as critiques of modernity, capitalism, technocracy or authority. This might all seem a disingenuous way of diverting attention away from science itself. On the contrary, it prompts us to ask a very real question: 'How might it be otherwise?' Could science really disentangle itself from the demands of the military, the government and the market; abandon its visions of progress and the control of nature; forsake its technocratic mentality and renounce its claims for the authority of experts? If so, then maybe we are right to distinguish between attacks on science and attacks on what might be called its historical circumstances. If not, then maybe there are grounds for opposition and saying that this is what science *is*. Even so, what is clear is that clashes over anti-science would be fought out in the arena of popular science and, as we shall see in the next chapter, around what it was that the public should understand science to be.

Note

1 In 2006 the prize was won by cosmologist and popularizer John D. Barrow.

Further reading

Carson, R. ([1962] 1999) *Silent Spring* with an afterword by L. Lear. London: Penguin.

Lewenstein, B.V. (1992) 'The meaning of "public understanding of science" in the United States after World War II', in *Public Understanding of Science*, 1: 45–68.

Roszak, T. ([1968] 1970) *The Making of a Counter Culture: Reflections on the Technocratic Society and its Youthful Opposition*. London: Faber and Faber.

Sarup, M. (1993) *An Introductory Guide to Post-Structuralism and Postmodernism*, second edition. Hemel Hempstead: Harvester Wheatsheaf.

Turney, J. (1998) *Frankenstein's Footsteps: Science, Genetics and Popular Culture*. New Haven, CT: Yale University Press.

5 | LITERACY AND LEGITIMATION

We would seem to be entering our own 'uncertain times', with the meaning of science contested every bit as much as it was in the period described in Chapter 1. The difference now, of course, is the status of science and the power that it wields. No longer does science have to struggle to establish its professional and institutional presence; instead the challenge is to re-establish its links with the public. The new post-war situation was noted in a Mass Observation report of 1947:

> After decades during which it was possible to live in a world which was becoming more and more subject to the rule of science without having the faintest idea of what science was; after doing this without any tangible evidence of evil consequences, it has suddenly been brought to people's notice that the nature of science, as opposed to its trappings, must be examined and understood . . . The alternative might be very nasty.
> (Mass Observation 1947: file 2489)

Once an understanding of science might have been seen as a matter of enlightenment or social advancement; now it might even be seen as a matter of survival. The need to increase the public's understanding of science would seem, therefore, to be a self-evident political truth. However, for all its importance – and it is important – in our own uncertain times it is equally important to be clear about just what it is that we are asking for – and why.

Two cultures

A common point of reference for most analyses of the relationship between science and the public is the idea of 'two cultures' put forward by C.P Snow in the 1950s. This is significant in itself because of the dualism within which the problem gets framed (see below), and although Snow was writing about Britain in particular he believed it was a problem which affected the whole of western civilization. Certainly it was taken up on both sides of the Atlantic even if only as a convenient label for something that had been recognized for a long time. It is worthwhile therefore to spend a little time to see what Snow's argument was.

One cannot but help get the impression that Snow did not quite fit in. Trained as a scientist, he gave up a career in research because the calculations upon which his work was based were shown to be faulty. Moving into science administration, he started to write novels about scientists and politicians, but his style was dismissed as stilted and pompous. While his career in government did advance (becoming Lord Snow and serving Harold Wilson as a Minister of State), Snow's legacy lies not in his work as scientist, novelist or administrator but in a phrase that he coined, 'The Two Cultures', which was the title of an essay given as the Rede Lecture in Cambridge in 1959 and published in the same year.

He starts by drawing on personal experience, saying that for the past thirty years he had been working with scientists as part of his job and mixing in literary circles as he tried to write his novels:

> It was through living among these groups and much more I think, through moving regularly from one to the other and back again that I got occupied with the problem of what, long before I put it on paper, I christened to myself as the 'two cultures'. For constantly I felt I was moving among two groups – comparable in intelligence, identical in race, not grossly different in social origin, earning about the same incomes, who had almost ceased to communicate at all, who in intellectual, moral and psychological climate had so little in common that instead of going from Burlington House or South Kensington to Chelsea, one might have crossed an ocean.
>
> (Snow 1959: 2)

The landmarks are British (the Royal Society at Burlington House; the Science and Natural History Museums at South Kensington; the artistic life centred on Chelsea) but Snow believed the split was more widespread, indeed, that the gap between the two cultures was greater than that between countries or continents – 'Greenwich Village talking precisely the same language as Chelsea, and both having about as much communication with MIT as though the scientists spoke nothing but Tibetan' (2). Although it might be particularly acute in England, the problem was one of the entire West:

I believe the intellectual life of the whole of western society is increasingly being split into two polar groups . . . at one pole we have the literary intellectuals, who incidentally while no one was looking took to referring to themselves as 'intellectuals' as though there were no others . . . Literary intellectuals at one pole – at the other scientists, and as the most representative, the physical scientists. Between the two a gulf of mutual incomprehension – sometime (particularly among the young) hostility and dislike, but most of all lack of understanding.

(Snow 1959: 3–4)

Across the divide each has a distorted image of the other. On the one hand, non-scientists see scientists as 'brash and boastful', 'shallowly optimistic, unaware of man's condition'. On the other, scientists see literary intellectuals as 'lacking in foresight, peculiarly unconcerned with their brother men, in a deep sense anti-intellectual, anxious to restrict both art and thought to the existential moment' (5). In addressing the charge of shallow optimism, Snow argues that there is a confusion between individual and social life. Individual life, the central concern of the literary intellectuals and the philosophy of existentialism which was popular at the time, is indeed tragic ('each of us dies alone'), but, says Snow, scientists 'see no reason why, just because the individual condition is tragic, so must the social condition be' (6) That is what is seen as 'optimism', a belief that something can be done to improve things and an impatience that it should be done. Snow's sympathies are clear. He is not just describing a split between two groups but taking sides, and in doing so paints a picture of a beleaguered community of scientists beset on all sides by enemies. For Snow, the scientific culture 'really is a culture' with 'common attitudes, common standards and patterns of behaviour, common approaches and assumptions' (9):

At the other pole, the spread of attitudes is wider . . . But I believe the pole of total incomprehension of science radiates its influence on all the rest. That total incomprehension gives, much more pervasively than we realise, living in it, an unscientific flavour to the whole 'traditional' culture, and that unscientific flavour is often, much more than we admit, on the point of turning anti-scientific.

(Snow 1959: 10–11)

Note how science is the 'real' culture and how the rest is only defined by its incomprehension and opposition to science. In the duality of 'two cultures', non-science is characterized through absence and antagonism, ignorance where there should be knowledge, darkness where there should be light. How many literary intellectuals, asks Snow, could describe the second law of thermodynamics? Yet this would be like asking whether they had read any Shakespeare.

How many know the meaning of mass and acceleration? Yet this would be like asking if they could read (15). However, it is 'traditional' culture, says Snow, which manages the western world.

The full title for Snow's essay is 'The Two Cultures and the Scientific Revolution'. It is divided into four sections and it is only the first section that concerns itself with the 'two cultures'. What is often not remarked upon is the fact that the bulk of the essay is about the 'scientific revolution' and exporting it across the globe. Taken as a whole, the essay is not so much about a cultural divide as about promoting one side of that divide. It is science, and in particular applied science, that he puts forward as the solution to the world's ills. In Snow's terms the 'scientific revolution' is the application of science to industry (what historians would now call the second industrial revolution, dating from the late nineteenth century with the development of new chemical and electrical industries). Snow confesses that even pure scientists are snobbish about applied science, industry and engineering, but the literary intellectuals are 'natural Luddites' who 'have never tried, wanted, or been able to understand the industrial revolution, much less accept it' (21). Nevertheless, in Snow's eyes it is industrialization that will save the world. 'For, of course, one truth is straightforward. Industrialisation is the only hope of the poor' (24).

As the essay proceeds it is easy to see Snow falling foul of the same shallow optimism that he said the scientists were accused of. The gap between rich countries and poor countries was growing, he said, and poverty was becoming more noticeable, but the solution was at hand. Technology was easy and only needed political will and enough engineers. 'Once the trick of getting rich is known, as it now is, the world can't survive half rich half poor. It's just not on' (40). As this was such an easy trick he expected all countries to industrialize and for the disparity between rich and poor to disappear by the year 2000. Helping the rest of the world transform itself through their own scientific revolution was the most important task for the rich countries and, for Snow, was the only way through the three menaces of nuclear war, over-population and the poverty gap. 'Since the gap between rich countries and the poor can be removed', he said, 'it will be' (44). What was needed for this worldwide scientific revolution was: firstly, capital (money and machines from nations, not private industry); secondly, trained scientists and engineers (who will muck in, do the job and get out); and finally an education programme (to nurture more scientists and engineers). In short, it was the ultimate technological fix with scientists and engineers whizzing around the world like a cross between Christian missionaries and comic book super-heroes.

The reaction to Snow's essay shows that he had struck a nerve, sometimes a very raw nerve. The lecture was soon translated into several languages including Hungarian, Polish and Japanese. In most cases comments on the lecture seemed to show widespread recognition of the problem that Snow had highlighted, even if there may not have been full agreement with the whole thesis. It has even been said that in the US Snow was regarded as a 'high priest' amongst those concerned with science and politics (see Gregory and Miller 1998: 50). However, not everyone was persuaded. The most scathing (and often personal) attack came from Cambridge literary critic F.R. Leavis who thought Snow to be 'portentously ignorant' (Watson 2000: 469). For Leavis, the widespread acceptance of the thesis was a depressing sign of the times characterized by 'blindness, unconsciousness and automatism. He doesn't know what he means and he doesn't know he doesn't know' (cited in Gregory and Miller 1998: 48). A more tempered critique came from the American literary critic Lionel Trilling who saw the clash between Snow and Leavis as a recent version of the one between T.H. Huxley ('Darwin's bulldog') and the poet and literary intellectual Matthew Arnold in the 1880s. While Trilling accused Leavis of bad manners for being so personal, he also thought that Snow had overstated his case. It was too simplistic, he said, to characterize the great variety of writers in such a 'cavalier' way (Watson 2000: 470).

The phrase stuck and the debate continues. This is reflected in the titles of books that attempt, in some way, to move the debate on. George Levine's edited collection *One Culture* (1987) tries to show the close relationship between science and literature; and more recently *The One Culture?* (2001), edited by Labinger and Collins, tries to develop a conversation to transcend the misunderstandings of the 'science wars' (see below). For present purposes the most interesting example of these modern echoes is to be found in John Brockman's book *The Third Culture* (1995). 'The playing field of American intellectual life has shifted', says Brockman. Traditional intellectuals with their education in Freud, Marx and modernism have become increasingly marginalized. Instead what is emerging is a 'third culture' consisting of 'those scientists and other thinkers in the empirical world who, through their work and expository writing, are taking the place of the traditional intellectual in rendering visible the deeper meanings of our lives, redefining who and what we are' (17). C.P. Snow had also written of a third culture when he revisited the problem a few years after his original lecture, but what Brockman has in mind is different. Snow had thought that the communications gap between the two cultures would close and this would bring a 'third culture'. Brockman thinks differently:

> Literary intellectuals are not communicating with scientists. Scientists are communicating directly with the general public. Traditional intellectual media played a vertical game: journalists wrote up and professors wrote down. Today, third-culture thinkers tend to avoid the middleman and

endeavor to express their deepest thoughts in a manner accessible to the reading public.

(Brockman 1995: 18)

In other words, this new, emerging, third culture is nothing other than – popular science.

If true, this is a very curious development. Certainly Brockman is right to point to the recent publishing success of 'serious' books on science. Similarly, John Carey, Professor of English at Oxford University, has argued that science writers like Carl Sagan, Richard Feynman, Stephen Jay Gould and Richard Dawkins 'have created a new kind of late twentieth century literature, which demands to be recognised as a separate genre, distinct from the old literary forms . . .' (Carey 1995: xiv). However, from earlier chapters it might be recalled that Robert Chambers's 'hybrid' book *Vestiges* has also been seen as creating a new genre of popular science; that later in the nineteenth century the redefinition of 'popular science' brought it closer to our modern understanding of popular*ized* science; and that this new sense enabled professional scientists to separate themselves further from the general public. Now, it seems, popular science is the very thing which transcends the old two cultures divide. Science is being brought direct to the public. If so, then two questions spring to mind. Are we really at the start of a new age when science is part of 'public culture' (Brockman 1995: 18), or is Brockman's vision of a third culture simply a vision of one culture (science) triumphant? And, if popular science is now so successful, why is there so much concern about scientific literacy and the 'public understanding of science'?

Science literacy and PUS

Less than two years before C.P. Snow gave his lecture on the two cultures, the US had heard something even more shocking. It was a simple message ('beep–beep–beep . . .') but it was loaded with meaning. It told Americans they were violated, threatened, second-rate. The radio transmission from Sputnik, the Soviet satellite launched in 1957, marked the start of the 'space race' and the US had a lot of catching up to do. The launch of their own satellite was brought forward several months only to explode on take-off, giving the Soviet press the opportunity to crow with headlines like 'Kaputnik!' and 'Stayputnik!' (Watson 2000: 484). There was more than injured pride at stake. The Soviets had shown that they had the technology to build rockets which were both powerful and accurate. If they could put a satellite into orbit they could equally put atomic bombs into New York, Chicago or Los Angeles. In this climate of fear science and technology suddenly became an issue of national importance in ways that it had not done before. Equally important, and equally frightening, was just how little science the average American knew. A survey by the National Association of Science Writers found that attitudes to science were generally positive, but levels of factual knowledge were low (Gregory and Miller 1998: 4). One response to Sputnik was to hype American science in the US press. A more substantial response came with the reorganization of science teaching and with it a concern for what would later be known as 'scientific literacy'.

Although there is widespread agreement that scientific literacy is a 'good thing', it is not at all clear what it is that everyone is agreeing on. Drawing on an earlier notion of literacy as the ability to read and write, scientific literacy can be seen as a similar ability, but an ability to do what? Science is littered with (mostly failed) attempts at defining itself and it is difficult to see what might unite the diversity of practices found in, for example, high-energy physics, palaeontology and genetics, let alone be seen as prerequisites for someone to be 'literate' in science. Far from giving guidance, work in the history and philosophy of science only shows how deep this problem goes. Even without such considerations we would still need to take into account the fact that science is both a body of knowledge and a set of practices. Would we expect our literate person to have skills in both, some knowledge or understanding of both product and process? Should the emphasis be on one or the other? However, when considering the question of why we should bother with science literacy, most answers place the emphasis elsewhere, on a third factor. To product and process should be added context. Our ideal science literates not only should have an understanding of what science knows and how it works but, more importantly, should be able to relate that understanding to their own life and the world around them.

It is through this contextual dimension that the perceived reasons *for* scientific literacy shape the definitions *of* scientific literacy. John Durant gives three major reasons why scientific literacy matters:

> *Cultural*: 'Science is the major intellectual achievement of modern western culture . . . It seems clear, therefore, that we have a responsibility to convey something of the world of science to everyone, if only so that people will feel "at home" in their culture.'
> *Practical*: 'The practical applications of science underpin not only modern agriculture and industry, but also modern transport, communications and health.' (Durant also adds shopping to this list of areas where a knowledge of science could be of practical use.)
> *Political*: '. . . many important political issues involve science and technology . . . thus scientific literacy becomes a precondition for informed

public debate, which is itself a precondition for truly democratic decision-making.'

(Durant 1991: 70–2)

Elsewhere, Durant (1993) gives three definitions of scientific literacy: 'knowing a lot of science' (i.e. science content), 'knowing how science works' (i.e. science as idealized procedure), and 'knowing how science really works' (i.e. science as social practice). Thus all Durant's reasons for scientific literacy can be encompassed within the third contextual definition of scientific literacy. Shen also offered a threefold typology (practical, cultural and civic), while the National Research Council proposes four reasons for and types of scientific literacy that can be seen as personal, cultural, civic and economic (National Research Council 1996; Miller 1998).

In all these cases the emphasis is on a contextual understanding of science to enable citizens to participate in democracy – what has been generally called civic scientific literacy. Civic scientific literacy is a central feature of Project 2061, an ambitious project from the American Association for the Advancement of Science (AAAS) to raise levels of scientific literacy in the US by the time of the return of Halley's Comet. Just what is involved in such civic science literacy can be seen in the AAAS's recommendations set out in its 'Science for all Americans'. The AAAS takes a broad definition of science literacy:

Science literacy – which encompasses mathematics and technology as well as the natural and social sciences – has many facets. These include being familiar with the natural world and respecting its unity; being aware of some of the important ways in which mathematics, technology, and the sciences depend upon one another; understanding some of the key concepts and principles of science; having a capacity for scientific ways of thinking; knowing that science, mathematics, and technology are human enterprises, and knowing what that implies about their strengths and limitations; and being able to use scientific knowledge and ways of thinking for personal and social purposes.

(AAAS 1989)

In shaping science curricula across the education system it recommends that the amount of science content be cut down so that what is taught can be taught better. It offers no prescriptions to science educators as to what should be taught, but suggests the following criteria for the content-cutting exercise:

Utility: Will the proposed content – knowledge or skills – significantly enhance the graduate's long-term employment prospects? Will it be useful in making personal decisions?
Social responsibility: Is the proposed content likely to help citizens

participate intelligently in making social and political decisions on matters involving science and technology?

The intrinsic value of knowledge: Does the proposed content present aspects of science, mathematics, and technology that are so important in human history or so pervasive in our culture that a general education would be incomplete without them?

Philosophical value: Does the proposed content contribute to the ability of people to ponder the enduring questions of human meaning such as life and death, perception and reality, the individual good versus the collective welfare, certainty and doubt?

Childhood enrichment: Will the proposed content enhance childhood (a time of life that is important in its own right and not solely for what it may lead to in later life)?

(AAAS 1989)

Clearly, scientific literacy is no easy option. It should be useful, enable us to be socially responsible and enrich our children; without it education would be incomplete, but with it we can ponder the meaning of life.

Extending the concept of scientific literacy to include a civic dimension has many attractions, not the least of which is that it directly addresses the problem of why we should want scientific literacy in the first place. However, not only does this make scientific literacy more difficult to define; it also makes it more difficult to measure. If we restrict ourselves to basic facts (e.g. atoms are bigger than electrons) and procedures (e.g. use of placebos in drug trials) it is fairly easy to check whether someone knows or does not know. If we want to see if a person is equipped to make personal, social and political decisions as well as tackle 'the enduring questions of human meaning', then a research methodology is not so obvious. It is not even clear what it is that we should be looking for. Jon D. Miller has probably done more than most to develop rigorous ways of testing scientific literacy and has also provided a useful overview of work in the field (Miller 1998). According to Miller,

civic scientific literacy should be conceptualized as involving three related dimensions: (1) a vocabulary of basic scientific constructs sufficient to read competing views in a newspaper or magazine, (2) an understanding of the process or nature of scientific inquiry, and (3) some level of understanding of the impact of science and technology on individuals and on society.

(Miller 1998: 205).

However, the third of these is of little use in cross-national comparisons because the content varies so much across different contexts. This may not be such a problem, Miller suggests, because a survey of empirical work appears to show agreement that we only need the first two anyway and that 'the desirability and feasibility of using a third dimension that reflects the social impact of science and technology in conceptualizing civic scientific literacy is still a point of some disagreement' (206). In other words, the dimension that we might regard as the most 'civic' (because it is the most contextual) is also the least useful and most debatable (because it is the most contextual). We are therefore left to measuring what Miller calls the 'construct vocabulary dimension' (i.e. facts) and the 'understanding of scientific enquiry dimension' (i.e. procedures). Respondents in surveys who achieve acceptable scores in both dimensions are said to be 'civic scientifically literate'.

From all the surveys in a range of countries consistently over time there is one thing that everyone seems to agree on – levels of scientific literacy are abysmally low. Whatever the definition, and however it gets measured, the result is the same: only a small portion of the population can be regarded as scientifically literate. Using the approach outlined above and based on material gathered from surveys across Europe in 1992 and in the US in 1995, Miller concludes that only 12 per cent of adult Americans and 5 per cent of Europeans can qualify as being civic scientifically literate. Within Europe the figures range from 10 per cent for the UK down to 1 per cent for Portugal (Miller 1998: 217). Earlier surveys in the US show a 5 per cent level of scientific literacy in 1985 and 7 per cent in 1979 (Miller 1987: 28–30). The latest figures from the National Science Foundation's *Science and Engineering Indicators* (published May 2004) are hardly encouraging. In the US one person in every four thinks the Sun goes round the Earth; in Europe the figure is one in three (National Science Foundation 2004).

By having such a clear and consistent message amidst so much diversity and uncertainty, attention naturally becomes focused on this failing. Conceptualizing what the public understands about science, therefore, becomes framed in terms of a deficit, a lack on the part of the public which has to be remedied. This certainly seems to have been the case in the UK with what has been called the 'movement' for the Public Understanding of Science, or PUS.

In 1983 the Royal Society set up an ad hoc group under the chairmanship of Walter Bodmer (Director of Research at the Imperial Cancer Research Fund). Its terms of reference asked it 'to review the nature and extent of public understanding of science and technology in the UK and its adequacy for an advanced industrialized democracy, to review the mechanisms for effecting the public understanding of science and technology and its role in society, [and] to consider the constraints upon the processes of communication and how they might be overcome'. The report it published in 1985 was highly influential and can be seen as the starting point for the Public Understanding of Science (PUS) movement:

A basic thesis of this report is that the better public understanding of science can be a major element in promoting national prosperity, in raising the quality of public and private decision-making and in enriching the life of the individual . . . Improving the public understanding of science is an investment in the future, not a luxury to be indulged in if and when resources allow.

(Bodmer 1985: 9)

There quickly followed a number of PUS initiatives, many of them promoted by the newly formed COPUS (Committee on the Public Understanding of Science) – a joint venture of the Royal Society, the Royal Institution and the British Association for the Advancement of Science. COPUS became the principal channel for activities to promote science including small grants for PUS research and funding for community based projects. It also hosted workshops to provide media training for scientists, awarded a prize for the best popular science book each year and in general acted as a convenient point of access for government consultation on science policy. Beyond COPUS the report also spurred on academic PUS activity. The Economic and Social Research Council (one of the major sources of academic funding in the UK) established a research programme in the public understanding of science. A new journal, *Public Understanding of Science*, was started in 1992, and two new chairs in public understanding of science were established in 1995 (at Oxford University and Imperial College London). The momentum was kept going by a government White Paper, *Realising Our Potential* (Cabinet Office 1993), which reinforced the recommendations of the Bodmer report. An annual jamboree of PUS events began in 1994 with the first Science, Engineering and Technology week bringing enthusiastic scientists to national TV and local shopping malls.

The importance of the Bodmer report in generating all this feverish activity should not be underestimated. As Steve Miller says, 'Britain's scientists were told that they had no less than a duty to communicate with the public about their work. From being an activity carried out by superannuated boffins or second-rate minds, popularizing science was *legitimized* by Bodmer' (Miller 2001: 115, original emphasis). In this respect, Bodmer set out to reverse the trend of scientists retreating into their laboratories when faced with what was seen to be declining public support. However, for the very same reason a different picture emerges, one in which we can see PUS not so much as an attempt to legitimize popularization as popularization as an attempt to legitimize science. Steve Fuller (1997) puts it vividly when he describes PUS as 'our latest moral panic'. It is a crisis of legitimation which, according to Brian Wynne, is of the scientists' own making:

In short, the re-emergence of the public understanding of science issue in the mid-1980s can be seen as part of the scientific establishment's anxious response to a legitimation vacuum which threatened the well-being and social standing of science. It is arguable that this legitimation vacuum, which manifests itself as the widely publicized and lamented public ignorance of science, is the direct result of the way that science in the past legitimated its harvest of public funds by *distancing* itself from the ordinary public ... [S]cience now finds itself hoist with its very own petard, namely the cultural alienation whose establishment it actively, if innocently, promoted.

(Wynne 1992: 38, original emphasis)

In previous chapters we saw how scientists established their authority by setting themselves apart; now it seems they are the victims of their own success. Despite this, the problem is not seen as one which lies within science but rather is seen to arise from public ignorance and poor communication. 'Questions such as those about whose interests are served by different kinds of science and scientific representation, and about the basis of trust and social accountability of different institutional forms of control and ownership of science, are effectively deleted' (Wynne 1992: 38; see also Irwin and Wynne 1996).

We can see, therefore, that a proper consideration of the problem of scientific literacy takes us far beyond simple questions about measuring the number of 'right' answers in a survey. Not only does it raise issues about the contexts for knowledge, but the very framing of the problem also raises issues about scientific legitimacy and authority. By accepting that authority we can see the problem as a concern for, and fear of, the public *ignorance* of science (though as an acronym I am not sure that 'PIS' is any better than 'PUS'). On the other hand, shifting our focus away from public ignorance leads us to question the nature of scientific authority. This reveals a fundamental dilemma faced by science. To maintain its authority it needs to be set apart from the general public, but to maintain its legitimacy it needs to appeal to the general public. Being set apart increases its alienation; making it more 'popular' undermines its authority. The domain of popular science is especially important because that is where science has to carry out this delicate balancing act. Equally important is how that domain is characterized; indeed, that is part of the balancing act. Is PUS nothing more than a public relations exercise; or maybe that is what it should be? What if the public were to understand science and *because* of that understanding decide to reject it? Is PUS an attempt to legitimize science, or could (should) popular science be something much more subversive, something which actively seeks to undermine the authority of science itself? No doubt PUS advocates would stress the value of scientific knowledge and the need for spreading it as widely as possible, but is this diffusion of useful knowledge just a twentieth-century reincarnation of the nineteenth-century SDUK (see Chapter 1)? If so it would only be natural to ask, what would now constitute *really* useful knowledge? The public understanding of history? Of politics? Of global capitalism?

Science wars (and 'anti-science')

Intended to be 'more than a metaphor, but less than a cultural map', Snow's concept of the 'two cultures' is suggestive without being too precise. As one scholar puts it, this gives it 'considerable interpretative flexibility' so that 'writers tend to transform it to mean what they currently happen to be debating' (Hultberg 1997: 211). As a consequence, the durability of the concept lies not so much in its usefulness as an analytical tool than in the ease with which it can be extended beyond its original domain. This is especially true when considering the public understanding of science. Moreover, although the problem identified by Snow provides a convenient and common reference point in such considerations, what is more important is the widespread (if tacit) acceptance of the dualism within which that problem is framed. To start with the dualisms set out in Snow's lecture we can see how science is contrasted with 'traditional culture', 'literary culture', 'literary intellectuals', 'intellectuals', 'Arts' and 'Culture'. Snow also sets up knowledge against ignorance, optimism against pessimism, and technology/industry against 'Luddites'. In all these binarisms, for Snow, it is the association on the side of science that is the privileged term. It is science that provides us with the right answers and, by inference, everything else leads us into error. There are two consequences to accepting this dualistic framing and its attendant privileging. First, the dualism enables us to move beyond Snow's original formulation, allowing us to contrast science with everything that is not science so that we can talk about science and humanities, science and religion, science and society, science and the public. Secondly, the privileging means that in each case the relationship between the two puts the second term in an inferior position so that to be 'not-science' means to be 'unscientific' or 'less than science'.

The dualism should also alert us to the interaction between the two sides. Snow wrote of 'incomprehension' and 'misunderstanding' between the two cultures but his privileging of science exposes his real concern as the misunderstanding of 'science' by 'literary culture', not the other way round. However, even accepting the dualistic framework one does not have to accept the exclusionary 'and' that sits in the middle. A whole range of other prepositions might be possible: not just science *and* literary culture but *in, for, against, with* or *as* literary culture (and, of course, vice versa for each one). Indeed, a good deal of work in the history of science might be characterized as a search for the most suitable preposition to describe science's relationship with its socio-cultural context. All seem applicable, but none quite fits. This is, perhaps, most clearly seen in studies of science and religion which have shifted from a simplistic conflict thesis to more nuanced, multi-faceted accounts (see Brooke 1991, and Lindberg and Numbers 1986 and 2003). Similar sensitivities need to be employed in considering the two cultures divide in whatever way it may be construed but particularly when the dualism is that of 'science' and the 'public'. Unfortunately in the early 1990s the misunderstanding between the two sides was given a more belligerent twist.

When Snow first put forward his thesis his focus was principally upon England, but he believed that it was a problem that bedevilled the whole of Western civilization. In 1963, when he revisited the problem with a 'second look', he acknowledged that in the US the divide was not so deep or unbridge-able, that universities in the states were running non-specialized classes in the sciences and that a new third culture was emerging from a 'mixed bag' that included history of science, social history, sociology, economics and psychology (Snow 1963: 65–7). It is ironic, therefore, that from this mixed bag came a book which would crack open the divide in new directions; that the humanities' examination of science would provoke fears that science was under attack; and that the ensuing 'science wars' would be fought most fiercely in the United States.

Thomas Kuhn's book *The Structure of Scientific Revolutions* was to have a profound effect on how people thought about science. It appeared in 1962 and argued that science does not progress through its own internal logic. Instead scientific disciplines pass through alternating phases of 'normal' science and 'revolutionary' science. Kuhn describes normal science as a puzzle-solving activ-ity within a dominant way of thinking or 'paradigm'. Puzzles which cannot be solved using the conceptual resources of the existing paradigm are simply put to one side as anomalies. Eventually the number of anomalies exposes the puzzle-solving limitations of the paradigm and forces the discipline into a more creative or revolutionary phase of activity. Erstwhile deviant theories are now given more consideration until a shift to a new paradigm allows normal science to proceed with a new set of puzzles and a new set of puzzle-solving techniques. A full account of Kuhn's book and its reception need not concern us here; suffice it to say that within the field of the sociology of science it caused its own paradigm shift in thinking about science. No longer should science be seen simply as a narrative of progress driven by its own rationality, but instead non-rational influences had to be taken into consideration. This was especially the case when addressing the question of how old paradigms were sustained, new paradigms were developed and the clash between the two resolved. In short, it opened up new possibilities for examining science as a social activity; not just the practices and institutions of science, but also the content of science. What such examinations revealed, for example in Latour and Woolgar's study of laboratory life, was how ordinary science was, how much it seemed to be a job like any other. More than that, sociologists in Edinburgh put forward what became known as the Strong Programme, which emphasized that not only was science as an institution influenced by society but also that scientific knowledge itself was socially constructed. For some it seemed a short step from *explaining* science in terms of its social context to *explaining it away* in terms of its social context. In this way, the emphasis on the social might be seen to undermine science's claim to be the 'truth', since whatever science had to say would no longer appear to be determined or constrained by physical reality but by social reality.

Throughout the 1970s and 1980s science and scientists were subjected to sociological scrutiny. By the early 1990s a range of factors brought matters to a head and scientists were prompted to respond. The general context for the response was provided by the debates, particularly fierce in the US, that came to be known as the 'culture wars'. In these debates about multiculturalism, Eurocentrism and the place of the Western Canon in the curriculum, the more 'conservative' faction saw themselves fighting the pernicious effects of post-modernism, cultural studies and political correctness. In this general climate of intellectual conflict, science suffered a number of specific blows. The **Challenger** disaster and problems with the **Hubble Space Telescope** prompted *Time* magazine to produce a special issue on 'Science under siege'. In 1993 the US Congress withdrew funding for the **superconducting supercollider** – a major, and superexpensive, project in particle physics. This was only the latest, and most high-profile, instance of the questioning or cutting of research budgets for science. In the 1980s, for example, Representative John Dingell's aggressive investigations of scientists and research institutions were part of a more general investigation of financial proprieties that included bank regulators, the insurance industry and cable TV companies (Toumey 1996: 32–3). Sociologists' claims about the ordinariness of science were certainly confirmed if the scientist were to be treated the same as an insurance salesman. When such reduced status was also accompanied by reduced budgets, it is small wonder that some scientists felt compelled to fight back.

The most notable (and probably the most inflammatory) response came with Paul R. Gross and Norman Levitt's *Higher Superstition: The Academic Left and its Quarrels with Science* (1994). The book is an attempt to rescue the 'academic left' from a misguided dislike of science. Such 'muddleheaded' ideas about science, they argue, come from literary criticism, social history and cultural studies, each informed or influenced by postmodernism, Marxism, feminism, multiculturalism and radical environmentalism. From this rag-bag of '-isms', or 'contiguous ideological field' as they call it, science criticism became 'a game of mix-and-match' where differences were played down for the sake of solidarity and in the interests of a common purpose 'which is to *demystify* science, to undermine its epistemic authority, and to valorize "ways of knowing" incompatible with it' (11, original emphasis). They do not deny that there is a relationship between science and culture or science and politics but the relationship is one where science is 'influenced' by these external factors, not 'driven' by them. Above all else, they say, science is a 'reality-driven enterprise ... Reality is the overseer at one's shoulder, ready to rap one's knuckles or to spring the trap into which one has been led by overconfidence, or by a too-complacent reliance on surmise ... Reality is the unrelenting angel with whom scientists have agreed to wrestle' (234). With its focus firmly on reality, science had taken little notice of the critiques of its underlying conceptual basis. There had been no rethinking of fundamental ideas or rearticulations of observational reality in response to criticisms from feminists, sociologists and postmodernists, nor was there likely to be: 'To put it bluntly, the probability that science will sooner or later take these critiques sufficiently to heart to change its fundamental way of knowing is vanishingly small' (236).

But if science will not be 'influenced, deflected, restricted, or even inconvenienced by these critics and those they influence', why worry? Why the need to respond? We should worry, they say, 'because unanswered criticism *must* in due course have effects' (236, original emphasis). The reason they give for this has echoes of Snow's Two Cultures: the postmodern science critics have high positions in notable universities with both political and intellectual influence – very much like Snow's vision of the British establishment being humanities-based. For Gross and Levitt, what makes matters worse is that those who have such high positions do not deserve them. Substantial careers had been built on insubstantial critiques simply because they were ideologically intoxicating:

> In sum, we are accusing a powerful faction in modern academic life of intellectual dereliction ... We allege that eagerness to praise a certain spectrum of work has disarmed skepticism and careful attention. Political sympathy has combined with professional vanity to give undue weight, prestige, and influence to a decidedly slender body of work.
>
> (Gross and Levitt 1994: 239)

If this were not insult enough to those in the humanities, Gross and Levitt push their attack even further. Scientists are 'deeply cultured people', they say, with an extensive range of knowledge of music, art, history, philosophy and literature. If the humanities department at MIT were to walk out, then faculty from the science departments would be able to fill the breach and could 'patch together a humanities curriculum, to be taught by the scientists themselves'. They simply leave it to the reader's imagination to consider what would happen if the situation were reversed.

It was an attack (or counter-attack) that was too strident to ignore. The culture wars were now joined by the 'science wars' and *Social Text* (one of the leading cultural studies journals) devoted a special issue to the conflict. The journal's editor Andrew Ross (1996) wrote that the science wars opened a 'second front' in Culture Wars: 'Seeking explanations for their loss of standing in the public eye and for the decline in funding from the public purse, conservatives in science have joined the backlash against the (new) usual suspects – pinkos, feminists, and multiculturalists of all stripes' (7). The special issue brought together contributions from many of Gross and Levitt's targets; it also included a late submission from Alan D. Sokal (1996a), professor of physics at New York University. Sokal's article pushed all the right buttons: arguing for a 'postmodern and liberatory science', accepting physical reality as a social and linguistic construct, undermining the privileged epistemological status of scientists, trying to expose scientific objectivity as an ideology of dominance, even making flattering references to the work of the journal's editors along the way. It drew on fashionable areas of physics (quantum mechanics, chaos theory, **relativity**) and fashionable aspects of postmodern theory (**transgression, deconstruction, indeterminism**). It made all the right noises with its language ('encoding', 'demystification', 'political praxis') and with its quotations (from Derrida, Lacan, Irigaray). It employed all the stylistic techniques that are the hallmark of much postmodern writing: puns, slicing words with brack(ets), 'ironic' quotation marks. It was also nonsense, a hoax. In amongst the right noises Sokal had planted a number of scientific absurdities (for example, that the number pi was not a universal constant). Sokal revealed the hoax in an article for *Lingua Franca* which appeared soon afterwards and explained that he had intended it as an 'experiment' to test the intellectual standards of those he was parodying. 'Did they meet the test? I don't think so' (Sokal 1996b). Ziauddin Sardar, who might normally be seen on the other side of the fence to Sokal, seems to agree: 'Sokal's hoax proves what many scholars already suspected: cultural studies has become quite meaningless, and anyone can get away with anything in the name of postmodern criticism' (Sardar 2000: 62).

The Sokal hoax made the front pages of several newspapers around the world (including the *New York Times, International Herald Tribune* and *Le Monde*) and the inside pages of many more. It was, perhaps, the most high-profile clash in the science wars, but there were other skirmishes too. In many respects popular science had become the chosen arena as academic battles erupted into the public domain. For example, Steven Weinberg's popular science book *Dreams of a Final Theory* (1992) can be seen as a thinly veiled defence of the supercollider project, and Lewis Wolpert's *Unnatural Nature of Science* (1992) took regular sideswipes at the constructionists and relativists. In the opposite corner Harry Collins and Trevor Pinch tried to popularize a sociological understanding of science with their book *The Golem: What Everyone Should Know about Science* (1993). In 1994 Wolpert and Collins had a 'fiery exchange' at the British Association's annual festival, prompting a special feature in the *Times Higher Education Supplement* on the question 'Is science a social construct?' (Irwin 1994). The contribution from Richard Dawkins was characteristically clear and robust:

> Lewis Wolpert is to be congratulated for standing up at the British Association and blowing the whistle on the chic drivel of the 'all knowledge is a social construct and merits equal attention' persuasion . . .
>
> Western science works . . . When you take a 747 to an international convention of sociologists or literary critics, the reason you will arrive in one piece is that a lot of western trained scientists and engineers got their sums right. If it gives you satisfaction to say that the theory of aerodynamics is a social construct that is your privilege, but why do you then entrust your air-travel plans to a Boeing rather than a magic carpet? As I have put it before, show me a relativist at 30,000 feet and I will show you a hypocrite.
>
> (Dawkins 1994: 17)

This public face to the science wars is especially important since it should be noted that in the UK some of the most high-profile and fiercest critics of the sociological perspective such as Dawkins and Wolpert were also leading players in the PUS movement – Dawkins as Professor of the Public Understanding of Science at Oxford, and Wolpert as chairman of COPUS. If nothing else the science wars raised the stakes, because in 'understanding science' what was it that the public should understand? What was science? A collection of facts? An access point to the 'truth'? Simply something that some people do? Most importantly, was it a social construction or not?

In the fog of war it was not always possible to see who was fighting whom. Not all scientists were science warriors and neither were all sociologists (if anything, there was a distinct lack of rallying around a humanities flag). Neither side presented a united front. On one side we can contrast Weinberg's vision of science as a search for 'beautiful theories' that resist falsification with Wolpert's where falsification is the only guarantee that you are actually doing science (Fuller 2000: 194). As for the sociologists, it was only a particular section of them who were concerned with the social construction of knowledge and even then we should distinguish between those wanting to show that science is inherently ideological and those who simply wanted to show science as not the fully rationalist endeavour that some philosophers of science claimed it to be (Segerstråle 2000). This problem of trying to find the enemy was one identified by Gross and Levitt who said that the greatest difficulty in putting together their response was the 'absence of a central body of doctrine' that they were trying to respond to. 'There is no intellectual core to the process by which the critics scrutinize and, for the most part, disparage science; thus there is no obvious target for a definitive rejoinder' (Gross and Levitt 1994: 10). It would appear that the common factor uniting those seen by Gross and Levitt as the enemy was that they were seen as the enemy by Gross and Levitt. It is probably for this reason that Andrew Ross, a favourite target for the warrior scientists, felt able to dismiss their criticisms as a 'conspiratorial fantasy' where '. . . class-soaked pronouncements about the return of the Dark Ages among the ill-educated masses are intended to reinforce the myth of scientists as a beleaguered and isolated minority of truth seekers, armed only with objective reasoning and standing firm against a tide of superstitions' (Ross 1996: 9, 11).

When the rhetoric is toned down a little, there is, I think, something to be said for Ross's assessment. The war seemed driven not by sociologists' malice or enmity, but by scientists' fear. What frightened them was a threat so indefinable it could only be labelled 'anti-science', and so nebulous that it may also have been non-existent. There is no evidence from numerous surveys that the public was (or is) anti-science. Reviewing decades of survey work on the public understanding of science, Jon D. Miller concludes:

> A substantial body of research from the end of World War II to the present indicates that an overwhelming majority of US adults are interested in science and technology, believe that it has contributed to our standard of living, and are willing to support it with government funding.
>
> (Miller 2004: 284)

Likewise, the first conclusion of a joint report on 'Science and the Public' from the Office of Science and Technology and the Wellcome Trust was that 'the British public is not anti-science'; it may not be as pro-science as in other countries but 'on balance, the British people are interested in science and enthusiastic about the benefits it brings' (Office of Science and Technology and Wellcome Trust 2000: 33). Nevertheless, a constant theme in the science wars (and before) was the perceived threat from an anti-science movement, not just from sociologists but from the public in general (Holton 1993b).

The following two examples are taken from the leading science journal *Nature*. In 1983 Isaac Asimov (scientist, popularizer and science fiction novelist) highlighted the dangers in a piece on 'Popularizing science':

> We must not view science and technology as either an inevitable saviour, or

as an inevitable destroyer. It can be either, and the choice is ours. A general public, utterly ignorant of science, led by rulers scarcely better informed, cannot be expected to make intelligent choices in this matter. The alternatives of salvation and destruction depend, in that case, upon the blind gropings of ignorance.

This is not to say that we must build a world of scientists. That would be beyond the abilities of popularisers. But at least let the public make up an intelligent and informed audience. Football games are watched by millions who cannot play the game themselves, or even direct one successfully – but who can at least understand enough to applaud and to groan at the proper places . . .

The difference to the public between a scientist and a magician is the difference between understanding and not understanding and that is also the difference between respect and admiration on the one side, and hate and fear on the other.

Without an informed public, scientists will not only be no longer supported financially, they will be actively persecuted.

(Asimov 1983: 119)

This second extract comes from the editor of *Nature*, John Maddox. Published at the height of the science wars, its rallying cry is clear in its title: 'Defending science from anti-science':

. . . science is docile in the face of what is really a torrent of attack. But is it not disgraceful that there should be such general and benign tolerance of astrology (and other mumbo-jumbo such as faith healing, water divining and spiritualism) apparently on the grounds that they are the harmless pursuits of people who are not scientists? Would other professionals, lawyers or accountants say, be as tolerant of public belief that undermined the integrity of their work – and potentially, their livelihood?

Religion is something else again . . . The idea that religion may be a way of organising one's appraisal of one's place in the world is not very different from what astrologers tell their clients. In other words, it may not be long before the practice of religion must be regarded as anti-science.

(Maddox 1994: 185)

It does not take too much analysing to see the extent of the fear. There is a 'torrent of attack' and the enemy is on all sides: 'mumbo jumbo', sociologists, literary critics, religion, astrology, faith healing, spiritualism, water divining. The financial support of science is under threat and scientists are in danger of being 'actively persecuted'. Lack of understanding has brought 'hate and fear' when understanding could bring 'respect and admiration'. The only objection to building 'a world of scientists' is a practical one: it would be 'beyond the abilities of popularisers'.

The science wars were not simply the Two Cultures at war. The warring parties were similar, but the differences can be equally important. As James Robert Brown has pointed out, in recent clashes it is:

> (1) the objectivity of science, rather than its cultural importance, that is principally at issue . . . (2) Snow was fighting for underdog science, whereas today science is anything but that . . . (3) Snow took his scientists to be predominantly on the [political] Left and the literati on the Right. Yet in much of the current science wars commentary, the very opposite is assumed.
>
> (Brown 2001: 7)

Such differences reveal how the political and cultural ground had shifted, but this is not to say that Snow's thesis was not a contributory factor or at least provided a conducive environment. The dualism of the Two Cultures, its persistence as a way of framing science's relationship with society, the abundance of evidence about public ignorance and a perceived threat from sociological scrutiny had all combined, it would seem, to produce a siege mentality. No longer was science confronted simply with an amorphous 'other' that was 'not science', but to be 'not science' was taken as being 'anti-science'. If you are not with us you are against us, and there was an awful lot of the world (the humanities, arts, religion, society, the public) that could be regarded as not science. The wars may have been *about* the social relations of science but they were also revealing *of* the social relations of science: its relationship with the academic left and debates over the curriculum; with government and its control over funding for the supercollider; with the public more generally and anxieties over scientific literacy. At least in part, the science wars 'reflected the lack of clarity in science's basic social contract at the end of the twentieth century' (Segerstråle 2000: 24–5), resulting from the emergence of a new 'postacademic science' with new sponsors, new rules, and new relationships between science, government and industry (see also Ziman 2000). As Ullica Segerstråle says, the question was who had the right (and the competence) to criticize science? It is this question that will be one of the themes in the next chapter.

Further reading

Gregory, J. and Miller, S. (1998) *Science in Public: Communication, Culture, and Credibility*. New York: Plenum.

Gross, P.R. and Levitt, N. (1994) *Higher Superstition: The Academic Left and its Quarrels with Science*. Baltimore, MD: Johns Hopkins University Press.

Lewenstein, B.V. (ed.) (1992) *When Science Meets the Public*. Washington, DC: American Association for the Advancement of Science.

Shamos, M.H. (1995) *The Myth of Scientific Literacy*, New Brunswick, NJ: Rutgers University Press.

Snow, C.P. (1963) *The Two Cultures and a Second Look*. London: New English Library.

Toumey, C.P. (1996) *Conjuring Science: Scientific Symbols and Cultural Meanings in American Life*. New Brunswick, NJ: Rutgers University Press.

6 | GOING CRITICAL

In February 2000 the UK's House of Lords Select Committee on Science and Technology reported that 'Society's relationship with science is in a critical phase.' Public interest in science was high, said the report, yet there was a basic lack of trust in science, especially science associated with government or industry. The language of the report was clear and emphatic: there was a 'crisis of confidence', a need for 'a sea-change' in the culture of UK science, and – a phrase the report used several times – 'a new mood for dialogue'. All this, it should be remembered, after fifteen years of intense activity in the 'public understanding of science' (or PUS). Indeed, the point (or the irony) was not lost on the select committee which reviewed the range of public understanding initiatives only to conclude that 'despite all this activity and commitment, we have been told from several quarters that the expression "public understanding of science" may not be the most appropriate label'. Not only was the efficacy of PUS being called into question but so too were the models upon which it was based. In considering the appropriateness (or otherwise) of the PUS label the report noted the views of many of its witnesses:

> It is argued that the words imply a condescending assumption that any difficulties in the relationship between science and society are due entirely to ignorance and misunderstanding on the part of the public; and that, with enough public-understanding activity, the public can be brought to greater knowledge, whereupon all will be well.
>
> (Select Committee on Science and Technology 2000: 3.9)

Sir Robert May told the committee that this was a 'rather backward looking vision'. The British Council even went so far as to call it 'outmoded and

potentially dangerous'. The select committee's report provided a useful, percep-
tive and timely overview of PUS, and clearly all was not well.

This chapter will look at the failings of PUS and consider alternative concep-
tions about the relationship between science and the public before suggesting a
way forward.

Deficit deficiencies

Although 'PUS' might be a peculiarly British label, what it represents is a dominant tradition in studies (and practices) of science communication. It can be
taken as an example of a common approach to be found on both sides of the
Atlantic. Indeed much can be traced back to the US in the 1950s and the work
of Warren Weaver who was a central figure in the attempts of the scientific
community to disseminate an appreciation of science to a wider public. Weaver
was a 'catalyst' for many of the public science activities and initiatives involving
the American Association for the Advancement of Science, the National Science
Foundation, the Rockefeller Foundation, the Sloan Foundation and the Council
for the Advancement of Science Writing (Lewenstein 1992a). Together with
Claude Shannon he was also the co-author of one of the most influential
models of communication. The Shannon and Weaver model of communication
takes a mathematical theory of how information is transmitted in physical
systems such as two connected telephones (Shannon was an engineer at the Bell
Telephone Laboratories) and applies it to all forms of interpersonal communication. As a transmission model it reduces communication to the simple
form of Sender–Message–Receiver and accounts for any disruption of the message through the action of 'noise' (e.g. the crackle on a telephone line). In
Weaver's concern for making science public and his transmission model of
communication we have the main elements of what would be the dominant
tradition in science communication for the rest of the century. The model of
Sender–Message–Receiver would easily translate as Scientist–Popularization–
Public, and improving science communication would become a problem of
reducing the amount of interference from noise or crackle.

The approach fed into (and fed off) concerns for scientific literacy throughout the 1950s, 1960s and 1970s, and was firmly established by the 1980s when
the Royal Society produced its report on the Public Understanding of Science
(see Chapter 5). Christopher Dornan was to characterize the approach as:

> . . . a camp of inquiry that operates with a rigidly linear model of the
> communication process. Scientists are the sources of information, the
> media are the conduit, and the public is the ultimate destination. The goal

is to minimize media interference so as to transmit as much information as possible with the maximum fidelity.

(Dornan 1989: 102)

By 1990 Stephen Hilgartner could refer to it simply as the 'dominant view':

The culturally-dominant view of the popularization of science is rooted in the idealized notion of pure, genuine scientific knowledge against which popularized knowledge is contrasted. A two-stage model is assumed: first, scientists develop genuine scientific knowledge; subsequently popularizers disseminate simplified accounts to the public. Moreover, the dominant view holds that any differences between genuine and popularized science must be caused by 'distortion' or 'degradation' of the original truths. Thus popularization is, at best, 'appropriate simplification' – a necessary (albeit low status) educational activity of simplifying science for non-specialists. At worst, popularization is 'pollution', the 'distortion' of science by such outsiders as journalists, and by a public that misunderstands much of what it reads.

(Hilgartner 1990: 519)

Nevertheless, the persistence of the transmission model in the face of mounting criticism is seen in the launch issue of the journal *Public Understanding of Science* in 1992, where Bodmer and Wilkins argued that what PUS activists needed was research to point them in the right direction. Their demand was simple: 'We need to know the most effective models to use to get messages across to a wide variety of target audiences' (Bodmer and Wilkins 1992: 7).

By the end of the 1990s criticisms of the dominant view were widespread yet, as Gregory and Miller noted in 1998, such criticisms 'have barely impacted on scientists' discussions of public understanding of science' (17). More than that, what seemed to be most common was not to think at all about how science is communicated:

In discussions of science, popularization and the public, talk is frequently of activity – of what one should do in order to achieve better or more public understanding of science. Rather less attention has been devoted to articulating the philosophies and models that inform and drive popularizing activities.

(Gregory and Miller 1998: 81)

Lacking such articulation, any understanding of popularization necessarily rests upon uncritical tacit assumptions. In this way the 'dominant view' might also be called the 'common-sense view', based as it is on simple assumptions taken from common-sense understandings of audiences, communication, the media, knowledge, culture, social interaction and so on. Lewis Wolpert, for example, might highlight the limitations of common sense to show the counter-intuitive 'unnatural nature' of science, yet he seemed quite happy to rely on that same common sense for his understanding of science communication.

Not only does the dominant model accord with common sense but it is also simple, generalizable and tries to deal with measurable entities. It is easy to see the appeal of the model for those with a scientific turn of mind. It was, after all, based on Shannon's work as an engineer and originally published as *A Mathematical Model of Communication*. It is almost like classical Newtonian physics in the way that it translates the communication process into a quantitative problem of cause and effect. There is a desired effect (more public understanding of science) and what needs to be worked out is an appropriate cause to bring it about. The public is seen as a target that needs to be hit and the 'effectiveness' of any cause (e.g. a particular PUS campaign) can be measured by the number of successful hits (e.g. increased levels of 'scientific literacy'). We should not, therefore, be surprised by its success or its longevity. However, as will be apparent from the select committee report mentioned earlier, it is also a model that is deeply flawed. If we take the standard or common-sense view described above we can see that it is characterized by:

1   a linear model of communication which focuses on the delivery of messages from source to receiver with effectiveness measured by the number of hits on target;
2   a deficit model of understanding where the public is conceived of as empty vessels which need to be filled with right answers to make good the deficit;
3   an unproblematic account of science as a body of uncontested knowledge or as objective inquiry with privileged access to truth.

On each of these three counts the view is open to question from many years' work within social studies of science and from cultural and media studies. In the previous chapter we saw how difficult it was to define scientific literacy, let alone measure it, so the extent to which the model is able to quantify science communication is certainly questionable. We could also point out how the model does not take into account:

• the context of communication (reading a book for an exam is different to reading the same book for pleasure);
• the importance of the medium (saying 'I love you' by email is not the same as saying it face to face);
• the relationship between sender and receiver (being told 'stop' is different when it comes from a politician, a doctor, a friend, an enemy).

What all these weaknesses reveal is a blindness to the importance of *meaning* in communication. The information a statement contains might remain the same, but its meaning can change with context, medium and relationship between people involved. In the transmissive model, the reader/listener/viewer is portrayed as passively receiving information, not as actively constructing meaning. This is an important point that will be returned to later, because the central feature in the development of a more critical understanding of science in public is a shift in focus from the transmission of information to the construction of meaning.

With its concerns for the accuracy of representations and the distorting effects of the media process, the traditional or dominant approach to science and the media can be placed 'firmly within the mainstream tradition of North American communication inquiry' (Dornan 1989: 102). However, an alternative approach to the media was being developed from the 1960s onwards, a more European 'critical' approach which centred on questions about ideology and the maintenance of hegemony. Within such critical analyses the concern was not so much with the impact of particular media messages, but more with the politics of signification, the struggle over meaning and the production of consent (Hall 1982; Dornan 1989). By the late 1980s, therefore, there was a rather curious state of affairs. There had been over two decades of critical attention given to science (see previous chapter) and over two decades of critical attention had been given to the media, but there was a surprising absence of critical attention given to science in the media. Writing at the end of the 1980s, Dornan was surprised at the absence, saying that media representations of science should 'be of considerable interest to those who seek to understand how consensus is engineered within liberal democracy'. As the embodiment of rational inquiry science presents itself as both the 'antithesis of ideology' and as the 'chief legitimating agent for political decisions'. This gives it a key role in the construction of consent, since 'only that which is universally accepted as necessary enters into the realm of effective ideology, and only that which escapes interrogation remains effective' (103). In other words, the very absence of critical examination should alert us to the power of that which is left unexamined. It would seem, therefore, that far from providing us with analytical tools the dominant view should instead be our object of inquiry.

The internal logic of the dominant view presents the public as ill-informed passive consumers of media misinformation. From a PUS perspective this lack of knowledge is identified as the problem that needs to be addressed – hence the concern for scientific literacy. By focusing on the public's deficiencies, the theoretical basis for PUS (and the dominant view it represented) soon came to be known as the 'deficit model'. However, by seeing the public as 'the problem' and looking to improved media coverage for 'the solution' there is an important, and obvious, element missing from the science–media–public equation. Framing the problem in this way leaves out any consideration of science itself, which is taken as a given, that which is true and right. Such an approach accepts the claims of science on its own behalf. 'It holds that science is indeed an inherently objective, rational and heroic endeavour, and that the project of science communication should be to affirm just this view in the popular understanding' (Dornan 1989: 102). This is not without ideological or political significance. As Simon Locke has argued, science needs to maintain public support but equally needs to maintain professional integrity and authority, to defend the boundary with the 'lay' public:

> One means of doing this is to accentuate the impoverished condition of public knowledge and the public's dependence on professional expertise. Hence the periodic revival of concern with public understanding, and the characteristic rhetoric aimed at 'assessing' the extent of and 'improving' the public's knowledge deficiency. The 'discovery' of such deficiency then justifies the experts' belief in their expertise and the call for support to raise the public standard . . .
>
> The deficit model is readily identifiable as the rhetoric of professional ideology, masking inequities of power in the language of democratization; citizenship through science comes at the price of expressing knowledge in ways acceptable to professional (natural) scientists – it is our way or not at all. Hence the presence of competing knowledge claims and knowledge bases are rejected as simply 'anti-science' . . .
>
> (Locke 1999: 78)

As with our discussions in the previous chapter, it would seem that, once again, we cannot extricate popular science (or in this case more particularly science communication) from wider issues of power, authority and the demarcation of what is science from what is not. Not only is science communication a site of struggle, so too is the *study* of science communication.

This political dimension is clearly brought out by Stephen Hilgartner (1990) who has shown that while the dominant view greatly oversimplifies the process of science communication it is a model that is politically useful for scientists. By providing a vocabulary for the boundary work of demarcating 'genuine' knowledge from 'popularized knowledge', 'real' science from 'popularized' science, it helps maintain 'an idealized view of genuine, objective, scientifically-certified knowledge' as the exclusive preserve of scientists (520). Scientists are thus given the authority to determine which popularizations are 'appropriate' and which are 'distortions', enabling them to give the authority of science to their own representations of science and discrediting those of others. Consequently, despite its limitations:

. . . the dominant view remains a useful political tool for scientific experts
. . . Most fundamentally, the dominant view sets aside genuine scientific
knowledge as belonging to a realm that cannot be accessed by the public,
but is the exclusive preserve of scientists. It thus buttresses the epistemic
authority of scientists against challenges by outsiders.

(Hilgartner 1990: 530)

In the previous chapter I argued how popularization might be seen as an
attempt to legitimize science; now we can see how a particular model for
popularization might be doing the same thing.

Talking with experts

At the eighth international conference of the Public Communication of Science
and Technology network (PCST8) held in Barcelona in 2004 I noticed one
striking commonality to many, if not most, of the presentations. Like the ritual-
istic confessing of sins at a revivalist meeting, paper after paper felt it necessary
to reject the old transmission or deficit model before moving on to the substance
of what was to be said. Within the science communication community it would
seem that the deficiencies of the model were now part of common knowledge,
something that everyone could agree on. Anti-deficit rhetoric provided common
ground where people could at least start from the same place even if in some cases
the paper that followed seemed heavily informed by the old way of thinking.
There was, however, still the question: 'what next?'

Fortunately, a number of other models and approaches have been waiting in
the wings. One of the most influential models, at least in terms of the language
it has provided for recent discussions, is that of Stephen Hilgartner's (1990)
analogy of science communication with a stream. For Hilgartner there are not
just two categories of science and non-science but a whole spectrum of knowledges and contexts for science. Upstream we find talking shop in the lab,
meetings or technical seminars. Downstream are textbooks and the tabloid
press. 'The point is simply that "popularization" is a matter of degree. The
boundary between real science and popularized science can be drawn at various
points depending on what criteria one adopts, and these ambiguities leave some
flexibility about what to label "popularization" ' (528). In addition, as Gregory
and Miller point out, the spectrum is not fixed: 'If a microbiologist reads a
newspaper feature article about food poisoning, does the article become a technical communication? If a sick layperson were to read up on the latest research
into his condition, are those academic papers now popularisations?' (Gregory
and Miller 1998: 87).

From media studies we could also take Stuart Hall's model of the circuit of communication. Hall analysed mass communication as a system of encoding and decoding messages, the meaning being read into any message not necessarily being the same as the meaning being read out of it. The circuit of communication links several 'moments' of encoding/decoding (production, circulation, distribution, consumption, reproduction), each opening up the possibility for the active interpretation of messages. In Hall's model communication is not to be understood in terms of the flow of information from sender to receiver, but as a feedback system that generates the construction of meanings (Hall 1980; see also Miller *et al.* 1998). Both Jonathan Topham (1998 and 2000) and James Secord (2000) have taken this idea of a communication circuit and applied it to the study of popular science. Topham sees readers, publishers and authors all providing feedback into a system centred on the production and consumption of popular science books in nineteenth-century Britain. James Secord's study of Robert Chambers's *Vestiges* emphasizes the importance of 'literary replication' whereby readers made sense of the book through their familiarity with associated reviews, pamphlets, advertisements and a range of other texts that the book generated.

Bruce Lewenstein (1995a) meanwhile prefers to use the analogy of a web in his account of the **cold fusion** controversy. The announcement by Martin Fleischmann and Stanley Pons in 1989 that they could produce fusion in a test tube not only generated a media frenzy but also exposed a network of relations through which scientists communicated. In Lewenstein's web we can see press conferences, lab reports, news programmes, emails, grant proposals, policy documents and seminars all interconnected and feeding into each other. Rather than a simple diffusion of science through the media to the public, information was flowing from all points in all directions (e.g. scientists were trying to replicate experiments on the basis of video recordings of TV news reports). A multidirectional model is also evident in Mike Michael's (2002) idea of popular science as a 'rhizome' (a term taken from the work of Deleuze and Guattari). The rhizome is a root system which can spread in all directions, join any point with any other, and regenerate if cut. Applied to popular science, says Michael, the imagery 'suggests that there is no easy differentiation between the expert and the popular, between the scientific and the lay, between the factual and the fictional' (370).

Streams, circuits, webs, rhizomes – each in its own way tries to break free from the old unidirectional linear model. What they all suggest is that in science communication the public has a part to play too. In recent years, this recognition that the public might have something to say has led to frequent calls for 'dialogue'. In contrast to the Royal Society's 1985 report focusing on public ignorance and media indifference, the House of Lords Select Committee report in 2000 is 'peppered with calls for dialogue, discussion, and debate' (Miller 2001: 117). In response, the aims of the Royal Society's *Science in Society Programme* were:

- to develop a widespread, innovative and effective system of dialogue with society;
- to involve society more positively in influencing and sharing responsibility for policy on scientific matters;
- to embrace a culture of openness in decision-making;
- to take account of the values and attitudes of the public;
- to enable the Society to promote the national science policy.

(Royal Society 2004: 8)

Indeed, 'dialogue' has been a buzzword in science policy circles for some time, with many researchers and practitioners preferring to talk of PEST (Public Engagement with Science and Technology) rather than PUS (Pitrelli 2003). We can see attempts at dialogue or PEST in a number of activities; both top-down (**consensus conferences, citizens' juries, science shops**) and bottom-up (e.g. lay experts from medical interest groups or advocacy groups such as Greenpeace or Friends of the Earth). In some cases public engagement has had an important effect upon government policy and scientific research: in 1987, for example, the Danish government decided not to fund projects on animal gene technology after reports from lay panels, and in the 1980s activists from the gay community were able to influence the process of research into AIDS.

Even so, one might still ask how far the new language of dialogue masks the old objective of public relations. To what extent is PUS dressed up as PEST? This is one of the main concerns expressed by James Wilsdon and Rebecca Willis (2004a) in *See-through Science*, their report for the think tank Demos. In their report they argue that scientists are faced with a crisis of trust because of the blurring of boundaries between science, business and politics. The response has been a call for more engagement and dialogue but, they say, 'engagement' can actually be used to close down debate by making it simply part of bureaucratic processes and by how questions are framed. Indeed, 'talk of engagement can backfire unless it has a demonstrable impact. Those whose engagement is being sought need to know that their participation will affect the policies and processes under discussion' (16). Moreover, even when the public is properly involved in a process of engagement, debates over science and technology are too often dominated by questions of risk assessment, asking simply whether a technology is safe rather than whether it is necessary. 'Possible risks are endlessly debated, while deeper questions about the values, visions and vested interests that motivate scientific endeavour often remain unasked or unanswered' (18). More fundamental questions are at stake in any new technology, they say:

'Who owns it? Who benefits from it? To what ends will it be directed?' (23). It should not be left to 'experts' to 'frame a question and slot in an engagement process to provide the answer . . . Instead, the public should help to decide the questions and the way in which a particular issue will be approached' (40–1).

Calls for engagement now come with a new language of 'horizon scanning' and 'upstream debate' (picking up on Hilgartner's stream analogy), of identifying potential problems and nipping them in the bud before they get too serious. This is particularly evident in the UK government's *Science and Innovation Investment Framework 2004–2014* and in the Royal Society's cautious report on **nanotechnology**. Nanotechnology, for example, is seen as the next big thing but there are also fears that it might be the 'next **GM**' and face the same kind of public opposition as did GM crops and foods. With more money being targeted at science and technology, 'advocacy of upstream debate', say Wilsdon and Willis, 'is clearly influenced by a desire to remove obstacles that might upset the innovation apple-cart' (20). However, upstream debate can also be an opportunity. Wilsdon and Willis express this clearly in a piece they wrote for the *Guardian*, published soon after their Demos report. It is worth quoting at length:

> One of the biggest lessons from GM is that it isn't only the risks of a new technology that cause concern. Controversies arise when people are unable to ask more fundamental questions: what is the technology for? Who owns it? Who will take responsibility if things go wrong – and can we trust them? These questions cannot be answered by committees of scientists or through technical risk assessments. The public must be involved from the start. Now, while nanotech is still in its infancy, is the time to start a proper public debate, with all of these questions on the table. Public views can then shape the direction of research in a meaningful way.
>
> Above all, we need to move away from the idea that new technologies are developed by scientists and then presented to the public as a done deal. Science and society must work together to shape the direction of a technology – with research processes opened up to scrutiny and debate, and assumptions challenged from the start. It is only through these new forms of 'upstream' public engagement that we will develop technologies that people want.
>
> This is a huge challenge. The temptation at every stage will be to fall back into the old ways of doing things – assuring safety, closing down debate, assuming that experts know best. But a new approach could offer the ultimate prize – science and technology that genuinely serves the common good.
>
> (Wilsdon and Willis 2004b)

True dialogue would give the public the freedom to set its own agenda, frame its own questions, make its own decisions. In effect, what needs to be examined is not just the processes of science communication and consultation but the whole system of deliberative democracy. Being informed is not enough; the public also needs to be empowered.

The need for empowerment has led David Dickson (2000), news editor at *Nature*, to suggest that calls for dialogue do not go far enough. A striking aspect of the report from the House of Lords, says Dickson, is that it 'avoids addressing a central factor in the debate, that of political power' (918). He welcomes the report's call for greater openness and dialogue but:

> . . . without additional attention to the political factors influencing, indeed frequently determining, the way science is used in society, there is unlikely to be a resolution of the tensions created by the distrust that originates from the exclusion of individuals from decision-making.
>
> (Dickson 2000: 918)

For Dickson, the public is well aware of the political dimension to science; indeed, that is what causes such distrust and not the activities of scientists themselves. During the **BSE** crisis of the early 1990s it is easy to see the British public distrusting government science advisers because they lied about the safety of eating beef, but 'what is frequently ignored is the public's (correct) perception that the lies originated in the influence of the beef industry over the Ministry of Agriculture, Fisheries and Food' (918). Similarly the critical attitude to GM foods is not mistrust of science but mistrust of multinationals and globalization. Since 'efforts to promote the public understanding of science clearly represent a bid to legitimize science-based growth strategies . . . any criticism of science is seen as a direct challenge to the paradigm that scientific progress leads inevitably to social progress' (919). The result is that:

> . . . the two sides in what is intended to be a dialogue appear to have different agendas, focus on different long-term goals, speak in different languages, and play the game according to different rules . . . All this points to the need for a new type of dialogue, one that acknowledges the true nature of such disputes, and allows space for creative criticism and politically-based challenges, rather than dismissing all such criticism and challenges as a manifestation of a lack of public 'awareness'.
>
> (Dickson 2000: 920)

PUS might promote the Enlightenment ideal of rational discourse, says Dickson, but it also encourages an opaqueness that 'helps to screen the political basis of this rationality' (922).

If political factors are a necessary contextual consideration then there is also an equally important intrinsic factor that needs to be taken into account – the nature of the dialogue itself. One criticism of the transmission model of communication was that it did not take into account the relationship between the sender and receiver. There is a danger that the same could happen with a dialogue model. Both sides may now be given a voice but this equality may just mask the real inequality of power that exists. As we have seen over the previous chapters, science has accrued an immense amount of authority and recognizing a need for dialogue will not make it go away. It is still the doctor that asks the patient to remove his clothes, not vice versa. It is still the scientific adviser that has better access to government circles and the media. Any success the public has had in engaging with science has been because the public has had to learn to engage with science on science's own terms. PEST is an invitation for the public to engage with science and not for science to engage with the public.

Furthermore, this asymmetry of power is accompanied by a more subtle inequality, what might clumsily be called an epistemological asymmetry. Science has 'facts': the public has 'opinions'. This is only a recent development and, as Bernadette Bensaude-Vincent (2001) has shown, one that is intimately linked to the history of popular science. For the ancient Greeks, she says, opinion (*doxa*) and science (*epistêmê*) were to be equally valued and as late as the eighteenth century a tradition of mundane science could be maintained at the same time as the notion of 'public opinion' was emerging. The development of science popularization in the nineteenth century might increase the separation of science from public, but it was only from the mid-twentieth century, she says, that opinion was devalued because of its association with the public's perceived 'ignorance'. Separation of science and opinion is now so complete that 'dialogue' is needed to bring the two together. It may be time, suggests Bensaude-Vincent, to revalue opinion and 'revive the ancient notion of *doxa* as a specific popular variety of knowledge that is more relevant than science in the sphere of political decisions' (110).

There is, however, another way to address the asymmetry – not by giving fresh value to opinion but by recognizing that there is knowledge and opinion on both sides. This is not just a recognition that scientists are the public too and so are equally entitled to have opinions, but an acknowledgement that *within* the practice of science different positions will be taken by different scientists. This might even be said to be an essential feature of scientific practice. Much is made of the fact that scientific knowledge is based on consensus, but the process of science is driven by dissent – rejecting old paradigms (in Kuhn's philosophy of science), falsifying theories (in Popper's philosophy of science) or simply trying to make a name for oneself (on scepticism and controversy see Ziman 2000: 246–88). It is especially important to remember this in the context of popular science: first, because scientific controversy brings scientific opinion into the public domain; secondly, because it is not uncommon for scientists to make a direct appeal to the public as a way of trying to resolve (or win) controversies within science (see Bucchi 1998); and finally, because it is where knowledge is still undecided and science is, as it were, still under construction that there is likely to be most public interest. If done properly, moving debates 'upstream' should expose these open areas even further. 'Controversy and uncertainty', says Steve Miller, 'are still regarded as things that should be kept within the scientific community . . . "Not in front of the children" is still the attitude. But this, too, has to change' (Miller 2001: 118). If we recognize that scientists have opinions then we should also recognize that the public has knowledge. Mention has already been made of 'lay experts', but are there other forms of lay knowledge and, perhaps, more importantly, what does it mean to be an expert?

We should begin with a word of warning from Steve Miller: 'the end of the deficit model does not mean there is no knowledge deficit'.

> If there is not a gap between what scientists and members of the general public know about science, then something is very wrong. We do not want a public understanding of science political correctness in which the very idea that scientists are more knowledgeable than ordinary citizens is taboo. Scientists and lay people are not on the same footing where scientific information is concerned, and knowledge, hard won by hours of research, and tried and tested over the years and decades, deserves respect.
>
> (Miller 2001: 118)

Valuing lay knowledge should not be at the expense of devaluing scientific knowledge. Nevertheless, the issue of lay knowledge does raise fundamental questions about the nature of expertise. Collins and Evans (2002) put the matter quite bluntly: 'If it is no longer clear that scientists and technologists have special access to truth, why should their advice be specially valued?' (236). More particularly, and something that will be returned to in the next chapter, how do we square specialist knowledge restricted to a few with democratic principles of rights for the many? 'Should the political legitimacy of technical decisions in the public domain be maximised by referring them to the widest democratic process, or should such decisions be based on the best expert advice?' (235–6).

In Chapter 2 we saw the separation of experience from expertise. Collins and Evans argue that the notion of expertise should now be extended to include 'experience-based experts'. However, this raises what they call the 'Problem of Extension'. Although science studies has shown that the notion of expertise should be extended beyond formally accredited scientists and technologists, how far should that participation extend? Justifying expansion also has to show where the limits are. The 'first wave' of science studies in the 1950s and 1960s had accepted the authority of science, locating all expertise in the scientific community. A 'second wave' of science studies from the 1970s onwards, building on Thomas Kuhn's work, placed a stronger emphasis on the social construction of knowledge and so blurred the distinction between scientific expertise and political rights. Collins and Evans now propose a 'third wave of science studies', which would re-establish the distinction between expert and non-expert but, crucially, the distinction would be based on expertise, not on whether an 'expert' is professionally accredited with the necessary qualifications and certificates. In this way non-certified experts would be 'experience-based experts', and as examples they cite Brian Wynne's study of Cumbrian sheep farmers arguing with government officials over the fallout from Chernobyl and the influence of AIDS activists on medical research.

Let me give a particularly dramatic illustration of experience-based expertise from my own work (largely unpublished but see Broks 1999).

Thousands of women in the US and the UK have XY (i.e. 'male') chromosomes. Androgen Insensitivity Syndrome (AIS) is a form of intersexuality where a foetus with XY chromosomes develops a female body. Such XY women usually have internal testes and no uterus, but externally the only signs of the condition are a lack of pubic and underarm hair and the absence of periods. It is likely that more than one in every 20,000 'male' births are affected (one study has put it as high as one in 2000), but it is quite probable that many women with XY chromosomes are never diagnosed, and of those women who have been diagnosed many never know because they are never told. The general belief is that the psychological shock would be too great so, with the best interests of the patient in mind, it has been a common practice for doctors not to disclose the true nature of the condition (see website of Androgen Insensitivity Support Group *www.medhelp.org/www/ais/*). Yet in those cases where the patient has been told (or has self-diagnosed), she often comes to know more about the condition than her doctor. Moreover, what is known (and more importantly how it is known) results in major disjunctions in the perspectives of doctor and patient.

	Doctor	*Patient*
Problem	not fully male	not fully female
Cause	faulty gene	presence of unwanted hormone
Concern	gender identity	coital adequacy, fertility
Experience of AIS	vicarious, via patient	lived, first-hand
Policy	secrecy	disclosure

There is, perhaps, no starker illustration of two perspectives looking at the same problem but from different directions. Is a person not fully male or not fully female? Where doctors see a failure to virilize and trace the problem back to a 'faulty' gene, XY women experience a failure to fully feminize and trace the problem back to the presence of an unwanted hormone which inhibits the development of uterus and tubes. Language makes the problem worse. Why should bits of biochemistry such as chromosomes and hormones be labelled as 'male'? Doctors see the male label and worry about gender identity, but XY women experience a female body and worry about infertility and sexual adequacy. Therein lies the major difference. For doctors, AIS is a condition to be known about only vicariously via their own or other patients, but for XY women it is a lived experience. Bringing such *experiential expertise* to complement the technical knowledge of the medical profession is now beginning to influence the care regime of patients (Simmonds 2003; Liao and Boyle 2004). More generally, the National Health Service in the UK is now embarked on a major initiative on the role of 'expert patients' in the self-management of chronic diseases (Department of Health 2001; see also Kerr *et al*. 1998).

The idea of lived experience has brought us a long way from the usual PUS concerns of effective messages and targeting audiences, but as an essential feature of cultural studies it is important for a proper *cultural* understanding of popular science. Nor should this be seen as an optional extra to the real business of science communication and the study of PUS. This is made perfectly clear in *Misunderstanding Science?*, a collection of essays edited by Alan Irwin and Brian Wynne (1996). In their introduction Irwin and Wynne begin by questioning the usual PUS premises: that public controversy arises because of public ignorance, that science offers a uniquely privileged view of the everyday world and that science is value-free. Instead they argue for the need to 'rethink and reconceptualise the relationship between "science" and the "public" ' (7):

> . . . only a properly sociological approach to contemporary science can give us a real insight into the issues of 'public understanding'. Otherwise, we are doomed to a sterile and even counter-productive juxtaposition of 'science' against 'non-science' rather than an appreciation of the diversity and social interdependence of different forms of science, knowledge and expertise.
>
> (Irwin and Wynne 1996: 8)

In this respect, particularly relevant is the way boundaries between 'science' and 'everyday knowledge' are established and maintained, and the way PUS presents an image of science as 'a unified, cleanly bounded, and clear body of knowledge and method' (7 and 8):

Rather than assuming from the beginning of discussion, therefore, that science unconditionally deserves privileged status, we need to consider just how relevant and important scientific understanding is within everyday life. To accept science as a key resource in public issues is radically different from accepting its automatic authority in *framing* what the issues are.

(Irwin and Wynne 1996: 8–9, original emphasis)

For Irwin and Wynne PUS was characterized by large-scale quantitative surveys and small-scale social qualitative research, with the assumption that the quantitative work provided an objective large-scale picture of reality and the qualitative work was simply there to colour in the details:

Questions about the meanings of 'science' to different social groups, and the possibility of unarticulated epistemological conflict and negotiations about the implicit social purposes of knowledge, were simply not conceived to be issues within this perspective. In other words, 'universal' science was not problematised. Qualitative social research on public understanding was seen only as intellectual embroidery within the 'objective' macro-social patterns revealed by large-scale surveys.

(Irwin and Wynne 1996: 216)

But these micro-scale responses to science are best understood:

. . . not by seeing them merely as local embellishments of life within the objective cosmopolitan parameters of scientific modernity, but as responses partly to the fundamental failures of those 'universal' modernist institutions, programmes, and promises even within their own instrumental terms.

(Irwin and Wynne 1996: 217)

In other words, micro-scale sociological research could show not merely public attitudes to science (the values that lay behind public 'ignorance') but that the public was questioning the very nature of science itself. Indeed, say Irwin and Wynne, a recurring theme of local studies is how matters of trust, powerlessness and contextually generated expertise become more significant than 'science' which 'as a category blurs into other areas of social practice and contestation'. This means that in contrast to PUS placing science centre-stage, local studies often reveal the 'disappearance' of science (12–13).

A Critical Understanding of Science in Public

When the report from the House of Lords select committee highlighted the failings of PUS it called instead for a 'broader approach'. However, it should be clear from the previous section that a proper understanding of science in the public domain takes us beyond the select committee's call for dialogue. Drawing on the kinds of studies referred to above, what can we say about the main features of our new perspective?

- It is *multi-directional*: no longer is science seen simply as diffusing downwards but in communication circuits and webs all points feed into and off each other.
- It is *contextual*: concerned not just with the context for the reception of science but also recognizing that science is contextualized too as is the relationship between science and the public. In this sense it is social, political and cultural, and in turn raises issues of trust, power and authority.
- It broadens the notion of *expertise*: boundaries between lay and experts are redefined to encompass lay experts and experienced-based expertise. In addition, values and opinions are accepted as varieties of knowledge and as essential parts of the science–public domain.
- It is concerned with *meanings*: the focus of attention is shifted away from informational content to that of meaning and how things mean. To paraphrase the song: it ain't what you think, it's the way that you think it.

As a way of encompassing all these features I want to suggest a new label and to characterize this new perspective as the Critical Understanding of Science in Public, or 'CUSP' (which also captures the sense of in between, not one or the other but both, at the edge, an interface, an interaction, a starting point, a meeting point).

What does CUSP entail? To put it crudely, where PUS looked to marketing strategies as a solution to PR problems, CUSP engages with the problematics of context, negotiation and interactivity. Moreover, these problematics should encompass both the public's understanding of science and our understanding of the science that is public. Appropriately, CUSP can be seen as having a double meaning (and aim):

1   a public with a critical understanding of science (a *critical understanding of science* in public, or CUS-P); and
2   a critical understanding of the science and its associated meanings that is generated in the public domain (a critical understanding of *science in public*, or CU-SP).

In each case, 'critical' is taken simply to be the kind of multi-directional, contextual understanding of expertise and meanings outlined above. In particular, it recognizes the other terms (science, understanding and public) as problematic, is sensitive to the subtleties of communication and, perhaps above all else, focuses on the construction of meaning. To my mind it is this shift in focus from information to meanings that is the most important aspect of CUSP. In some ways it might even be seen as encapsulating the other aspects, so it is worth spending a little time exploring this further.

Let us begin with a question: could a computer ever do science? At first glance the simple response might be along the lines of 'maybe not at the moment, but one day with the advance of computer technology anything could be possible, including a computer being able to do science'. However, we may prefer a different answer if we see the question not as one about the ability of computers but as one about the nature of science. Is there something about science which in principle makes it something a computer will never be able to do? The distinction is often made between science as process and science as product, between science as objective, rational methodology and science as a body of knowledge. On the face of it we might be able to think of a computer being able to do both and, indeed, do it much more efficiently than a human scientist. We can, for instance, easily imagine a computer equipped with suitable robotic peripherals being able to make measurements and observations, record data, perform calculations, draw graphs and so on. We could even imagine a computer carrying out experiments, mixing chemicals and growing cells in culture or even designing experiments to obtain better measurements, data and calculations. In short, the computer would be able to generate, process and record vast quantities of information, but does this amount to science? No matter how rational and objective the process and no matter how much information was produced there would still be something missing. We would still be left with the question: what does it mean? Science, perhaps above all else, is a search for meaning. By this I do not want to imply that science is a search for purpose in the universe (though historically that has often been the case), but simply that science is a way that we *make sense* of the world. Moreover, if we are able to make sense of the world it is because we are able to *make it make sense* to us within our own sense-making environment or culture. Only when we can talk of computers having their own culture will we be able to talk about a computer being able to do science (and then only with reference to its own culture, not ours).

A useful way of trying to understand how we make sense of the world around us is the idea of 'seeing as'. The act of seeing is very rarely a simple matter of light entering the eye. Objects are not just seen, they are *seen as* something. We do not just see a spray of brown lines dotted with spots of green but rather these shapes and colours are *seen as* a tree. (The philosophically inclined might want to argue further that concepts such as 'brown', 'lines', 'spots' and 'green' are also varieties of seeing as). Moreover, what things are seen as is often context-dependent. For example, the same knife might be seen as a kitchen implement or a weapon depending on the context. Likewise in science, *seeing as* is often theory-dependent; according to the geocentric Ptolemaic model of the universe, dawn would be seen as a moving sun, but in the heliocentric Copernican system would be seen as a moving Earth. We could pursue this idea deeper and deeper into the philosophy of science (a good place to start is Hanson 1958) and the issues it raises have provoked much debate, but for present purposes I only want to note that for something to make sense it needs to be seen as something. This is as true for the process of science as it is for our own personal encounters with the world around us and equally true for how we make sense of the political, social and cultural world as it is for how we make sense of the natural world. If science is how we make sense of the world, then popular science is how we make sense of science and from previous chapters we can note how science can be *seen as* radical, useful, religious, modern, postmodern and so on.

Now, let us take these ideas of 'making sense' and 'seeing as' and see how we might apply them to our critical understanding of science in public. We can begin with how we might produce a critical reading of a popular science text. There are a number of levels at which the text can be read:

1   *Raw science content.* If this were our concern we might be interested in checking how accurate or true the information was (we might dispute just how 'raw' such science is, but for now we can leave aside such philosophical discussions).
2   How the science is *framed*. This is the first level of 'seeing as'. When we look at the raw content what are we expected to *see* it *as*? At this level we could examine such things as the use of language, metaphor and imagery.
3   *Critical.* What does it mean and how does it get to mean what it means? This is the second level of 'seeing as'. What should the framing at level 2 be seen as? At this level we can relate the level-two framing to wider issues and debates.

It is worth noting immediately how questions within the PUS perspective were often confined to level 1. How much information did the public have? Was the information accurate? Did the public give the right information in response to questions? Yet public discourse is probably most often at level 3. What does this mean for me? How should I understand it? What other cultural resources can I call on to help me understand it?

To see how this approach works in practice we can take a famous (or infamous) passage from *The Selfish Gene* by Richard Dawkins (1989). In it he describes the relationship between genes and our bodies and behaviour:

Now they swarm in huge colonies, safe inside gigantic lumbering robots, sealed off from the outside world, communicating with it by tortuous indirect routes, manipulating it by remote control. They are in you and in me; they created us body and mind; and their preservation is the ultimate rationale for our existence. They have come a long way, those replicators. Now they go by the names of genes, and we are their survival machines.

(Dawkins 1989: 19–20)

At the level of raw content we could examine this for information about genes and bodies. At the level of framing we could highlight examples of the imagery employed by Dawkins. For example, bodies are *seen as* 'lumbering robots' manipulated by genes. At the critical level we could explore how the language of 'robots' could be *seen as* an attack on our own sense of self and relate this to wider discussions about free will and identity.

There are, of course, more ways of taking a critical approach than the one suggested here but it does give some indication of where such a perspective can take us. A concern for meaning can be found in much of the work referred to in previous chapters. In addition one could also point to a useful collection of essays on *The Literature of Science* edited by Murdo William McRae (1993), which sees science as embedded in the culture which enables it and subjects popular science texts to rhetorical, linguistic and historical analyses (see also Locke 2002, Myers 2003 and Wyatt 2004). This kind of literary analysis of popular science texts is frequently a feature of a critical approach. Baudouin Jurdant (1993), for example, compares the popularization of science with the writing of autobiographies and argues that:

> . . . popularization of science is more concerned with the construction of a mythical background for laypeople to provide meanings to the world around them, than with a proper transmission of scientific knowledge that could challenge experts' monopoly on the definition of reality.
>
> (Jurdant 1993: 370)

Similarly, such a concern for textual analysis often brings with it an interest in the construction of narrative to the analysis of popular science. Curtis (1994), for example, has examined the narrative form in popular science, Landau (1991) has compared the narrative of human evolution to the tales of heroes in folklore, and Turney (2001) has examined the narrative knowledge needed to understand cosmology as an evolutionary epic.

There are, however, three aspects to the concern for meaning that are particularly pertinent to a critical approach: the way that meanings are generated, the way popular science acts as a space where those meanings are contested, and the active role the public plays in the construction of popular science. It may be worthwhile, therefore, to take a closer look at examples of each of these.

A critical understanding of the generation of meanings is clearly illustrated by Nelkin and Lindee (1995) in their study of how the gene has become a cultural icon. Exploring a wide range of sources (from books, TV and radio to jokes, lyrics and clichés), they found that the images and narratives of the gene in popular culture reflect and convey a message of 'genetic essentialism' which 'reduces the self to a molecular entity, equating human beings, in all their social, historical, and moral complexity, with their genes' (2). It is a view of the human condition that draws on earlier eugenic ideas about heredity and presents DNA as 'a secular equivalent of the Christian soul' (2). Thus, the meaning of the gene goes beyond the domain of the biologists:

> The gene of popular culture is not a biological entity. Though it refers to a biological construct and derives its cultural power from science, its symbolic meaning is independent of biological definitions. The gene is, rather, a symbol, a metaphor; a convenient way to define personhood, identity and relationships in socially meaningful ways. The gene is used, of course, to explain health and disease. But it is also a way to talk about guilt and responsibility, power and privilege, intellectual or emotional status. It has become a supergene, used to judge the morality or rightness of social systems and to explore the forces that will shape the human future.
>
> (Nelkin and Lindee 1995: 16)

The scientific legitimacy of any image, they argue, is less important than the use which is made of it:

> How do scientific concepts serve social ideologies and institutional agendas? Why do certain concepts gain social power to become the focus of significant popular and scientific attention? And what role do scientists play in shaping the appropriation of such concepts?
>
> (Nelkin and Lindee 1995: 4–5)

It was no coincidence that the popular appropriation of genetics intensified just as scientists were mapping the human genome, 'for in presenting their research to the public, scientists have been active players in constructing the powers of the gene' (5). The result is that the gene has become 'both a scientific concept and a powerful social symbol' with 'a cultural meaning independent of its precise biological properties' (2).

However, more important (in the present context of illustrating a 'CUSP' approach) is what they have to say about how this 'cultural construction of the gene' arises at the interface of science and the public:

> The point of our analysis is not to identify popular distortions of science or to debunk scientific myths. The interesting question is not the contrast

between scientific and popular culture; it is how they intersect to shape the cultural meaning of the gene.

(Nelkin and Lindee 1995: 4)

A similar case is made by José van Dijck (1998) who sees genetics as 'a continuous site of contestation' where the 'hegemonic meaning of genetics' is forged through the multi-layered process of popularization (3). In the popular representation of genetics, she says:

> Images are never mere illustrations of scientific practices, and neither are imaginations mere reflections of people's anxieties in relation to science and technology. Images and imaginations . . . are rhetorical tools in the construction of a public meaning.

(van Dijck 1998: 197)

Megan Stern (2003, 2004) extends these ideas to all of science. 'Science', she says, is not a fixed point of reference but a 'working title' in a state of flux that is 'produced between, rather than within, discourses' (2003: 151). She suggests that:

> . . . the most productive route for understanding the meaning of science may not be to look at specific sites of scientific activity or their representa-tions by scientists or cultural critics . . . but rather at the interplay between them. If science can never be properly located, this may be because its cultural and other meanings are generated between locations and, as such, are constantly changing.

(Stern 2003: 150)

In this way popular science becomes a useful starting point because it is 'neces-sarily hybrid', operating at 'a crossroads between genres' (2003: 151) – and here we do well to remind ourselves of what Secord says about *Vestiges* in Chapter 1.

The generation of meanings at the interface of science and public is also central to Constance Penley's (1997) study of NASA and *Star Trek*, but with an extra important emphasis – popular science is not just something that is given to the public, but is something that the public creates for itself. Taken together, NASA and *Star Trek* represent the actual and fictional realization of 'going into space' which, says Penley, 'has become the prime metaphor through which we try to make sense of the world of science and technology' (4–5). She presents both NASA and *Star Trek* as being engaged in a process of writing themselves and in turn being rewritten by each other and by the fan cultures associated with them. The result is a 'blended cultural text' she calls NASA/TREK and which can be seen as part of a 'large, ongoing popular engagement with issues of science and technology' (4). This is a far cry from the anxieties about public ignorance and lack of interest. In Penley's NASA/TREK the public are very much actively engaged in constructing their own popular science which should be accepted on its own terms, although, as she says, 'Recognizing and accepting this popular will to do science does not come easy, especially when "the experts" start from the assumption that most citizens are shamefully ignorant of scientific issues' (5).

However, if we do recognize the public creating its own popular science and we do accept it on its own terms, then we have a vision of popular science markedly different from that of science literacy surveys and PUS. This is clearly the case with a particular form of rewriting *Star Trek* known as 'slash fiction' – a form of pornography written by female fans in which the main characters of the series (Kirk/Spock, or K/S) are reimagined as lovers. For Penley, however, NASA/TREK is the kind of popular science we should aspire to:

> It is a collectively elaborated story that weaves together science and science fiction to help write, think, and launch us into space. Popular science involves the efforts of scientists, science writers, and scientific institutions to attract interest and support for advancing science and technology. Popular science includes the many science fiction television shows (and fewer films) that offer a personalised, utopian reflection on men and women in space. Popular science is fictional work that carries on this reflection. Popular science is ordinary people's extraordinary will to engage with the world of science and technology. Popular science wants us to go into space but keep our feet on the ground. Popular science envisions a science that boldly goes where no one has gone before but remains answerable to human needs and social desires. Popular science, fully in the American Utopian tradition, proposes that scientific experimentation be accompanied by social and sexual experimentation. Popular science insists that we are, or should be, popular scientists one and all.
>
> (Penley 1997: 9–10)

Not only are we all popular scientists but 'a slashed NASA/TREK is popular science at its best' since it provides 'a much needed utopian narrative' that imagines 'new forms of sexual and racial equality, democracy, and a fully human relation to the world of science and technology' (148). Thus, through CUSP, Penley and the pornographic couplings of Kirk and Spock we have clearly come a long way from seeing popular science as the capability (or incapability) of the public to give right answers.

Further reading

Bell, D. (2005) *Science, Technology and Culture*. Maidenhead: Open University Press.

Irwin, A. and Wynne, B. (eds) (1996) *Misunderstanding Science? The Public Reconstruction of Science and Technology*. Cambridge: Cambridge University Press.

McRae, M.W. (ed.) (1993) *The Literature of Science: Perspectives on Popular Scientific Writing*. Athens, GA: University of Georgia Press.

Nelkin, D. (1995) *Selling Science: How the Press Covers Science and Technology*. New York: W.H. Freeman.

Nelkin, D. and Lindee, M.S. (1995) *The DNA Mystique: The Gene as Cultural Icon*. New York: W.H. Freeman.

Penley, C. (1997) *NASA/TREK: Popular Science and Sex in America*. London: Verso.

Scanlon, E., Whitelegg, W. and Yates, S. (eds) (1999) *Communicating Science: Contexts and Channels*. London: Routledge.

Van Dijck, J. (1998) *Imagenation: Popular Images of Genetics*. Basingstoke: Macmillan.

CONCEPTUAL SPACE

What kind of model would be appropriate for the kind of critical understanding outlined in the previous chapter? In what ways should we think about the contextualized interactivity of science and public? How can we reframe our understanding of popular science to take into account the way it is constituted by the struggles around it? What follows is not so much an answer as a speculative suggestion.

From the history given in the first four chapters we can see that:

1   *Popular science generates different meanings.* Not only do these meanings change over time, but alternate meanings will co-exist at the same historical conjuncture. We have seen, for example, how in the formative period of the early nineteenth century it took on radical, religious or utilitarian aspects. Later it was to be a vehicle for technological utopianism, a wide variety of Darwinisms, and the popularization of efficiency, rationality and modernity. Finally, we saw how it might also be associated with counter-cultural critiques of technocracy, a search for mystical enlightenment and the postmodern interest in uncertainty, instability and ambivalence.

2   *These meanings can be linked to political and social struggles.* We could, for example, point to the 'legal ideology of science' and its search for a technological fix to social problems, or to the dissemination of 'useful knowledge' as a way to ensure social stability. Later, the triumph of scientific naturalism would mark the triumph of the professionalization of science, and the subsequent demands for efficiency and planning would see a shift in focus, from the state promoting science to science

promoting the state. Oppositional voices might be heard in the demand for 'really useful knowledge' and in the concerns for responsibility and public accountability.

3   *In these struggles popular science is a form of mediation between public and experts.* The 'invention' of popular science in the early nineteenth century helped define science by excluding the public. The legitimation of knowledge by an appeal to experience would be replaced by legitimation through an appeal to expertise. The professionalization of expertise would entail the redefinition of popular science as that science which is 'popular-ised'. In a modern 'disembedded' society the function of such populariza-tions is to build a sense of trust between experts and public. However, scientists have been the victims of their own success. The distancing that is needed to maintain their authority is the very thing which undermines their legitimacy in the eyes of the public.

Furthermore, this history invites us to reframe current concerns about the public understanding of science (Chapters 5 and 6) such that:

4   *In studying popular science our concern should be with meanings not information.* The dualism of two cultures is inadequate and divisive. Although there is no clear and generally accepted definition, the reasons given *for* scientific literacy shape the definitions *of* scientific literacy. Consequently, the dominant model of science communication is itself a legitimation of science and as such should be an object of critical study. A more critical understanding of science in public (CUSP) would entail a shift in attention from the transfer of information to the construction of meaning.

It is in picking up this final point and considering what might be an appropriate way of thinking about CUSP that we move into a more speculative realm. The traditional view of popularization sees science as a gift to be handed over like a package or, as Bucchi describes it, 'a conception of public communication of science as benevolent alms-giving' (1998: 2). In the previous chapter we saw how this unidirectional linear model has been challenged and what might be called a second generation of models proposed which emphasize the two-way process of dialogue and engagement. What I want to suggest now is a third generation model which can go beyond this passing back and forth of information to think in terms of contextualized interactivity and so be able to give a critical account of the construction, proliferation and negotiation of meanings.

Spaces, spheres and boundaries

Elsewhere I have argued that popular science is best seen not as a conduit for messages but as a 'forum' where what is popular meets what is scientific (Broks 1993 and 1996). I now want to develop this spatial imagery further with the idea of 'conceptual space' as a new model for understanding how the meanings of scientific knowledge are challenged and negotiated. I want to shift from thinking about ideas as objects that get passed from person to person and see if it is possible to start thinking about them as spaces. We are already familiar with spatial imagery. Academics 'locate' their work within a particular subject 'area' and 'orientate' themselves with respect to other researchers in the 'field'. There are disciplinary 'boundaries' and 'frontiers' of knowledge. In the rhetoric of science spatial metaphor is a powerful and pervasive presence with its imagery of discovery, surveying, breaking new ground and so on (see for example Jenkins 1998). Moreover, through our experience of cyberspace we are becoming increasingly familiar with non-physical spaces where things happen and people interact. Indeed, so familiar is the spatial metaphor that I often have doubts about whether there really is something new to say. Yet, it is an idea that seems to be abandoned as soon as anyone writes about popular science. Scientists may well have their own subject area in a particular field and see themselves as pushing back the frontiers of knowledge, but as soon as the public become involved it seems that knowledge as a place to be explored becomes transformed into knowledge as a package that can be handed over. I want to see what happens if we take the spatial metaphor seriously and, as a consequence, see what happens to our understanding of popular science.

Let us begin with Oppenheimer's Reith lecture on *Science and the Common Understanding* (1953). Oppenheimer, who headed the scientific team in the Manhattan Project, likened science to a house:

> It is a vast house indeed . . . There is no central chamber, no one corridor from which all others debouch . . . It is a house so vast that there is not and need not be complete concurrence on where its chambers stop and those of the neighbouring mansions begin.
>
> It is not arranged in a line nor a square nor a circle nor a pyramid, but with a wonderful randomness suggestive of unending growth and improvisation. Not many people live in the house, relatively speaking – perhaps if we count all its chambers and take residence requirements lightly, one tenth of one per cent of all the people in this world – probably, by any reasonable definition, far fewer. And even those who live here live elsewhere also, live in houses where the rooms are not labelled atomic theory or genetics or the internal constitution of the stars, but quite

different names like power and production and evil and beauty and history and children and the word of God.

We go in and out; even the most assiduous of us is not bound to this vast structure. One thing we find throughout the house: there are no locks; there are no shut doors; wherever we go there are signs and usually the words of welcome. It is an open house, open to all comers.

(Oppenheimer 1953: 92–4)

Immediately we get the impression of science as a sprawling, rambling enterprise, an 'open house' with no need for agreement on where its boundaries are and complete freedom of movement within and around it. However, the imagery also immediately prompts questions. How true is it that there are no locks or shut doors when, for the most part, science is controlled by the military, the government and multinational corporations? Why is the place so empty? Just how welcoming are scientists to letting everyone come in and mess up the furniture? And what will the neighbours think, especially with that lack of concern over where the property ends?

It is this last question which raises a central issue in science studies: the problem of demarcation. Where – and note the spatial imagery – do we draw the line between what is science and what is not? The problem is as important as it is intractable for it raises a second question: *how* do we decide where to draw the line? In other words, how do we define science, particularly with respect to everything else? Here it is worth recalling from previous chapters the important role that popular science has played in carrying out that demarcation. In recent years it has also taken the attention of scholars within science studies in their explorations of 'boundary work', 'boundary objects' and 'trading zones'. For example, an examination of boundary work might show the ways that through social, cultural and political action boundaries are maintained between those who have authority to make knowledge claims and those who do not. Boundary objects, on the other hand, act as bridges across the boundaries that might otherwise separate a variety of groups (such as professionals, amateurs, administrators) by providing a common focus even though each group may imbue the object with different meanings. Similarly, trading zones are areas where a common simplified language can enable communication between different groups (for instance across disciplinary boundaries) despite other disagreements elsewhere (see Star and Griesemer 1989; Galison 1997; Gieryn 1999; Sismondo 2004). It might also be pointed out that talk of spaces, boundaries and bridges becomes more than a metaphor in the emerging field of knowledge domain visualization with its attempts to produce maps of all this (Chen 2003).

Oppenheimer's house of science is the starting point for Charles Alan Taylor's (1996) analysis of the problem of demarcation. Taylor takes a non-essentialist approach, that is, rather than trying to uncover some essential quality with which we can define what science is (an enterprise which has a long history of failure) he examines how science sets itself apart through its own rhetoric. Since such rhetoric will always be employed in, and often in response to, specific social and historical circumstances 'the identity of science is a product not of its ontological difference, but rather of its contextual connectedness' (7). His account, therefore, 'calls for a recognition of the inescapable symbiosis of what traditionally we have called the technical and the public, the internal and the external, or the natural and the cultural' (9). It is this symbiotic, contextual interconnectedness that leads Taylor to describe the system as a 'rhetorical ecology', such that what science is '. . . is a consequence of particular, historical episodes in which the constituents of the ecosystem stabilize' (8). In this way, spatial metaphors not only invite us to think about boundaries but also, and more importantly, to think about the network of interactions needed to sustain any ecosystem. Thus, with spatial imagery our attention is drawn away from objects to the spaces between them, from things to relationships. If we are then to think of popular science as part of a conceptual ecosystem we might then also have to conclude that there is no such *thing* as popular science – which is by no means a trivial conclusion in our efforts to understand it.

If there is no such thing as popular science what are we trying to understand? An analogy with E.P. Thompson's (1968) famous description of class might be a suitable way of explaining what I have in mind. There was, said Thompson, 'an ever-present temptation to suppose that class is a thing', or to think of the working class that 'it' exists (10). However, this 'it' does not exist. 'If we remember that class is a relationship, and not a thing, we cannot think in this way' (11):

> By class I understand a historical phenomenon, unifying a number of disparate and seemingly unconnected events, both in the raw material of experience and in consciousness. I emphasise that it is a *historical* phenomenon. I do not see class as a 'structure', nor even as a 'category', but as something which in fact happens (and can be shown to have happened) in human relationships.
>
> (Thompson 1968: 9)

The same might be said, I would argue, for popular science: it is not a thing, nor a category but a historical phenomenon that happens in human relationships. In the end, for Thompson, class is 'defined by men as they live their own history' (11), and the same might be said of popular science, as we have seen in the way it has been defined, redefined and struggled over. Such fluidity need not evade analysis if we see class as 'embodied in real people and in a real context', so too with popular science which we might see manifest in certain activities, behaviours and attitudes or embodied in specific objects or practices (e.g.

books, exhibitions or consultations with an expert). Indeed, it may be that as we understood the nineteenth century through the language of class, we shall have to develop a new language of knowledges and expertise to understand the twenty-first.

Thus, if we take the spatial metaphor seriously we are led towards a radical reframing of popular science in terms of boundaries, contexts, ecologies and relationships. There is, however, one further analogy I want to consider: an analogy with urban space. Oppenheimer has something like this in mind for his house of science when he writes that 'it does not appear to have been built upon any plan, but to have grown as a great city grows' (Oppenheimer 1953: 92). Similarly, Wittgenstein once wrote about language that it could '. . . be seen as an ancient city: a maze of little streets and squares, of old and new houses with additions from various periods, and this surrounded by a multitude of new boroughs with straight regular streets and uniform houses' (Wittgenstein 1958: 8). Substitute 'ideas' for 'language' and you have something close to my vision of 'conceptual space' except what I want to add is the dynamic quality of what people do in and with cities.

Like urban space, conceptual space is the result of design, history and use. It can be created, opened up, closed down. As urban space shapes what we do and how we live, so conceptual space shapes what we think and how we think it. In both cases we interact with the space and transform it for ourselves as it, in turn, transforms us. Our thoughts can be as habitual as the way that we move through a city: always taking the same route (or making the same argument, joining the same ideas), or revisiting the same places and avoiding others (our pet hobby-horses or things we prefer not to think about). Some places are more functional and only visited when needed (as is much of science for the public); other places are simply for pleasure (as much of science is not for the public). More particularly, with both urban and conceptual space we should note that:

1 *Space can be created and closed down.* The more open and accessible a space the greater the variety of use and the less control there is over it.
2 *We interact with space.* Urban space shapes what we do and how we do it; equally, space may be used in ways other than intended.

To close down a space restricts what we can do there. Walls, fences and security systems can keep close control over the use of urban space to ensure that it is used properly (albeit at the expense of freedom of movement): epistemological walls and academic security systems can equally ensure that ideas are used properly (albeit at the expense of freedom of thought). Conversely, the more open a space the more open it is for a variety of uses. Public parks can be spaces for ball games, jogging, picnics, lovers' trysts, walking the dog: music and novels can spark our imaginations and take us on flights of fancy. Finally, and for popular science what often seems most important, space can be used in ways that diverge from original intentions (much to the dismay of local authorities and science communicators). A handrail is designed to increase safety, but skateboarders 'grind' down them to increase risk; bridges are built to carry traffic, but provide shelter for the homeless; or, more simply, we might use a shop as a shortcut from one street to another. Equally we might look to the ragbag collection that has sheltered under the name of 'Darwinism' or to the popular appropriations of chaos theory or quantum theory.

The analogy could be pushed further, but it is enough to see how the idea of conceptual space reframes our understanding of popular science. No longer is there a simple boundary between science and the public, nor any simple line of communication between them. Instead we can see the open spaces where not everything is done or thought for rational or rationalized ends, and restricted spaces, fenced off and policed, where only the persevering few are able to venture. Thus, our new concern (in CUSP) should be with access to spaces, with freedom of movement, with helping people to navigate and showing them different routes, with opening up the conceptual environment and constructing enabling architectures. For example, if we translate this into science policy we may have to distinguish between, first, an 'open door' policy with the public invited in and scientists retaining control, and secondly, an 'open space' policy where the science goes out and the public do what they like with it. The first (difficult enough as it is for many scientists) limits the public's access to science; the second (though more 'popular') limits science's influence over what gets released. The dilemma highlights a very real problem for scientists since the desire to make science more public may conflict with an equally strong desire to control the meanings that the public construct.

Just how deep the problem goes can be seen if we return to the image of humans as 'lumbering robots' that Richard Dawkins uses in his book *The Selfish Gene* and which we looked at in the previous chapter. Dawkins is one of the great popularizers of the modern age. Not only is he a professor of the public understanding of science, but his numerous books (highly readable, clear and provocative) show him to be a master of the art. Yet he seemed surprised that his image of human robots could be seen differently from the way that he had intended. In a note to the second edition of the book Dawkins tried to explain and justify himself:

> This purple passage (a rare – well, fairly rare – indulgence) has been quoted and requoted in gleeful evidence of my rabid 'genetic determinism'. Part of the problem lies with the popular, but erroneous, associations of the word 'robot'.
>
> (Dawkins 1989: 270)

As Andrew Brown has commented, 'Who is he to tell us what the erroneous associations of "robot" are?' (Brown 1999: 40). What Dawkins associates with the word 'robot' may differ from what the public has in mind, but that does not make the popular associations erroneous. Indeed, it makes Dawkins sound rather like Lewis Carroll's Humpty-Dumpty who tells Alice, 'When I say a word it means whatever I want it to mean.' Consequently, *contra* Dawkins, the problem lies not with those popular meanings that have a general currency, but rather with the expectation that a more circumscribed set of associations should be accepted. In other words, the problem lies in the expectation that there can be some measure of control over the meanings of an idea once it is placed in the public domain. Unfortunately, the problem is exacerbated by the very thing that makes communication possible – the use of a common language. As Steven Shapin has pointed out:

> To the extent that scientific statements are couched in, or even appear to be couched in, ordinary public language, problems may be endemic. On the one hand, scientists may decide that certain scientific conceptions simply cannot be expressed in the public language. On the other hand, scientists' endeavours to use that public language may involve metaphors and analogies whose resonances they cannot expect to hold in place and control.
>
> (Shapin 1990: 997)

It is then a question of control. To open up conceptual spaces means to lose control over them. The challenge for scientists is not just whether they are able to do this but whether they are willing. It is also a challenge that must be faced by democracy.

Science and democracy

With only a few exceptions, until the mid-nineteenth century 'democracy' was a 'strongly unfavourable term', especially at the time of the French Revolution when Burke thought that a perfect democracy was 'the most shameless thing in the world'. Democracy, in the sense of direct rule by the people, was thought of as nothing more than uncontrolled rule by the mob, or, as we might now say, mob-rule. Indirect rule by the people (or representative democracy) developed as a modified form in the United States, but it was only from the mid-nineteenth century that the term lost some of its revolutionary overtones. By the twentieth century it was so prized as an ideal that it became the common claim of rival traditions across the political spectrum (Williams 1976: 82–7). Consequently, as we have seen in previous chapters, in the early nineteenth century respectable science sought to distance itself from democracy's radical associations. The French Revolution provided an all too clear example of what 'democracy' meant and so the legitimation of respectable science was to be found in appeals to its piety and utility. By the twentieth century, however, the consolidation of science's position within the state naturally meant the legitimation of science through appeals to the state's ideals, in particular 'democracy', which was by now seen as a favourable term. The growing respectability of the democratic ideal and the desirability of its representative form match, step by step, the rise in status of science and the enhanced prestige of its experts. However, as we have also seen in previous chapters, the rise of the expert was at the expense of public participation in science. What we see, then, is science's appeals to democracy becoming more common at the same time as science itself was becoming less 'democratic', that is, as it increasingly disenfranchised the public by excluding them from the scientific enterprise. Not surprisingly, on close inspection the relationship of science with democracy turns out to be an uneasy partnership.

It has often been suggested that science is inherently democratic. Jacob Bronowski (1964), for example, thought that an ethic for science would arise naturally from its own practice. There were no technical or philosophical rules for doing science, he argued; instead the conditions for the practice of science were to be found in its values, 'independence and originality, dissent and freedom and tolerance' (68). Thus, dissent and tolerance were not only essential conditions *of* science; they were also essential preconditions *for* science. 'The society of scientists must be a democracy. It can keep alive and grow only by a constant tension between dissent and respect; between independence from the views of others, and tolerance for them' (69). This liberal pluralist vision was particularly attractive in the West at the height of the Cold War, its clearest – and most often cited – spokesman, Karl Popper. In large part, Popper's 'open society' was the product of his philosophy of science, a philosophy which emphasized the provisional quality of scientific knowledge. Not only was science vulnerable to the development of new ideas, he argued, but that was how it should be; true science opened itself to be proven wrong and much scientific activity was directed towards such falsification. Consequently, only democracy offered the possibility for an 'open society' because only democracy embodied these provisional qualities, could see society simply as work in progress, would have the 'openness' to admit to mistakes and so have the necessary flexibility to make improvements based on experience. Nor was Popper alone in such views, as Steve Fuller (1997) notes: 'most democratic theorists in the Western tradition . . . have regarded the form of critical inquiry that characterizes science as the model of the ideal polity' (4). However, Fuller also immediately points out a major problem for this approach, and one which relates directly to our concern for popular science. The problem is '. . . whether the model is limited to an elite whose internal divisions mirror the interests in society at large or whether the model can be extended to include everyone's direct participation' (4). In short, should our democracy (and science) be participatory or representative?

Far from the easy equation of science and democracy, it might even be that science poses a threat to democracy and we might have to consider how the two could be reconciled. Steven Turner (2001), for example, highlights two problems that scientific expertise poses for liberal democratic theory. The first is the problem of equality: whether it violates the conditions of rough equality presupposed by democratic accountability giving power to those privileged to possess the expertise which others cannot control, acquire or share. The second is the problem of neutrality: 'whether the state can preserve its neutrality in liberal "government by discussion" while subsidizing, depending on, and giving special status to, the opinions of experts and scientists' (123). Indeed, even though the liberal democratic state is supposed to be neutral:

> . . . the state not only protects and subsidizes science, it attends to the opinions of science, which is to say it grants science a kind of authority, and reaffirms this authority by requiring that regulations be based on the findings of science or on scientific consensus, and by promoting the findings of science as fact.
>
> (Turner 2001: 124)

The problems are compounded by low levels of scientific literacy, as Christopher P. Toumey (1996) says: 'Scientific thinking can hardly enhance democratic culture when barely anyone can think scientifically' (38). Nevertheless, Toumey looks to American democratic culture for what he calls 'democratic science':

> . . . a matrix of cultural conditions (including values, meanings, symbols, judgements, and the opinions of nonscientists) in which both the style and the content of science are shaped by direct and indirect democratic processes, including elections, referenda, legislation, litigation, consensus, and compromise. Nonscientists' understandings of science intersect with the expertise of credentialed scientists, and scientific thought is subject to extrascientific considerations. The subject matter is science, but the framework is American democratic culture.
>
> (Toumey 1996: 41)

In some respects, Toumey's 'matrix of cultural conditions' seems to have much in common with Habermas's 'public sphere', but there are important differences. In Habermas's analysis ([1962] 1989), the public sphere developed in the eighteenth century as a mediation between private interests (family, work, everyday life) and the power of the state. Initially constituted through public discourse in newspapers, journals, coffee houses and political societies it was associated with, and eventually institutionalized by, the rise of bourgeois liberal democracy. In both Toumey and Habermas, therefore, we can see an appeal to public debates within a framework of democratic culture. However, for Habermas the public sphere was in decline from the late nineteenth century onwards to be replaced by the spectator politics of welfare state capitalism. Toumey's democratic science, on the other hand, is very much concerned with the present day, making reference to the recent development of consensus conferences and science shops as important ways that science can contribute to the democratic process. More importantly, whereas for Habermas the central feature of the public sphere is rational–critical debate, for Toumey democratic science encompasses values, symbols and a plurality of meanings, making it 'politically gracious and hermeneutically promiscuous' (56).

Habermas looks to the open and unrestricted communication between experts, politicians and the public as a way of reviving the public sphere and realizing the Enlightenment ideal of a rational society. As such, it is a model of deliberative democracy that gives a central role to the relationship between science and public. Not surprisingly we can see it being taken up as part of that move from the Public Understanding of Science to the Public Engagement with Science and Technology but, as Elam and Bertilsson (2003) argue:

> As a basis for the 'democratic turn' in PUS, and its self-mutation into PES, deliberative democracy provides a model of democracy where scientists have good chances of appearing before others as already model scientific citizens. By valuing rationality, reserve, selflessness and powers of argumentation, deliberative democracy is a democratic politics played out on scientists' home turf.
>
> (Elam and Bertilsson 2003: 242)

This takes us back to the asymmetries of science–public dialogue that were discussed in Chapter 6 – asymmetries of power, authority and epistemology. If we want to examine science and democracy with the kind of model that was proposed in that chapter (multi-directional, contextualized, broadens notion of expertise and concerned with meanings), then we need to move beyond the rational debates of Habermas's public sphere.

Much of what we need can be found in the analysis of Nowotny *et al.* (2001) and their attempts to 'rethink' science. The organizing perspective for their rethinking is the increasing contextualization of science. The history they present contrasts the period of growth, predictability and planning in the quarter century after the Second World War with the period of uncertainty at the end of the century (the turning points being the oil crisis of the 1970s and the collapse of communist regimes in the 1980s). Society in this new period of uncertainty (what they call 'Mode-2 society') is characterized by pluralism, diversity, volatility and transgressivity as the boundaries between the domains of private, public, market, culture and media are broken down. In short, it is the type of society we saw in Chapter 4 and which is often analysed in terms of post-industrialism and postmodernity. Furthermore, with Mode-2 society comes Mode-2 science – contextualized science that arises from the closer interaction of science and society, and the emergence of socially distributed expertise. In turn, increasing contextualization demands that we 'rethink' science as it moves from the production of reliable knowledge to the production of socially robust knowledge. It also means that the formulation of scientific problems and solutions has moved from institutional sites within government, industry and universities out into what they call the '*agora*':

> The *agora* is the public space in which 'science meets the public', and in which the public 'speaks back' to science. It is the domain (in fact, many domains) in which contextualization occurs and in which socially robust knowledge is continually subjected to testing while in the process it is becoming more robust. Neither state nor market, neither exclusively private nor exclusively public, the *agora* is the space in which societal and scientific problems are framed and defined, and where what will be accepted as a 'solution' is being negotiated.
>
> (Nowotny *et al*. 2001: 247)

The *agora* was the city centre in ancient Greece. Often translated as 'market-place' it was more than simply a site for commercial transactions. It was a meeting place; a cultural centre; a social hub; a place of gossip, news and intrigue; a place filled with hustle, bustle and noise. This is where, metaphorically speaking, science has to survive. Nowotny *et al*., however, do not see this as a threat to science but rather as a great opportunity. Moving science into the *agora* will mean, amongst other things:

- raising questions about social justice, economic equality and the democratization of knowledge as we face the challenge of how to cope with the proliferation of uncertainties;
- finding flexible strategies to explore the unknown implications of a contextualized science;
- seeing people as active agents in generating contexts;
- seeing the 'social' as a key resource of creativity and innovation rather than an intrusion into science;
- valuing trust as an even more scarce and precious resource in the social distribution of expertise.

Science in the *agora* certainly seems to be a way forward in our thinking (or rethinking) about science in public.

The *agora* also picks up the spatial imagery of the previous section. How can we apply this way of thinking (forum, conceptual space, *agora*) to the problem of science and democracy? After all, the ancient Greek *agora* might be seen as the birthplace of democracy. Could our conceptual *agora* help us develop a conceptual democracy? It is with this in mind that I want to put forward one final speculative suggestion. Rather than try to see science as an essential part of a democratic society that attempts to share power, could we not see science as an essential part of a 'demosophic' society that attempts to share knowledge? As democracy is a system to manage power, balancing individual interests through collective rule, so demosophy would be a system to manage knowledge, balancing individual experiences through collective wisdom. In the clamour and confusion of the *agora* where knowledge is contextualized, uncertain, contested we would certainly need formal and informal institutional machinery to bring some degree of epistemological order, much as democracy has formal and informal institutional machinery to bring some degree of political order. Indeed, when we say that democracy does or does not work most often we are passing judgement on the machinery of democracy rather than democracy itself. Rarely is the democratic principle itself questioned. Can the same be said for the sharing of knowledge as it is for the sharing of power? Can there be a similar acceptance of the demosophic principle at the same time as there is a rigorous examination of the machinery that puts that principle into practice? But is this not a pernicious form of relativism with all its attendant dangers? Maybe not. A fully functional demosophic society is no more likely to fragment into epistemological anarchy than a fully functional democratic society will break down into political anarchy. Each is based on a collective individualism. As we maintain legal institutions to deliver 'justice', so we need scientific institutions to deliver the 'truth', even though justice and truth may not ultimately be obtainable. We need, therefore, to hold to our ideals of justice and truth while recognizing the imperfections of our systems to deliver them. We must not confuse what ought to be with what is.

It has taken centuries of cultural, social, economic and political struggle to develop the mechanisms and institutions that enable the sharing of power in a democratic society (nor should we see that struggle as complete or current institutions as any more than work in progress). We should, perhaps, expect an equally long struggle to develop the cultural, social, economic and political machinery for the sharing of knowledge in a demosophic society. A proper understanding of popular science will help us do that.

Further reading

Gieryn, T.F. (1999) *Cultural Boundaries of Science: Credibility on the Line*. Chicago, IL: University of Chicago Press.

Habermas, J. ([1962] 1989) *The Structural Transformation of the Public Sphere: An Inquiry into a Category of Bourgeois Society*. Cambridge: Polity Press.

Nowotny, H., Scott, P. and Gibbons, M. (2001) *Re-thinking Science: Knowledge and the Public in an Age of Uncertainty*. Cambridge: Polity Press.

Smith, C. and Agar, J. (eds) (1998) *Making Space for Science: Territorial Themes in the Shaping of Knowledge*. Basingstoke: Macmillan.

GLOSSARY

American Association for the Advancement of Science (AAAS): founded in 1848, the AAAS seeks to 'advance science and serve society' by acting as educational institution, professional association and spokesperson for science.

Anthropocentricism: from a human-centred perspective or for a human-centred purpose; for example, as seen in the belief that the world was specifically created for the benefit of humans.

Anthropomorphism: giving human qualities to non-human entities. Often seen in descriptions of animal behaviour.

British Association for the Advancement of Science: founded in 1831 to promote the interests of scientific progress and communication. Now known simply as the BA, the association's annual meetings have become festivals to promote public interest in science.

BSE: bovine spongiform encephalopathy, a degenerative and fatal neurological disease of cattle and popularly known as 'mad cow disease'. In the 1990s there was much discussion over whether it could be passed to humans, causing a variant form of Creutzfeldt-Jakob disease, which is the human equivalent.

Challenger: name of space shuttle carrying the first civilian into space, but which exploded soon after lift-off in 1986.

Chaos theory: field of mathematics and physics that exposes the simple, deterministic rules that underlie seemingly random and complex behaviour.

Citizens' jury: similar to **consensus conference**.

Cold fusion: the idea that nuclear energy can be released through electro-chemical reactions without the need for massive nuclear reactors and very hot temperatures.

Interest in cold fusion was sparked in 1989 by the much-disputed claims of Stanley Pons and Martin Fleischman that this had been achieved.

Consensus conference: a form of public participation in science policy where members of the public are selected to act as a lay panel examining a specific issue related to science and technology. Expert witnesses are usually called to make presentations and be cross-examined.

Deconstruction: a form of literary criticism associated with the philosopher Jacques Derrida (1930–2004), which exposes how the logic of a text invites its own refutation. This is often achieved through subverting the conceptual oppositions upon which a text is based (e.g. mind–body, nature–culture).

Epistemology: branch of philosophy concerned with the study of knowledge (e.g what it is and how it can be achieved); sometimes used in the sense of 'a way of knowing'.

Eugenics: the attempt to improve the quality of a 'race' through selective breeding. Now seen as highly controversial and highly ideological, not least because of its focus on race and the means by which 'improvement' would be achieved (ranging from welfare support for those seen as 'healthy stock' to eliminating those deemed to be 'unfit').

Fractal geometry: branch of mathematics that deals with the self-similarity of patterns and structures at different orders of magnification.

GM: genetically modified, as in 'GM crops' or 'GM food'. The manipulation of genetic material to alter the function of cells in an organism (e.g. to increase resistance to disease).

Hubble Space Telescope: powerful optical telescope in orbit around the Earth. Launched in 1990, it was initially plagued by technical problems but has since produced stunning images of the universe.

Indeterminism: the belief that not all events are necessary or inevitable. In the social sciences and philosophy indeterminism emphasizes the role of free will in history. It is often conflated with 'indeterminacy', the principle in physics which states that it is not possible to know precisely both the position and momentum of a particle.

Lyceum movement: educational movement built upon and coordinating local groups organizing debates, public lectures, libraries and museums.

Malthusian: stemming from the ideas of the Rev. Thomas Malthus (1766–1834), who argued that the increase in population will always outstrip the increase in resources to feed it.

Materialism: the belief that the world is made of nothing but matter in motion.

Mesmerism: also known as animal magnetism and named after the work of Franz Anton Mesmer (1734–1815), who believed that the 'magnetic fluid' in people could be manipulated to produce a range of physical and mental sensations. Can be regarded as an early form of hypnotism.

MIT: Massachusetts Institute of Technology.

Nanotechnology: technology on a microscopic scale ('nano' = a millionth of a milli-metre). The extremely small scale of nanotechnology has generated fears that it could interfere with biological processes.

Natural theology: the study of nature as the product of God's design. Conversely, by pointing out design in nature it provides a means to show the existence and attributes of God.

Paradigm: in the analysis of Thomas Kuhn (1922–1996), a set of beliefs, theories and techniques that enable scientists to examine and explain the world. Over time this set of beliefs will be found to be inadequate and a new set will emerge to replace it.

Phrenology: the study of character and mental faculties through examining the surface of the skull.

Quantum physics: study of sub-atomic phenomena based on the idea that energy can only come in discrete packets or 'quanta'. The nature of quantum phenomena raises questions about the relationship between cause and effect as well as what it is possible to know about the world.

Reductionism: a form of explanation that breaks down complex phenomena into their less complex constituent parts which in turn can be broken down into their con-stituent parts. For example, explaining psychology in terms of biology, biology in terms of chemistry, chemistry in terms of physics.

Relativism: the belief that knowledge, ideas and values are essentially dependent upon the specific circumstances of time and place in which they are held, thereby denying the existence of absolute criteria for truth, morality or ethics.

Relativity: the principle that there is no absolute, privileged position from which to view the world and that all observations are relative to an observer's specific frame of reference. In the work of Albert Einstein (1879–1955), the principle gives rise to the Special Theory of Relativity which forces us to reconsider the relationship of space and time, and to the General Theory of Relativity which extends these ideas to include gravity. Not to be confused with **relativism**.

Royal Institution (RI): founded in 1799 to foster science as an agent of technological progress, the RI continues to play a major role in popularizing science, most notably with a series of Christmas lectures.

Royal Society: one of the world's leading scientific organizations; established in London in 1660.

Science shop: a term used to describe a range of projects that enable universities to provide scientific information for citizen groups such as trade unions or residents' associations.

Smithsonian Institution: major educational and research institution with associated museums; founded in 1846.

Society for the Diffusion of Useful Knowledge (SDUK): founded in 1826, largely at the instigation of Lord Brougham, the SDUK acted as an intermediary between authors and publishers for several ambitious series of cheap educational publications. The Society was wound up in 1848.

Superconducting supercollider: a multi-billion dollar particle accelerator that would have enabled physicists to examine the fundamental nature of matter. The project was cancelled by Congress in 1993.

Teleology: explaining phenomena by reference to the goal towards which the phenomena are working. Thus a teleological account of a natural process would see it as determined by its ultimate purpose. By extension, teleology can then appeal to the ultimate purpose of nature and the universe as a whole (e.g. as established by God).

Transgression: going beyond accepted boundaries, for example between disciplines or conceptual oppositions (see also **deconstruction**).

BIBLIOGRAPHY

AAAS (American Association for the Advancement of Science) (1989) *Science for All Americans*. Washington, DC: American Association for the Advancement of Science.

Allan, S. (2002) *Media Risk and Science*. Buckingham: Open University Press.

Allan, S. (2006) When worlds collide: reporting the realities of Hiroshima, in H. Nossek, P. Sonwalkar and A. Sreberny (eds) *Political Violence and the News Media*. Cresskill, NJ: Hampton Press.

Alsop, S. (1999) Understanding understanding: a model for the public learning of radioactivity, *Public Understanding of Science*, 8: 267–84.

Androgen Insensitivity Syndrome Support Group (2006) www.medhelp.org/www/ais.

Anonymous (1906) Science as Sherlock Holmes, *Cassell's Saturday Journal*, 18 April.

Appleyard, B. (1992) *Understanding the Present: Science and the Soul of Modern Man*. London: Pan.

Asimov, I. (1983) Popularising science, *Nature*, 30 November.

Barnes, B. (1972) On the reception of scientific beliefs, in B. Barnes (ed.) *Sociology of Science*. Harmondsworth: Penguin.

Barnes, B. and Shapin, S. (eds) (1979) *Natural Order: Historical Studies of Scientific Culture*. London: Sage Publications.

Barrow, L. (1986) *Independent Spirits: Spiritualism and English Plebeians*. London: Routledge and Kegan Paul.

Barton, R. (1998a) 'Huxley, Lubbock, and Half a Dozen Others': professionals and gentlemen in the formation of the X Club, 1851–1864, *Isis*, 89: 410–44.

Barton, R. (1998b) Just before nature: the purposes of science and the purposes of popularization in some English popular science journals of the 1860s, *Annals of Science*, 55: 1–33.

Basalla, G. (1976) Pop science: the depiction of science in popular culture, in G. Holton and W. Blanpied, *Science and its Public: The Changing Relationship*. Boston, MA: D. Reidel.

Bauman, Z. (1992) *Intimations of Postmodernity*. London: Routledge.

Bauman, Z. (2000) *Liquid Modernity*. Cambridge: Polity Press.

Bauman, Z. (2005) *Liquid Life*. Cambridge: Polity Press.

Begley, S. (1998) Science finds God, *Newsweek*, 27 July.

Bell, D. (2005) *Science, Technology and Culture*. Maidenhead: Open University Press.

Bellamy, E. ([1888] 1984) *Looking Backward 2000–1887*. Harmondsworth: Penguin.

Bensaude-Vincent, B. (2001) A genealogy of the increasing gap between science and the public, *Public Understanding of Science*, 10: 99–113.

Berman, Marshall (1983) *All That is Solid Melts into Air: The Experience of Modernity*. London: Verso.

Berman, Morris (1978) *Social Change and Scientific Organisation: The Royal Institution 1799–1844*. London: Heinemann Educational.

Best, S. (1991) Chaos and entropy: metaphors in science and postmodern social theory, *Science as Culture*, 2: 188–226.

Bloom, A. (1987) *The Closing of the American Mind*. London: Simon and Schuster.

Bloom, H. (1994) *The Western Canon: The Books and School of the Ages*. London: Macmillan.

Bodmer, W. (1985) *The Public Understanding of Science*. London: Royal Society.

Bodmer, W. (1986) *The Public Understanding of Science: The 17th J.D. Bernal Lecture*. London: Birkbeck College.

Bodmer, W. and Wilkins, J. (1992) Research to improve public understanding programmes, *Public Understanding of Science*, 1: 7–10.

Bowler, P. (1975) The changing meaning of 'Evolution', *Journal of the History of Ideas*, 36: 95–114.

Bowler, P. (2001) *Reconciling Science and Religion: The Debate in Early-twentieth-Century Britain*. Chicago, IL: University of Chicago Press.

Bowler, P.J. (1983) *The Eclipse of Darwinism: Anti-Darwinian Evolution Theories in the Decades around 1900*. Baltimore, MD: Johns Hopkins University Press.

Bowler, P.J. (1987) *Theories of Human Evolution: A Century of Debate 1844–1944*. Oxford: Basil Blackwell.

Brockman, J. (1995) *The Third Culture: Beyond the Scientific Revolution*. New York: Simon and Schuster.

Brogan, H. (1999) *The Penguin History of the USA* (second edition). London: Penguin.

Broks, P. (1988) Science and the popular press: a cultural analysis of British family magazines 1890–1914. Unpublished PhD thesis, University of Lancaster.

Broks, P. (1993) Science, media and culture, *Public Understanding of Science*, 2: 123–39.

Broks, P. (1996) *Media Science Before the Great War*. London: Macmillan.

Broks, P. (1999) Trust me – I'm a patient, *Wavelength*, May: 8–10.

Broks, P. (2003) The authority of science and the postmodern reformation, *Interdisciplinary Science Reviews*, 28: 76–82.

Bronowski, J. (1964) *Science and Human Values*. Harmondsworth: Penguin.

Brooke, J.H. (1979) The natural theology of the geologists: some theological strata, in L.J. Jordanova and R. Porter (eds) *Images of the Earth: Essays in the History of the Environmental Sciences*. Chalfont St Giles: British Society for the History of Science.

Brooke, J.H. (1991) *Science and Religion: Some Historical Perspectives*. Cambridge: Cambridge University Press.

Brown, A. (1999) *The Darwin Wars: The Scientific Battle for the Soul of Man*. London: Simon and Schuster.

Brown, J.R. (2001) *Who Rules in Science: An Opinionated Guide to the Wars*. Cambridge, MA: Harvard University Press.

Brown, R.H. (1998) *Toward a Democratic Science: Scientific Narration and Civic Communication*. New Haven, CT: Yale University Press.

Bruce, R.V. (1987) *The Launching of Modern American Science, 1846–1876*. New York: Alfred A. Knopf.

Bucchi, M. (1998) *Science and the Media: Alternative Routes in Scientific Communication*. London: Routledge.

Bucchi, M. (2004) *Science in Society: An Introduction to Social Studies of Science*. London: Routledge.

Burnham, J.C. (1987) *How Superstition Won and Science Lost: Popularizing Science and Health in the United States*. New Brunswick, NJ: Rutgers University Press.

Burrow, J.W. (1966) *Evolution and Society: A Study in Victorian Social Theory*. Cambridge: Cambridge University Press.

Bush, V. (1945) *Science – The Endless Frontier*. Washington, DC: Government Printing Office.

Cabinet Office (1993) *Realising Our Potential: A Strategy for Science, Engineering and Technology*. London: Her Majesty's Stationery Office.

Cantor, G. and Shuttleworth, S. (eds) (2004) *Science Serialized: Representations of the Sciences in Nineteenth-century Periodicals*. Cambridge, MA: MIT Press.

Cantor, G., Dawson, G., Gooday, G., Noakes, R., Shuttleworth, S. and Topham, J.R. (eds) (2004) *Science in the Nineteenth Century Periodical: Reading the Magazine of Nature*. Cambridge: Cambridge University Press.

Capra, F. (1982) *The Turning Point: Science, Society and the Rising Culture*. London: Flamingo.

Capra, F. ([1975] 1983) *The Tao of Physics: An Exploration of the Parallels between Modern Physics and Eastern Mysticism*, second edition. London: Flamingo.

Capra, F. (1997) *The Web of Life: A New Synthesis of Mind and Matter*. London: Flamingo.

Cardwell, D.S.L. (1972) *The Organisation of Science in England*. London: Heinemann.

Carey, J. (ed.) (1995) *The Faber Book of Science*. London: Faber and Faber.

Carson, R. ([1962] 1999) *Silent Spring* with an afterword by L. Lear. London: Penguin.

Channel 4 (1995) *God Only Knows*, produced by N. Kent, and directed by P. Webber.

Chant, C. (ed.) (1989) *Science, Technology and Everyday Life 1870–1950*. London: Routledge.

Chen, C. (2003) *Mapping Scientific Frontiers: The Quest for Knowledge Visualization*. London: Springer-Verlag.

Clarke, I.F. (1979) *The Pattern of Expectation, 1644–2001*. London: Jonathan Cape.

Collins, H. (1987) Certainty and the public understanding of science, *Social Studies of Science*, 17: 689–713.

Collins, H. and Evans, R. (2002) The third wave of science studies: studies of expertise and experience, *Social Studies of Science*, 32: 235–96.

Collins, H. and Pinch, T. (1993) *The Golem: What Everyone Should Know About Science*. Cambridge: Cambridge University Press.

Collins, P. (1981) The British Association as public apologist for science, 1919–1946, in R. Macleod and P. Collins (eds) *The Parliament of Science: The British Association for the Advancement of Science 1831–1981*. Northwood: Science Reviews.

Cooter, R. (1979) The power of the body: the early nineteenth century, in B. Barnes and S. Shapin (eds) *Natural Order: Historical Studies of Scientific Culture*. London: Sage Publications.

Cooter, R. (1984) *The Cultural Meaning of Popular Science*. Cambridge: Cambridge University Press.

Crosland, M (1987) The image of science as a threat: Burke versus Priestley and the 'Philosophic Revolution', *British Journal for the History of Science*, 20: 287–307.

Curtis, R. (1994) Narrative form and normative force: Baconian story-telling in popular science, *Social Studies of Science*, 24: 419–61.

Darnton, R. (1990) *The Kiss of Lamourette: Reflections in Cultural History*. London: Faber and Faber.

Davies, P. (1992) *The Mind of God: Science and the Search for Ultimate Meaning*. London: Penguin.

Dawkins, R. (1989) *The Selfish Gene*, second edition. Oxford: Oxford University Press.

Dawkins, R. (1994) The moon is not a calabash, *Times Higher Educational Supplement*, 30 September.

Dawson, G. (2004) The *Review of Reviews* and the new journalism in late-Victorian Britain, in G. Cantor, G. Dawson, G. Gooday, R. Noakes, S. Shuttleworth and J.R. Topham (eds) *Science in the Nineteenth Century Periodical: Reading the Magazine of Nature*. Cambridge: Cambridge University Press.

Department of Health (2001) *The Expert Patient: A New Approach to Chronic Disease Management for the 21st Century*. London: Department of Health.

Desmond, A. (1987) Artisan resistance and evolution in Britain, 1819–1848, *Osiris*, 3: 77–110.

Desmond, A. (1989) *The Politics of Evolution: Morphology, Medicine and Reform in Radical London*. Chicago, IL: University of Chicago Press.

Dickson, D. (2000) Science and its public: the need for a 'third way', *Social Studies of Science*, 30: 917–23.

Dornan, C. (1989) Science and scientism in the media, *Science as Culture*, 7: 101–21.

Duncan, P.D. (1980) Newspaper science: the presentation of science in four British newspapers during the interwar years 1919–1939. Unpublished MPhil thesis, University of Sussex.

Durant, J. (ed.) (1985) Darwinism and divinity: a century of debate, in J. Durant (ed.) *Darwinism and Divinity: Essays on Evolution and Religious Belief*. Oxford: Basil Blackwell.

Durant, J. (1991) Why scientific literacy matters, *Science Communication in Europe*, report of Ciba Foundation discussion meeting. London: Ciba Foundation.

Durant, J. (1993) What is scientific literacy?, in J. Durant and J. Gregory (eds) *Science and Culture in Europe*. London: Science Museum.

Durant, J. (1995) A new agenda for the public understanding of science, Inaugural lecture, Imperial College, London.

Elam, M. and Bertilsson, M. (2003) Consuming, engaging and confronting science: the emerging dimensions of scientific citizenship, *European Journal of Social Theory*, 6: 233–51.

Ellegård, A. (1958) *Darwin and the General Reader: The Reception of Darwin's Theory in the British Periodical Press*. Göteborg: Gothenburg Studies in English.

Evans, G.A. and Durant, J. (1989) Understanding of science in Britain and the USA, in R. Jowell, S. Witherspoon and L. Brook (eds) *British Social Attitudes: Special International Report*. Aldershot: Gower.

Fürsich, E. and Lester, E.P. (1996) Science journalism under scrutiny: a textual analysis of 'Science Times', *Critical Studies in Mass Communication*, 13: 24–43.

Fuller, S. (1997) *Science*. Buckingham: Open University Press.

Fuller, S. (2000) Science studies through the looking glass: an intellectual itinerary, in U. Segerstråle (ed.) *Beyond the Science Wars: The Missing Discourse about Science and Society*. Albany, NY: State University of New York Press.

Fyfe, A. (2002) Publishing and the classics: Paley's *Natural Theology* and the nineteenth-century scientific canon, *Studies in History and Philosophy of Science*, 33: 729–51.

Galison, P. (1997) *Image and Logic: A Material Culture of Microphysics*. Chicago, IL: University of Chicago Press.

Gardner, C. and Young, R. (1981) Science on TV: a critique, in T. Bennett, S. Boyd-Bowman, C. Mercer and J. Woollacott (eds) *Popular Television and Film*. London: British Film Institute and Open University Press.

Giddens, A. (1990) *The Consequences of Modernity*. Cambridge: Polity Press.

Gieryn, T.F. (1999) *Cultural Boundaries of Science: Credibility on the Line*. Chicago, IL: University of Chicago Press.

Gillispie, C.G. (1959) *Genesis and Geology: The Impact of Scientific Discoveries upon Religious Beliefs in the Decades before Darwin*. New York: Harper and Row.

Gillott, J. and Kumar, M. (1995) *Science and the Retreat from Reason*. London: Merlin.

Gilman, S. (1985) *Difference and Pathology: Stereotypes of Sexuality, Race and Madness*. New York: Cornell University Press.

Golinski, J. (1992) *Science as Public Culture: Chemistry and Enlightenment in Britain, 1760–1820*. Cambridge: Cambridge University Press.

Gould, S.J. (1977) *Ontogeny and Phylogeny*. Cambridge, MA: Belknap Press.

Gould, S.J. (1991) *Wonderful Life: The Burgess Shale and the Nature of History*. London: Penguin.

Graves, R. and Hodge, A. (1941) *The Long Week-end: A Social History of Great Britain 1918–1939*. London: Faber and Faber.

Greene, J.C. (1958) Science and the public in the age of Jefferson, *Isis*, 49: 13–25.

Gregory, F. (1986) The impact of Darwinian evolution on protestant theology in the nineteenth century, in D.C. Lindberg and R.L. Numbers (eds) *God and Nature:*

Historical Essays on the Encounter between Christianity and Science. Berkeley, CA: University of California Press.

Gregory, J. and Miller, S. (1998) *Science in Public: Communication, Culture, and Credibility*. New York: Plenum.

Gross, P.R. and Levitt, N. (1994) *Higher Superstition: The Academic Left and its Quarrels with Science*. Baltimore, MD: Johns Hopkins University Press.

Habermas, J. (1970) *Toward a Rational Society: Student Protest, Science and Politics*, translated by J.J. Shapiro. Boston, MA: Beacon Press.

Habermas, J. ([1962] 1989) *The Structural Transformation of the Public Sphere: An Inquiry into a Category of Bourgeois Society*. Cambridge: Polity Press.

Hales, M. (1982) *Science or Society? The Politics of the Work of Scientists*. London: Pan.

Hall, S. (1980) Encoding/decoding, in S. Hall, D. Hobson, A. Lowe and P. Willis (eds) *Culture, Media, Language*. London: Hutchinson.

Hall, S. (1982) The rediscovery of 'ideology': return of the repressed in media studies, in M. Gurevitch, T. Bennett, J. Curran and J. Woollacott (eds) *Culture, Society and the Media*. London: Methuen.

Handlin, O. (1965) Science and technology in popular culture, *Daedalus*, 94: 156–70.

Hanson, N.R. (1958) *Patterns of Discovery: An Inquiry into the Conceptual Foundations of Science*. Cambridge: Cambridge University Press.

Harris, N. (1990) *Cultural Excursions: Marketing Appetites and Cultural Tastes in Modern America*. Chicago, IL: University of Chicago Press.

Haskell, T.L. (ed.) (1984) *The Authority of Experts: Studies in History*. Bloomington, IN: Indiana University Press.

Hawking, S. (1988) *A Brief History of Time: From the Big Bang to Black Holes*. New York: Bantam.

Hawking, S. (1996) *The Illustrated A Brief History of Time*, updated and expanded edition. New York: Bantam.

Hawking, S. and Mlodinow, L. (2005) *A Briefer History of Time*. New York: Bantam.

Hayles, K. (ed.) (1991) *Chaos and Order: Complex Dynamics in Literature and Science*. Chicago, IL: University of Chicago Press.

Haynes, R.D. (1994) *From Faust to Strangelove: Representations of the Scientist in Western Literature*. Baltimore, MD: Johns Hopkins University Press.

Henson, L., Cantor, G., Dawson, G., Noakes, R., Shuttleworth, S. and Topham, J.R. (eds) (2004) *Culture and Science in the Nineteenth Century Media*. Aldershot: Ashgate.

Hilgartner, S. (1990) The dominant view of popularization: conceptual problems, political uses, *Social Studies of Science*, 20: 519–39.

Hobsbawm, E.J. (1977) *The Age of Capital 1848–1875*. London: Abacus.

Hobsbawm, E.J. (1987) *The Age of Empire 1875–1914*. London: Weidenfeld and Nicolson.

Hobsbawm, E.J. (1994) *Age of Extremes: The Short Twentieth Century 1914–1991*. London: Michael Joseph.

Hofstadter, R. (1955) *Social Darwinism in American Thought*. Boston, MA: Beacon.

Hogben, L. (1938) *Science for the Citizen*. London: George Allen and Unwin.

Hollinger, D.A. (1984) Inquiry and uplift: late-nineteenth-century American academics and the moral efficacy of scientific practice, in T.L. Haskell (ed.) *The Authority of Experts: Studies in History and Theory*. Bloomington, IN: Indiana University Press.

Holton, G. (1993a) Can science be at the centre of modern culture?, *Public Understanding of Science*, 2: 291–305.

Holton, G. (1993b) *Science and Anti-science*. Cambridge, MA: Harvard University Press.

Holton, G. and Blanpied, W. (eds) (1976) *Science and its Public: The Changing Relationship*. Boston Studies in the Philosophy of Science, 33. Dordrecht and Boston: D. Reidel.

Horgan, J. (1997) *The End of Science: Facing the Limits of Knowledge in the Twilight of the Scientific Age*. London: Little, Brown.

Hultberg, J. (1997) The two cultures revisited, *Science Communication*, 18: 194–215.

Huxley, A. ([1932] 1977) *Brave New World*. London: Granada.

Huxley, J. ([1926] 1937) *Essays in Popular Science*. London: Penguin.

Hynes, S. (1968) *The Edwardian Turn of Mind*. London: Oxford University Press.

Inge, T.M. (ed.) (1981) *Handbook of American Popular Culture*, Volume 3. Westport, CT: Greenwood Press.

Inkster, I. (1976) The social context of an educational movement: a revisionist approach to the English mechanics' institutes, 1820–50, *Oxford Review of Education*, 2: 277–307.

Inkster, I. (1979) London science and the seditious Meetings Act of 1817, *British Journal for the History of Science*, 12: 192–6.

Inkster, I. (1981) Seditious science: a reply to Paul Weindling, *British Journal for the History of Science*, 14: 181–7.

Inkster, I. and Morrell, J. (eds) (1983) *Metropolis and Province: Science in British Culture, 1780–1850*. Philadelphia, PA: University of Pennsylvania Press.

Irwin, A. (1994) Science's social standing, *Times Higher Education Supplement*, 30 September.

Irwin, A. and Wynne, B. (eds) (1996) *Misunderstanding Science? The Public Reconstruction of Science and Technology*. Cambridge: Cambridge University Press.

Jasanoff, S., Markle, G.E., Petersen, J.C. and Pinch, T. (1995) *Handbook of Science and Technology Studies*. London: Sage Publications.

Jenkins, A. (1998) Spatial imagery in nineteenth-century representations of science: Faraday and Tyndall, in C. Smith and J. Agar (eds) *Making Space for Science: Territorial Themes in the Shaping of Knowledge*. Basingstoke: Macmillan.

Johnson, R. (1979) 'Really Useful Knowledge': radical education and working-class culture, 1790–1848, in J. Clarke, C. Critcher and R. Johnson, *Working-Class Culture: Studies in History and Theory*. London: Hutchinson.

Jones, A.H. (1981) Medicine and the physicians in popular culture, in T.M. Inge (ed.) *Handbook of American Popular Culture*, Volume 3. Westport, CT: Greenwood Press.

Jurdant, B. (1993) Popularization of science as the autobiography of science, *Public Understanding of Science*, 2: 365–73.

Kelley, R.T. (1993) Chaos out of order: the writerly discourse of semipopular scientific texts, in M.W. McRae (ed.) *The Literature of Science: Perspectives on Popular Scientific Writing*. Athens, GA: University of Georgia Press.

Kerr, A., Cunningham-Burley, S. and Amos, A. (1998) The new genetics and health: mobilizing lay expertise, *Public Understanding of Science*, 7: 41–60.

Kevles, D. (1995) *In the Name of Eugenics: Genetics and the Uses of Human Heredity*. Cambridge, MA: Harvard University Press.

Kuhn, T.S. (1962) *The Structure of Scientific Revolutions*. Chicago, IL: University of Chicago Press.

Kumar, K. (1987) *Utopia and Anti-utopia in Modern Times*. Oxford: Blackwell.

Labinger, J.A. and Collins, H. (eds) (2001) *The One Culture? A Conversation about Science*. Chicago, IL: University of Chicago Press.

LaFollette, M. (1990) *Making Science Our Own: Public Images of Science 1910–1955*. Chicago, IL: University of Chicago Press.

Landau, M. (1991) *Narratives of Human Evolution*. New Haven, CT: Yale University Press.

Laurent, J. (1984) Science, society and politics in late nineteenth-century England: a further look at mechanics' institutes, *Social Studies of Science*, 14: 585–619.

Lederman, L. (1993) *The God Particle*. London: Vintage.

Levere, T.H. (1984) Dr. Thomas Beddoes (1750–1808): science and medicine in politics and society, *British Journal for the History of Science*, 17: 187–204.

Levine, G. (ed.) (1987) *One Culture: Essays in Science and Literature*. Madison, WI: University of Wisconsin Press.

Lewenstein, B.V. (1992a) The meaning of 'public understanding of science' in the United States after World War II, *Public Understanding of Science*, 1: 45–68.

Lewenstein, B.V. (ed.) (1992b) *When Science Meets the Public*. Washington, DC: American Association for the Advancement of Science.

Lewenstein, B.V. (1995a) From fax to facts: communication in the cold fusion saga, *Social Studies of Science*, 25: 403–36.

Lewenstein, B.V. (1995b) Science and the media, in S. Jasanoff, G.E. Markle, J.C. Petersen and T. Pinch (eds) *Handbook of Science and Technology Studies*. London: Sage Publications.

Lewenstein, B.V. (2002) How science books drive public discussion. Paper for the conference Communicating the future: best practices for communication of science to the public, held at the National Institute of Standards and Technology, Gaithersburg, MD.

Liao, L.M. and Boyle, M. (2004) Surgical feminising: the right approach?, *The Psychologist*, 17: 459–62.

Lightman, B. (1997) The voices of nature: popularizing Victorian science, in B. Lightman (ed.) *Victorian Science in Context*. Chicago, IL: University of Chicago Press.

Lightman, B. (2004) Scientists as materialists in the periodical press: Tyndall's Belfast Address, in G. Cantor and S. Shuttleworth (eds) *Science Serialized: Representations of the Sciences in Nineteenth-century Periodicals*. Cambridge, MA: MIT Press.

Lightman, B. (ed.) (1997) *Victorian Science in Context*. Chicago, IL: University of Chicago Press.

Lindberg, D.C. and Numbers, R.L. (eds) (1986) *God and Nature: Historical Essays on the Encounter between Christianity and Science*. Berkeley, CA: University of California Press.

Lindberg, D.C. and Numbers, R.L. (eds) (2003) *When Science and Christianity Meet*. Chicago, IL: University of Chicago Press.

Locke, S. (1999) Golem science and the public understanding of science: from deficit to dilemma, *Public Understanding of Science*, 8: 75–92.

Locke, S. (2002) The Public Understanding of Science – a rhetorical invention, *Science, Technology and Human Values*, 27: 87–111.

Lyotard, J-F. ([1979] 1984) *The Postmodern Condition: A Report on Knowledge*, translated by G. Bennington and B. Massumi. Manchester: Manchester University Press.

McEvoy, J.P. and Zarate, O. (1995) *Stephen Hawking for Beginners*. Trumpington: Icon.

Macleod, R. and Collins, P. (eds) (1981) *The Parliament of Science: The British Association for the Advancement of Science, 1831–1981*. Northwood: Science Reviews.

McRae, M.W. (ed.) (1993) *The Literature of Science: Perspectives on Popular Scientific Writing*. Athens, GA: University of Georgia Press.

Maddox, J. (1994) Defending science from anti-science, *Nature*, 17 March.

Mass Observation (1940) Treatment of science: survey of magazines, papers and books, Report 432.

Mass Observation (1941) Everyday feelings about science: report on panel replies, Report 951.

Mass Observation (1945) The atom bomb: analysis of panel replies, Report 2277.

Mass Observation (1947) Where is science taking us? Public view of science and the impact of the atom bomb, Report 2489.

Mellor, F. (2003) Between fact and fiction: demarcating science from non-science in popular physics books, *Social Studies of Science*, 33: 509–38.

Michael, M. (2002) Comprehension, apprehension, prehension: heterogeneity and the public understanding of science, *Science, Technology and Human Values*, 27: 357–78.

Michael, M. and Carter, S. (2001) The facts about fictions and vice versa: public understanding of human genetics, *Science as Culture*, 10: 5–32.

Miller, D., Kitzinger, J., Williams, K. and Beharrell, P. (1998) *The Circuit of Mass Communication: Media Strategies, Representation and Audience Reception in the AIDS Crisis*. London: Sage Publications.

Miller, J.D. (1987) Scientific literacy in the United States, *Communicating Science to the Public*, report of Ciba Foundation conference. London: Ciba Foundation.

Miller, J.D. (1998) The measurement of civic scientific literacy, *Public Understanding of Science*, 7: 203–23.

Miller, J.D. (2004) Public understanding of, and attitudes toward scientific research: what we know and what we need to know, *Public Understanding of Science*, 13: 273–94.

Miller, S. (2001) Public understanding of science at the crossroads, *Public Understanding of Science*, 10: 115–20.

Moore, J.R. (1979) *The Post-Darwinian Controversies: A Study of the Protestant Struggle to Come to Terms with Darwin in Great Britain and America, 1870–1900*. Cambridge: Cambridge University Press.

Morrell, J. and Thackray, A. (eds) (1981) *Gentlemen of Science: Early Years of the British Association for the Advancement of Science*. Oxford: Clarendon Press.

Morrell, J. and Thackray, A. (eds) (1984) *Gentlemen of Science: Early Correspondence of the British Association for the Advancement of Science*. London: Royal Historical Society.

Morris, W. ([1890] 1984) *News From Nowhere and Selected Writings and Designs*. Harmondsworth: Penguin.

Morus, I.R. (1993) Currents from the underworld: electricity and the technology of display in early Victorian England, *Isis*, 84: 50–69.

Myers, G. (1985) Nineteenth century popularisers of thermodynamics and the rhetoric of social prophecy, *Victorian Studies*, 29: 35–66.

Myers, G. (1990) The double helix as icon, *Science as Culture*, 9: 49–72.

Myers, G. (2003) Discourse studies of scientific popularization: questioning the boundaries, *Discourse Studies*, 5: 265–79.

National Research Council (1996) *National Science Education Standards*. Washington, DC: National Academy Press.

National Science Foundation (2004) *Science and Engineering Indicators*. Washington, DC: National Science Foundation.

Nelkin, D. (1995) *Selling Science: How the Press Covers Science and Technology*. New York: W.H. Freeman.

Nelkin, D. and Lindee, M.S. (1995) *The DNA Mystique: The Gene as Cultural Icon*. New York: W.H. Freeman.

Nieman, A. (2000) The popularisation of physics: boundaries of authority and the visual culture of science. Unpublished PhD thesis, University of the West of England.

Nowotny, H., Scott, P. and Gibbons, M. (2001) *Re-thinking Science: Knowledge and the Public in an Age of Uncertainty*. Cambridge: Polity Press.

Office of Science and Technolgy and the Wellcome Trust (2000) *Science and the Public: A Review of Science Communication and Public Attitudes to Science in Britain*. London: Department of Trade and Industry.

Oldroyd, D.R. (1980) *Darwinian Impacts: An Introduction to the Darwinian Revolution*. Milton Keynes: Open University Press.

Oppenheimer, J.R. (1953) *Science and the Common Understanding*, BBC Reith Lecture. London: Scientific Book Club.

Paley, W. ([1802] 1837) Natural theology, in *The Works of William Paley*. Edinburgh: Peter Brown.

Parrinder, P. (1972) *H.G. Wells: The Critical Heritage*. London: Routledge and Kegan Paul.

Paul, D. (1995) *Controlling Human Heredity, 1865 to the Present*. Atlantic Highlands, NJ: Humanities Press.

Penley, C. (1997) *NASA/TREK: Popular Science and Sex in America.* London: Verso.

Perkin, H. (1969) *The Origins of Modern English Society 1780–1880.* London: Routledge.

Pion, G.M. and Lipsey, M.W. (1981) Public attitudes toward science and technology: what have the surveys told us?, *Public Opinion Quarterly*, 45: 303–16.

Pitrelli, N. (2003) The crisis of the 'public understanding of science' in Great Britain, *Journal of Science Communication*, 2 (1): 1–9.

Porter, R. (ed.) (1992) *The Popularisation of Medicine, 1650–1850.* London: Routledge.

Porush, D.S. (1993) Making chaos: two views of a new science, in M.W. McRae (ed.) *The Literature of Science: Perspectives on Popular Scientific Writing.* Athens, GA: University of Georgia Press.

Reid, R. and Traweek, S. (eds) (2000) *Doing Science + Culture.* London: Routledge.

Rennison, N. (ed.) (2000) *Waterstone's Guide to Popular Science Books.* Brentford: Waterstones.

Rodgers, M. (1992) The Hawking phenomenon, *Public Understanding of Science*, 1: 231–4.

Rose, H. and Rose, S. (1970) *Science and Society.* Harmondsworth: Pelican.

Ross, A. (1991) *Strange Weather: Culture, Science and Technology in the Age of Limits.* London: Verso.

Ross, A. (ed.) (1996) *Science Wars.* London: Duke University Press.

Rossiter, A.P. ([1939] 1945) *The Growth of Science.* London: Penguin.

Roszak, T. ([1968] 1970) *The Making of a Counter Culture: Reflections on the Technocratic Society and its Youthful Opposition.* London: Faber and Faber.

Royal Society (2004) *Science in Society: Report 2004.* London: Royal Society.

Rudwick, M.J.S. (1982) Charles Darwin in London: the integration of public and private science, *Isis*, 53: 184–206.

Russell, C. (1983) *Science and Social Change 1700–1900.* Basingstoke: Macmillan.

Rydell, R.W. (1984) *All the World's a Fair: Visions of Empire at American International Expositions, 1876–1916.* Chicago, IL: University of Chicago Press.

Rydell, R.W. (1993) *World of Fairs: The Century of Progress Expositions.* Chicago, IL: University of Chicago Press.

Sagan, C. (1983) *Cosmos: The Story of Cosmic Evolution, Science and Civilization.* London: Futura.

Sagan, C. (1997) *The Demon-Haunted World: Science as a Candle in the Dark.* London: Headline.

Sardar, Z. (2000) *Thomas Kuhn and the Science Wars.* Duxford: Icon.

Sarup, M. (1993) *An Introductory Guide to Post-Structuralism and Postmodernism*, second edition. Hemel Hempstead: Harvester Wheatsheaf.

Scanlon, E., Whitelegg, W. and Yates, S. (eds) (1999) *Communicating Science: Contexts and Channels.* London: Routledge.

Schama, S. (1989) *Citizens: A Chronicle of the French Revolution.* Harmondsworth: Penguin.

Searle, G.R. (1971) *The Quest for National Efficiency: A Study in British Politics and Political Thought, 1899–1914.* Oxford: Basil Blackwell.

Secord, A. (1994) Science in the pub: artisan botanists in early nineteenth century London, *History of Science*, 32: 269–315.

Secord, J.A. (1989) Extraordinary experiment: electricity and The creation of life in Victorian England, in D. Gooding, T. Pinch and S. Schaffer (eds) *The Uses of Experiment: Studies in the Natural Sciences*. Cambridge: Cambridge University Press.

Secord, J.A. (2000) *Victorian Sensation: The Extraordinary Publication, Reception, and Secret Authorship of* Vestiges of the Natural History of Creation. Chicago, IL: Chicago University Press.

Secord, J.A. (2004) Knowledge in transit, *Isis*, 95: 654–72.

Segal, H.P. (1985) *Technological Utopianism in American Culture*. Chicago, IL: Chicago University Press.

Segerstråle, U. (ed.) (2000) *Beyond the Science Wars: The Missing Discourse about Science and Society*. Albany, NY: State University of New York Press.

Select Committee on Science and Technology (House of Lords) (2000) *Science and Society*. London: HMSO.

Shamos, M.H. (1995) *The Myth of Scientific Literacy*. New Brunswick, NJ: Rutgers University Press.

Shapin, S. (1990) Science and the public, in R.C. Olby, G.N. Cantor, J.R.R. Christie and M.J.S. Hodge (eds) *Companion to the History of Modern Science*. London: Routledge.

Shapin, S. and Barnes, B. (1977) Science, nature and control: interpreting mechanics' institutes, *Social Studies of Science*, 7: 31–74.

Shattock, J. and Wolff, M. (eds) (1982) *The Victorian Periodical Press: Samplings and Soundings*. Leicester: Leicester University Press.

Sheets-Pyenson, S. (1985) Popular science periodicals in Paris and London: the emergence of a low scientific culture, 1820–1875, *Annals of Science*, 42: 549–72.

Shinn, T. and Whitley, R. (eds) (1985) Expository science: forms and functions of popularization, *Sociology of the Sciences*, Volume 9. Dordrecht and Boston: D. Reidel.

Simmonds, M. (2003) Patients and parents in decision making and management, in A. Balen *et al.* (eds) *Paediatric and Adolescent Gynaecology*. Cambridge: Cambridge University Press.

Sismondo, S. (2004) *An Introduction to Science and Technology Studies*. Oxford: Blackwell.

Smart, B. (1993) *Postmodernity*. London: Routledge.

Smith, C. and Agar, J. (eds) (1998) *Making Space for Science: Territorial Themes in the Shaping of Knowledge*. Basingstoke: Macmillan.

Smith, F.B. (1979) *The People's Health, 1830–1910*. London: Croom Helm.

Smith, W. and Higgins, M. (2003) Postmodernism and popularisation: the cultural life of chaos, *Culture and Organization*, 9: 93–104.

Snow, C.P. (1959) *The Two Cultures and the Scientific Revolution*. Cambridge: Cambridge University Press.

Snow, C.P. (1963) *The Two Cultures and a Second Look*. London: New English Library.

Sokal, A.D. (1996a) Transgressing the boundaries: towards a transformative hermeneu-
tics of quantum gravity, *Social Text*, 46/47: 217–52.

Sokal, A.D. (1996b) Throwing a spanner in the text, *The Times Higher Education
Supplement*, 7 June.

Sokal, A.D. and Bricmont, J. (1997) *Intellectual Impostures* (published in US as
Fashionable Nonsense). London: Profile.

Star, S.L. and Griesemer, J.R. (1989) Institutional ecology 'translations' and boundary
objects: amateurs and professionals in Berkeley's Museum of Vertebrate Zoology,
1907–39, *Social Studies of Science*, 19: 387–420.

Stead, W.T. (1906) My system, *Cassells Magazine*, August.

Stebbing, L.S. ([1937] 1944) *Philosophy and the Physicists*. Harmondsworth: Penguin.

Stepan, N. (1982) *The Idea of Race in Science: Great Britain 1800–1960*. London:
Macmillan.

Stepan, N. (1986) Race and gender: the role of analogy in science, *Isis*, 77: 261–77.

Stern, M. (2003) A brief history of Stephen Hawking: making scientific meaning in
contemporary Anglo-American culture, *New Formations*, 49: 150–64.

Stern, M. (2004) *Jurassic Park* and the movable feast of science, *Science as Culture*, 13:
347–72.

Stocklmayer, M., Gore, M.G. and Bryant, C. (eds) (2001) *Science Communication in
Theory and Practice*. Dordrecht: Kluwer Academic Publishers.

Street, B. (1985) Reading the novels of Empire: race and ideology in the classic 'tale
of adventure', in D. Dabydean (ed.) *The Black Presence in English Literature*.
Manchester: Manchester University Press.

Street, B.V. (1975) *The Savage in Literature: Representations of 'Primitive' society in
English Fiction 1858–1920*. London: Routledge and Kegan Paul.

Taylor, C.A. (1996) *Defining Science: A Rhetoric of Demarcation*. Madison, WI:
University of Wisconsin Press.

Taylor, G.R. (1968) *The Biological Time-Bomb*. London: Thames and Hudson.

Thompson, A.M. ('Dangle') (1910) Uses of science, *The Clarion*, 30 December.

Thompson, E.P. (1968) *The Making of the English Working Class*. Harmondsworth:
Pelican.

Toffler, A. (1970) *Future Shock*. Toronto, ON: Bantam.

Topham, J.R. (1992) Science and popular education in the 1830s: the role of the
Bridgewater Treatises, *British Journal for the History of Science*, 25: 397–430.

Topham, J.R. (1998) Beyond the 'common context': the production and reading of the
Bridgewater Treatises, Isis, 89: 233–62.

Topham, J.R. (2000) Scientific publishing and the reading of science in nineteenth-century
Britain: a historiographical survey and guide to sources, *Studies in the History and
Philosophy of Science*, 31: 559–612.

Toumey, C.P. (1996) *Conjuring Science: Scientific Symbols and Cultural Meanings in
American Life*. New Brunswick, NJ: Rutgers University Press.

Turner, F.M. (1974) *Between Science and Religion: The Reaction to Scientific Naturalism
in Late Victorian England*. New Haven, CT: Yale University Press.

Turner, F.M. (1978) The Victorian conflict between science and religion: a professional dimension, *Isis*, 69: 356–76.

Turner, F.M. (1980) Public science in Britain, 1890–1919, *Isis*, 71: 589–608.

Turner, S. (2001) What is the problem with experts?, *Social Studies of Science*, 31: 123–49.

Turner, S. (2003) The third science war, *Social Studies of Science*, 33/4: 581–611.

Turney, J. (1998) *Frankenstein's Footsteps: Science, Genetics and Popular Culture*. New Haven, CT: Yale University Press.

Turney, J. (2001) Telling the facts of life: cosmology and the epic of evolution, *Science as Culture*, 10: 225–47.

Van Dijck, J. (1998) *Imagenation: popular images of genetics*. Basingstoke: Macmillan.

Waddington, C.H. ([1941] 1948) *The Scientific Attitude*. London: Penguin.

Waites, B. (1989) Social and human engineering, in C. Chant (ed.) *Science, Technology and Everyday Life 1870–1950*. London: Routledge.

Watson, P. (2000) *A Terrible Beauty: A History of the People and Ideas that Shaped the Modern Mind*. London: Weidenfeld and Nicolson.

Weinberg, S. (1992) *Dreams of a Final Theory: The Search for the Fundamental Law of Nature*. London: Vintage.

Weinberg, S. (2001) *Facing Up: Science and its Cultural Adversaries*. Cambridge, MA: Harvard University Press.

Weindling, P. (1980) Science and sedition: how effective were the acts licensing lectures and meetings, 1795–1819?, *British Journal for the History of Science*, 53: 139–53.

Wells, H.G. ([1927] 1958) *Selected Short Stories*. London: Penguin.

Wells, H.G. ([1933] 1967) *The Shape of Things to Come*. London: Corgi.

Werskey, G. (1988) *The Visible College: A Collective Biography of British Scientists and Socialists of the 1930s*. London: Free Association Books.

'The Whatnot' (1898) Spiritualism and things: a chat with Dr Russell Wallace, *The Clarion*, 22 January.

White, M. and Gribbin, J. (1992) *Stephen Hawking: A Life in Science*. London: Viking.

Whitley, R. (1985) Knowledge producers and knowledge acquirers: popularization as a relation between scientific fields and their publics, in T. Shinn and R. Whitley (eds) *Expository Science: Forms and Functions of Popularization. Sociology of the Sciences*, Volume 9. Dordrecht and Boston: D. Reidel.

Williams, R. (1976) *Keywords: A Vocabulary of Culture and Society*. London: Fontana.

Wilsdon, J. and Willis, R. (2004a) *See-through Science: Why Public Engagement Needs to Move Upstream*. London: Demos.

Wilsdon, J. and Willis, R. (2004b) Techno probe, *Guardian*, 1 September.

Winter, A. (1994) Mesmerism and popular culture in early Victorian England, *History of Science*, 32: 317–43.

Winter, A. (1997) Orthodoxies and heterodoxies in the early Victorian life sciences, in B. Lightman (ed.) *Victorian Science in Context*. Chicago, IL: University of Chicago Press.

Wittgenstein, L. (1958) *Philosophical Investigations*, second edition. Oxford: Basil Blackwell.

Wolpert, L. (1992) *The Unnatural Nature of Science*. London: Faber and Faber.

Woodlief, A.M. (1981) Science in popular culture, in T.M. Inge (ed.) *Handbook of American Popular Culture*, Volume 3. Westport, CT: Greenwood Press.

Worboys, M. (1981) The British Association and empire: science and social imperialism 1880–1914, in R. Macleod and P. Collins (eds) *The Parliament of Science: The British Association for the Advancement of Science, 1831–1981*. Northwood: Science Reviews.

Wyatt, S. (2004) Danger! Metaphors at work in economics, geophysiology, and the internet, *Science, Technology and Human Values*, 29: 242–61.

Wynne, B. (1979) Physics and psychics: science, symbolic action and social control in late Victorian England, in B. Barnes and S. Shapin (eds) *Natural Order: Historical Studies of Scientific Culture*. London: Sage Publications.

Wynne, B. (1992) Public understanding of science research: new horizons or hall of mirrors?, *Public Understanding of Science*, 1: 37–43.

Wynne, B. (1995) Public understanding of science, in S. Jasanoff, G.E. Markle, J.C. Petersen and T. Pinch (eds) *Handbook of Science and Technology Studies*. London: Sage Publications.

Yeo, R. (1984) Science and intellectual authority in mid-nineteenth century Britain: Robert Chambers and the *Vestiges of the Natural History of Creation, Victorian Studies*, 28: 5–31.

Yeo, R. (1993) *Defining Science: William Whewell, Natural Knowledge, and Public Debate in Early Victorian Britain*. Cambridge: Cambridge University Press.

Young, R.M. (1970) The impact of Darwin on conventional thought, in A. Symondson (ed.) *The Victorian Crisis of Faith*. London: SPCK.

Young, R.M. (1980) Natural theology, Victorian periodicals and the fragmentation of a common context, in C. Chant and J. Fauvel, *Darwin to Einstein: Historical Studies on Science and Belief*. Harlow: Longman.

Ziman, J. (2000) *Real Science: What It Is and What It Means*. Cambridge: Cambridge University Press.

Zochert, D. (1974) Science and the common man in ante-bellum America, *Isis*, 65: 448–73.

Zukav, G. (1979) *The Dancing Wu Li Masters: An Overview of the New Physics*. London: Fontana.

Zukav, G. (1990) *The Seat of the Soul: An Inspiring Vision of Humanity's Spiritual Destiny*. London: Rider.

INDEX

AAAS, *see* American Association for the Advancement of Science
abuse of science, 72
Acquired Immune Deficiency Syndrome, *see* AIDS
Adams, J., 6
AIDS (Acquired Immune Deficiency Syndrome), 126, 131
AIS, *see* Androgen Insensitivity syndrome
Aleksander, I., 89–90
Allan, S., 74–5
American Association for the Advancement of Science (AAAS), 62, 103–4, 119
American system of manufacture, 26–7, 54
Androgen Insensitivity Syndrome (AIS), 131–2
anthropocentrism, 32, 36
anthropomorphism, 32, 36
Anticipations, 66
Anti-Jacobin Review and Magazine, The, 6
anti-science, 94, 98, 114–16, 123
Arnold, M., 35
artisan botanists, 18–19
Ascent of Man, The, 89
Asimov, I., 114–15
Association of British Science Writers, 88
atheism, 7

Attenborough, D., 88, 89
authority of science, 23, 38, 87–8, 107–8, 123–4, 130, 151

BAAS, *see* British Association for the Advancement of Science
Bache, A.D., 30
Bauman, Z., 53–4, 72, 86
Beddoes, T., 6, 27
Begley, S., 93
Bell, D., 141
Bellamy, E., 54
Benjamin, W., 42
Benn, A.W., 38
Bensaude-Vincent, B., 129
Bentham, J., 13, 14
Berman, Marshall, 52, 53, 72
Berman, Morris, 13
Bernal, J.D., 64, 80
Best, S., 94
Bodmer, W., 105–6
Bodmer, W. and Wilkins, J., 120
boundary work, 132–3, 145
Bowler, P., 46, 93
Brave New World, 82–4, 85, 86
Bridgewater Treatises, The, 20–1
Brief History of Time, A, 89, 93
Brightwen, E., 35
British Association for the Advancement of Science (BAAS), 31, 56, 62
British Science Guild, 56–7

DOMESTICATION OF MEDIA AND TECHNOLOGY
Maren Hartmann, Thomas Berker, Yves Punie and Katie Ward (eds)

This book provides an overview of a key concept in media and technology studies: domestication. Theories around domestication shed light upon the process in which a technology changes its status from outrageous novelty to an aspect of everyday life which is taken for granted. The contributors collect past, current and future applications of the concept of domestication, critically reflect on its theoretical legacy, and offer comments about further development.

The first part of *Domestication of Media and Technology* provides an overview of the conceptual development and theory of domestication. In the second part of the book, contributors look at a diverse range of empirical studies that use the domestication approach to examine the dynamics between users and technologies. These studies include:

- Mobile information and communications techologies (ICTs) and the transformation of the relationship between private and the public spheres
- Home-based internet use: the two-way dynamic between the household and its social environment
- Disadvantaged women in Europe undertaking introductory internet courses
- Urban middle-class families in China who embrace ICTs and view them as instruments of upward mobility and symbols of success

The book offers valuable insights for both experienced researchers and students looking for an introduction to the concept of domestication.

Contributors
Maria Bakardjieva, Thomas Berker, Leslie Haddon, Maren Hartmann, Deirdre Hynes, Sun Sun Lim, Anna Maria Russo Lemor, David Morley, Jo Pierson, Yves Punie, Els Rommes, Roger Silverstone, Knut H. Sørensen, Katie J. Ward.

Contents
Introduction – I. Theory and History – Exploring Domestication Today – Domestication: The social performance of technology – Empirical Studies Using the Domestication Framework – Domestication Run Wild: From the Moral Economy of the Household to the Mores of a Culture – And Where is the Content? Media as technological objects, symbolic environments and individual texts – II. Theory & Application – Fitting the internet into our lives: what IT courses have to do with it – Domestication, Home and Work – Making a 'Home': the domestication of information and communication technologies in Single Parents' households – From cultural to information revolution: ICT domestication by middle-class Chinese families – Domestication at work in small businesses – III. Summary – Domesticating Domestication?

2005   240pp   0 335 21768 0 (Paperback)   0 335 21769 9 (Hardback)

SCIENCE, TECHNOLOGY AND CULTURE

David Bell

> An excellent introduction to some key debates in the cultural study of science and technology. David Bell is the ideal guide for non-science students, his gentle, engaging, friendly voice leading the reader through cultural issues surrounding everything from fridges and synth-pop to space exploration and nuclear war.
>
> David Gauntlett, Professor of Media and Audiences,
> Bournemouth University

Using the tools and approaches of cultural studies, David Bell provides an engaging introduction to the study of science and technology. Equipping readers with an understanding of science and technology as aspects of culture, the book encourages them to think about the roles and affects that science and technology have on everyday life.

Topics include:

- Representations of science and scientists in popular films
- Contests over amateur, fringe and pseudo-science
- Domestic technologies and household gender politics

The book features numerous topical case studies, from UFOs and nuclear war to the MMR vaccine, microwave ovens, New Agers, cars running on water, low-carb diets and astrology.

Science, Technology and Culture is key reading for students in cultural studies, media studies, sociology, and science and technology studies.

Contents

Series Editor's Foreword – Acknowledgements – Science, Technology . . . and Culture? – Thinking about Science and Culture – Thinking about Technology and Culture – Screening (and Singing) Science and Technology – The Moon and The Bomb – Ufologists, Hobbyists and Other Boundary Workers – Pause and Rewind – Glossary of Key Terms – References – Index.

176pp 0 335 21326 X (EAN: 9 780335 213269) (Paperback)
     0 335 21327 8 (EAN: 9 780335 213276) (Hardback)

MEDIA, RISK AND SCIENCE

Stuart Allan

- How is science represented by the media?
- Who defines what counts as a risk, threat or hazard, and why?
- In what ways do media images of science shape public perceptions?
- What can cultural and media studies tell us about current scientific controversies?

Media, Risk and Science is an exciting exploration into an array of important issues, providing a framework for understanding key debates on how the media represent science and risk. In a highly effective way, Stuart Allan weaves together insights from multiple strands of research across diverse disciplines. Among the themes he examines are: the role of science in science fiction, such as *Star Trek*; the problem of 'pseudo-science' in *The X-Files*; and how science is displayed in science museums. Science journalism receives particular attention, with the processes by which science is made 'newsworthy' unravelled for careful scrutiny.

The book also includes individual chapters devoted to how the media portray environmental risks, HIV-AIDS, food scares (such as BSE or 'mad cow disease' and GM foods) and human cloning. The result is a highly topical text that is invaluable for students and scholars in cultural and media studies, science studies, journalism, sociology and politics.

Contents

Series editor's foreword – Introduction: media, risk and science – Science fictions – Science in popular culture – Science journalism – Media, risk and the environment – Bodies at risk – News coverage of AIDS – Food scares: mad cows and GM foods – Figures of the human: robots, androids, cyborgs and clones – Glossary – References – Index.

256pp   0 335 20662 X (EAN: 9 780335 206629) (Paperback)

WHAT IS THIS THING CALLED SCIENCE?
AN ASSESSMENT OF THE NATURE AND STATUS OF SCIENCE AND ITS METHODS

Alan Chalmers

Reviews of the previous edition:

> In this academic bestseller – indeed, one of the most widely read books ever written in the history and philosophy of science – Alan Chalmers provides a refreshingly lucid introduction . . . Drawing on illuminating historical examples, he asks and answers some of the most fundamental questions about the nature of science and its methods.
>
> Ronald L. Numbers, William Coleman Professor of the History of Science and Medicine, University of Wisconsin at Madison

> Crisp, lucid and studded with telling examples . . . As a handy guide to recent alarums and excursions (in the philosophy of science) I find this book vigorous, gallant and useful.
>
> *New Scientist*

- What is the characteristic that serves to distinguish scientific knowledge from other kinds of knowledge?
- What is the role of experiment in science?
- What is the role of theory in science?

In clear, jargon-free language, the third edition of this highly successful introduction to the philosophy of science surveys the answers of the past hundred years to these central questions. This edition has been enriched by many new historical examples and the early chapters have been reorganised, re-ordered and amplified to facilitate the introduction of beginners to the field. The third edition includes new chapters on the new experimentalism; the Bayesian approach to science; the nature of scientific laws; and recent developments in the realism/anti-realism debate.

Contents

Preface – Introduction – Science as knowledge derived from the facts of experience – Observation as practical intervention – Experiment – Deriving theories from the facts: induction – Introducing falsificationism – Sophisticated falsificationism: novel predictions and the growth of science – The limitations of falsificationism – Theories as structures I: Kuhn's paradigms – Theories as structures II: Research programmes – Feyerabend's anarchistic theory of science – Methodical changes in method – The Bayesian approach – The new experimentalism – Why should the world obey laws? – Realism and anti-realism – Epilogue – Bibliography – Index.

288pp   0 335 20109 1 (Paperback)
Not available in Australia, Asia, South America and North America.